HOW MUCH

FOR A HAPPY

ENDING?

From domestic abuse survivor, to dominatrix, to sex
therapist and everything in between!

S.E. WINTERS

To Mum. We've done some things. I'm always doing stuff... with you by my side, cheering me on. You're my best friend and biggest supporter. Oh, and you made me grow like this, so there!

Also to my kids — hopefully you'll only read this after I've been eaten by worms, so you can't kill me for it. Sorry if I'm an embarrassing mum, but I reckon you're secretly proud of me too.
Thanks for being my reasons for everything.

CONTENTS

ACKNOWLEDGEMENTS

Thanks to everyone who helped to support me in the writing of this book. Thanks to my husband for believing in me. Thank you especially for all the coffee and submitting to my demands of silence whilst I was typing away until way past midnight, pulling my funny concentrating face.

Thanks to Fluffy-go-slow for giving me a head start on the five-year project and participating in some of the funnier memories. It would've been a lonely road without the double act.

Lady L of Tooltastic Towers, thank you for devouring my manuscript like you didn't know me, encouraging me with supportive feedback and being one of the only people I trusted to read about my antics with no judgement.

Lord Mentalist of The Shed, thank you for a grown-up (I use that term loosely) and helpful perspective on my project. You're in the wrong job.

Thanks to my Goth girl for the idea. You know which one. The funniest things are the misfortunes of others, and all that!

Thank you Playground Witch for your estate-isms. Did anyone tell you you're funny as f*ck?

Basil, for reading halfway through as a Beta Reader. It's the thought that counts, and that's pretty impressive for a stoner. Thanks for a male perspective on my work.

Thanks to Gwen Grant, who inspired me all those years ago with her trilogy of children's books. If I hadn't picked up your books, I would never have picked up my pen.

Finally, I feel like I should be dignified and say something like, "Thanks to the men who hurt me, for moulding me into a warrior." Therefore, please accept the shit off my shoe as a token of my gratitude.

PROLOGUE

I was standing in the queue at the school gates, waiting for my nine-year-old son, Morgan, to come out. It was a cold, drab and blustery autumn day. The leaves crunched under my stilettos as I shuffled about and pulled the furry collar of my coat around my neck, to keep the warmth in. Underneath I only had on a thin, white, low-buttoning blouse. *Maybe I should've worn a cardy.* This wasn't really the weather for sheer tights either, I thought as I looked down at my American Tan coloured legs, covered just above the knees by a tight, black and grey pinstripe pencil skirt. If the traffic hadn't been so busy, I would've been able to stop by my house to run in and shove some jeans on before driving up to school. I scratched the back of my head where a kirby-grip was digging into my scalp because I had pinned my French pleat up too tightly. *Come on, Miss Smith,* I silently willed Morgan's teacher. It was ten past three, and she was five minutes behind time already. *I could've bloody got changed after all.*

"Oh, hi Sinead," said a voice from behind me.

I turned to see Morgan's friend's mum standing right at the back of me. She was a plump lady, a few years older than me, with a pink, makeup-free, friendly face and wild, frizzy, auburn hair. She always dressed in khaki cargo pants and baggy t-shirts and was one of those mums who clearly only shopped at Next[1], and was all for her kids. As

---

[1] A popular clothes shop, frequented by the upper working classes, selling modest, classy, play-it-safe clothing. They make the best suck-in-your-wobbly-bits jeans, like, ever.

1

in, the type that could be found standing in the same little clique in the same place every morning after dropping her boy off, talking about nothing else but children. You know, the perfect parent sort. I didn't know her very well, but we were always at the same kids' birthday parties and had engaged in small talk a few times. She was nice enough, I guess. She had lent me a teddy once for Morgan to use when I'd forgotten to bring his in for the annual Teddy Bear's Picnic. That's the kind of mum I was; constantly rushing around at the last minute, always disorganised and chasing my tail. Well, today I was on time for a change.

"You look smart today. I like that lipstick. I'm never brave enough to wear red. In fact, I never have time to put makeup on at all with running around after the little monster all the time. Have you been somewhere nice?"

Not anywhere a lady like you would class as 'nice'.

"Thanks. Oh no, I've just been to work, that's all. I just fancied a change of colour to cheer myself up with the weather being so lousy."

"Oh, well, you look dead posh in your work clothes. What is it you do, again?"

I shifted uncomfortably and looked at my watch, pretending I hadn't heard the question. I felt a tap on my shoulder.

"What do you do?"

Oh, bugger off with your questions! Quick, Sinead, think. I looked at her blankly as the cogs in my mind whirred round at high speed.

"Erm…"

Prostitute. Escort. Sex worker. Adult entertainer. Mistress. What was I? Was I really any of those things? A prostitute is someone who has sex for money. I didn't do that. The word 'escort' conjured up images of women being paid for their company, taken to fancy restaurants and maybe sleeping with the client afterward. Nope; not me either. Adult entertainer, then? Well, I entertained, in a way; but the title made me think of pornographic films. I definitely wasn't a Porn star. *Hmm.* Sex worker, perhaps? No way. That was too close to the bone, and it sounded seedy. It may have been the most fitting, but it didn't sound nice at all. It made me think of drug-addled girls, soliciting their wares on street corners. When I was at work, I was inside, cosy and warm. I had a kettle and central heating and could nip to the toilet whenever I wanted. I called the shots. No Pimp for me, thank you! I wasn't vulnerable or exploited, was I? How about 'Dominatrix'? That sounded pretty cool. No, not sure this kind of mum would understand…

"Oh sorry, I was miles away then. Nothing interesting, I work in, erm, public relations." I smiled.

It was kind of true. I worked in relations with certain members of the public, anyway. What's a little truth-bending between friends? At that moment the shrill sound of the school bell rang out, right on cue. Saved by the bell.

Thank fuck for that.

CHAPTER 1

It's grim up north

My name is Claudette De Marco. I'm twenty-five, tall and statuesque, with flaxen blonde, long flowing locks. I have the most beautiful emerald green eyes that you ever saw, and I'm a skinny size eight. I'm also filthy rich and have a social calendar that Paris Hilton would be jealous of…

And I'm a shit liar. This isn't the secret diary of a high-class London call girl, and I really should tell the truth, shouldn't I?

Okay. My name is Sinead Emma Winters; I'm in my early forties, I have dark brown, just-under-boob-length, wavy hair, brown eyes, and I'm a curvy size ten to twelve when I abstain from eating too many pies. I've got an hourglass figure – well, apart from in the winter when I'm shaped more like a conical flask. I'm always getting told that I look young for my age. I think it must be because of how I carry myself. I take good care of my skin nowadays, I wear up-to-date clothes and still speak in the same dialect that I did when I was a teenager. I have a young outlook and listen to modern chart music as well as the old stuff. The youngest anyone has ever guessed my age to be is twenty-six, but it was in a dark nightclub, so I'm not sure that counts. I'm a short-arse, so I wear stiletto-heeled boots a lot because I'm afraid of looking fat and stumpy. Never mind though, you can't win 'em all. I'm not quite Bridget Jones, so I'm happy enough with my lot. My mum says I'm like a teenage boy's wet dream, so that'll do for me.

Is it bad to say that I'm pretty good looking? During my life I've used my pretty face to scrape through many a potential fuck-up by the skin of my teeth. Not that I'm not smart – I am. A 'clever little git', my dad would say (although I think he meant I was an opinionated, cheeky bugger). I'm no brainiac, and being a swot would have been social suicide at school, but I did well enough to get by. I can outwit idiots (although it hasn't always been that way!) and I can articulate myself pretty well. Oh, and I am a master at using my sexuality to get what I want, thanks to my mum's genes.

In our house, we grew up watching a dog-eared The Young Ones[2] VHS box set, on repeat. That's probably where I get my bawdy sense of humour from. My good attributes are that I'm empathic, compassionate, a good friend, a great listener, a near-perfect partner and a bloody good mum. I like to keep a tidy home and I value family time. My bad points... Oh, Christ. I'm opinionated, fickle, sometimes selfish, impulsive, short-tempered, horrendously impatient, slightly passive-aggressive and I've made some very poor choices in life. I can also be over-analytical; especially when my period is imminent.

I'm a very lucky wife and mother of two, and we live in a very ordinary, modest terraced house. My hobbies include writing in my trusty diary, cooking, watching horror films, gossiping with my friends, and spending quality time with my long-suffering other half and my wonderful kids. I work part-time as a Psychotherapist, and I'm a housewife for the rest of the time. Pretty normal stuff, really. If you scratched the surface, though, you'd see that my life was about as far removed from normal as you could get. I've done things that

---

[2] A popular, politically incorrect 1980s comedy TV sitcom about four misfits living together in student accommodation.

would make a nun blush (I did actually wear a nun's habit once, but for less than innocent purposes). My current life is now worlds away from how I was afraid it may turn out. We all have the odd skeleton in our closet, don't we? Mine just have a bit more meat on the bone than most. I now realise that the older you get, the less shameful it seems to be when you admit to daring exploits in your younger years.

Perhaps when I'm an old lady, I'll be entertaining my fellow nursing home residents with a twinkle in my eye, and they'll chuckle at my tales and say,

"By heck, lass, you haven't half lived!"

It'll sure beat watching Countdown[3] re-runs and playing solitaire, anyway. I'll never be laying on my deathbed, stating, "I wish I had…" or even, "I wish I hadn't", that's for sure. Let me explain…

Mum, Dad and I lived in a half red brick, half rendered semi-detached council house, in an ex mining town in the north of England. We had eleven cats, forty-odd rats, a chinchilla, a dog, a pair of gerbils, a snake and a few tropical fish. The living room boasted a feature wall with My Little Pony wallpaper and a little built-in bar. The kitchen was pillar box red and white and had a big Snoopy poster. At the top of the stairs was one of those massive, cheesy-but-trendy-at-the-time Athena posters, with a hot guy balancing a baby on his muscular arm. You know the one.

In the hallway was a big chest freezer that I suspect my parents had nicked from the back of Jack Fulton's discount frozen food shop. In it were teetering piles of Tesco Value burgers, oven chips, and not much

---

[3] Countdown is a daytime television game-show involving mind-boggling word and number tasks.

else. Our house was in a constant state of disarray and looked like a burglary crime scene. Things often got lost amid the clutter. Even the pets weren't safe. We once heard a muffled, "Miaow!" and after a much-confused ransacking session of the whole house, Mum finally discovered one of our cats in there, glistening with frost and shivering. Maybe Dad had put it in there earlier, to go with the chips for tea, to save a few bob. Tomcat and chips. *Yum.*

Each year, the Christmas tree would be carried out of the cellar, where it lived alongside the rats that my parents bred. Still decorated from the year before, it smelled fusty and carried a complex network of dusty cobwebs. On January 5th, like clockwork, they would carry it back down the cellar steps – still fully erect and covered in baubles, not to resurface until the following year.

In my parents' bedroom was a big, red poster, pinned to the wall above their bed. I've since seen them for sale in the tourist shops on Blackpool front. Peppered with images of Kama Sutra positions, star-sign titles were written underneath each picture. I felt uncomfortable whenever I entered their bedroom, as this poster was difficult for my eyes to avoid. I wasn't sure what it was about, but I knew it was something my young eyes shouldn't be looking at. The people had no clothes on, and no clothes meant one thing to me. That one thing was 'shame', as I was about to discover.

The first time I heard my parents having sex, muffled moans awoke me, and I opened my eyes to see what was going on. My room was empty. The moans grew louder, and I strained to hear where they were coming from. It was Mum. Yes, that was definitely my mum. Dad let out a series of aggressive-sounding grunts, as Mum's moan tapered off. *Oh, my gosh! Dad's hurting Mum!* I knew he had a temper, and Mum definitely seemed to be in distress. *What should I do?* Rooted to my mattress, I tried to process what was happening. Then I heard a loud giggle, and Dad saying, "You liked that, didn't you?"

"Oh, yeah!" she sighed, and they both laughed.

Okay, so let me get this straight – Dad was hurting Mum, and she liked it. I felt confused and upset. I heard their bedroom door creak open, and Mum clumsily padding barefoot to the toilet. I heard it flush, and Mum walking back to bed. I drifted off back to sleep and stored the memory on an imaginary shelf in my childish mind. Love meant pain, and pain meant boundless joy.

My parents were cool and edgy. Mum, ever-changing like a chameleon, was a punk in those days. Dad looked very much like Ozzy Osbourne, and funnily enough, his favourite band was Black Sabbath. Dad was also in a rock band. He wrote songs and played the drums; and the house was always full of fashionable teenage lads, wearing eyeliner and sporting crimped hair.

Dad worked for a man called Jimmy who owned a mattress company in a neighbouring industrial town. The family were a bit posh. His daughter, Sadie and I attended the same school. Because I was an only child, I was always grateful if someone made friends with me, and I hung on Sadie's every word.

Is it wrong to call a six-year-old a bitch? Well, Sadie was, so I don't care. She never tired of telling me that our car actually belonged to her dad, and she enjoyed humiliating me daily in the playground. I was a quiet, shy kid; so, I did whatever she told me to do. Isn't it funny how the most painful and shameful memories can sit in one's mind for so long? I remember as clear as day when we once went to the factory with our dads. We could mess about in the big office whilst they talked business in the room next door; so, we played hide and seek under the desks. The desks were the sort which has drawers at each side, and a cut-out gap in the middle where a swivel chair would fit. We were running about the place, laughing raucously, when out of the blue Sadie barked: "Take your clothes off!"

"What?"

"You heard what I said. Take your clothes off now, or I'll tell my dad you were hitting me."

No way! I didn't want to.

"Take them off, now!"

I did as she said, like the obedient little pet that I was.

"Now get under the desk and stay there until I say you can come out."

I scurried under the desk and curled up as small as I could in the gap meant for the chair. Sadie skipped off, whistling without a care in the world. I crouched there, trying in vain to cover with my chubby little palms what modesty I had left. My heart thudded as I heard the staff gossiping and laughing together, whilst on their tea break in the room next door. The sound was growing louder as it came closer, and it terrified me that they could come in and rumble me. How would I explain why I was sitting there, sans clothing, like a little weirdo? I felt ashamed for the first time that I can remember, and that was a theme that spanned from my childhood, into my adult life. My peers just couldn't resist taking the piss out of me. I was like Sadie's little gimp. She loved the control; even at such a young age. Definitely a little Dominatrix in the making. She systematically bullied the Hell out of me until my parents moved me to another school when I was almost seven years old. Bye-bye, six-year-old Satan!

Around the same age, Mum and Dad bought me some dolls made popular by the cartoon series, 'Jem and the Rock Stars'. The dolls were punky and unconventional, like my parents. I used to play with them upstairs in my bedroom and act out disturbing scenes. One such scenario was: The bad doll would shut the good doll in what I called 'the hot room' and gradually turn up the temperature. The good doll would become so uncomfortable, that she would have to strip out of her glam rock style outfit. She would cower in the corner of the hot room, naked, sweating and feeling helpless and embarrassed. The bad doll would look on in smug satisfaction, and I enjoyed playing both parts.

Nobody knew that I played these games in private, and I felt embarrassed and confused about them, but couldn't help myself. They came to me naturally, and I felt good and bad simultaneously. Perhaps I was acting out the emotions and lack of control that I felt regarding my childhood friendships? Whatever the reason, I was already developing an unhealthy interest in domination and submission.

I heard my parents arguing now and again. I remember I once awoke to shouting and I could hear Dad telling Mum she had to take her wedding ring off. My dad could be lovely, but sometimes he would just be mean for the sake of it and I feared his temper. One time, I'd gone to bed, and I woke up needing the toilet. I got up quietly, went for a wee and climbed back into bed. Dad must have heard the toilet flush, and like lightening, he shot up the stairs. He flew into my bedroom, grabbed my arm and yanked me with force off the top bunk of my bed. He pulled up my nightie and slapped my leg. It really hurt. I was tiny, and he had hands like spades. The floor seemed a long way down to me, and I felt shaken and confused as to what I had done wrong. Eyes flashing with rage, Dad shouted that I had got out of bed on purpose to wind him up. Was he pissed off with Mum for something and using this as an excuse to get rid of his tension and rage? I'll never know. But that night he was scarily angry.

I couldn't predict when Dad would be in a bad mood and what would annoy him next about my behaviour. Just like my abusive boyfriends in later life, he would alternate between violence and compassion. He would do the sweetest things for me sometimes. He had a kids' chair re-upholstered for me as a surprise once. I loved it. Another time he shouted me from my bed and told me to come downstairs. Mum was out somewhere, and I assumed I was in trouble again, as was so often the case. When I got downstairs, he told me to come and sit next to him in my new chair. I did as he had instructed, and felt something hard underneath me. I stood up, looked down, and saw a Mars Bar on the seat! I felt so special because I could sit downstairs, watching grown-up programmes, eating a grown-up Mars Bar with my dad.

This inconsistent parenting style became very normal to me and helped to form my values in a much-skewed way. This was how a man should behave – just like my wonderful dad. My future choice of male partners reflected this, and I became attracted to some extremely aggressive and abusive Jekyll and Hyde characters in adulthood.

I enjoyed being around boys at school, and I wanted to be close to them all the time. On my first day at school when I was almost five, I latched onto a boy called Chrissy. I told him I loved him and sat behind him on the carpet, at story time, with my hands up his jumper, stroking his stomach. He would let me put my hands down his trousers even though I knew I shouldn't. I wanted to cuddle him all the time and make him love me. I pestered the poor little lad to death and chased him in the playground at break times. He eventually grew fed up with it, and hit me in the face, telling me to leave him alone. I was heartbroken. Couldn't he see that I loved him? I followed a similar pattern with boys the whole way through primary school, and the more they ignored and rejected me – the more I wanted to be around them. Unavailable men – the story of my sodding life.

We moved house when I was nearly eight years old and went to live in another house on a bigger estate. I was glad to get away from Sadie and the other kids in the area, and I loved my new school. I didn't get bullied there; and I found the best friend in the world, Louise. She lived across the road from me, so we would walk to school together. She was a skinny, petite lass with orange freckles, bright ginger, bobbed hair, and a big smile that could melt ice-pops. We're still best friends now, although our lives have turned out very differently.

CHAPTER 2

20 years BC (Before Corruption)

We were seen as the scrubbers[4] of the street, as everyone else there had bought their council houses. The neighbours hated us because our house reeked of animals, our lawn resembled a jungle, our cats were always shitting in their gardens, and I looked like a street urchin in my second-hand, ill-matched clothes. Have you ever seen the TV series, Shameless?[5] Well, if you can imagine that, then you're close to visualising our family. The house looked all right at first, and morphed over the passing years into a place that even a tramp might turn his nose up at. Mum had spent ages proudly decorating my bedroom with trendy pink and grey striped wallpaper, and matching curtains. As the years wore on, my bed had seen better days and eventually had to be propped up at one side with old Smash Hits and Jackie Christmas annuals. When they finally gave way, there was nothing for it, other than to remove the base. I slept on a spiky mattress on the floor for a few years, until Mum and Dad could afford to buy me a new bed.

Mum was cool, and revelled in being called that by my mates. They all wanted a mum like mine. She used to walk me up to school in the mornings, in her sprayed-on jeans and a t-shirt that had the slogan: 'Don't walk on the grass, smoke it' emblazoned across the

---

[4] Scruffy, unclean, unkempt. Usually as a result of poverty.

[5] A TV comedy sitcom about skint, dysfunctional families who live on a fictional council estate on the outskirts of Manchester.

front. Her hair was a wild mishmash of pink, green, purple and orange, and she stood out a bloody mile in contrast to the other parents. We attracted lots of stares, and Mum would grin back, smugly and sarcastically. She liked the attention, and said she didn't care what those boring sods thought when they were looking down on her. She couldn't bear to be seen as ordinary.

Mum would playfully smack my dad's bum, and call him 'Big Boy'. Whatever that meant, I hadn't a clue. He would raise his eyebrows twice in quick succession, conveying his best version of come-to-bed eyes. She would ambush him in the hallway, as he was en route to the kitchen, and they would wrap themselves around each other, their tongues hungrily intertwining. I watched with interest, although slightly embarrassed by their display. French kissing. I was learning fast. The porn mags littered about inside Dad's perpetually open wardrobe helped me to understand a little more; along with the Sunday Sport[6] lovelies who graced the pages of the newspapers scattered next to the toilet. I had never known that it was possible to eat a banana in so many ways, and it was a shame that I had to wipe my arse on the fruit in question. We often ran out of toilet paper. Mum would buy a pack of four rolls, and when they ran out, that was it. Like a clothing sale, it was a 'when it's gone, it's gone' situation. We would then have no choice but to resort to using torn-off squares of the tabloids. How ironic that I would one day work topless for these newspapers. I never managed to get a photo with a banana, though. # *Life goals.*

Mum oozed sex appeal from every orifice. In one of our family photograph albums, she had proudly displayed an image of herself posing provocatively in a sexy playsuit. Underneath was the caption,

---

[6] A British newspaper, containing very little news, and an abundance of tits.

written neatly in Biro: "Me pretending to be a page three girl."[7] I didn't know what that meant, but she looked glamorous and happy with her bright, beaming smile and seductive facial expression. I didn't know what one was, but I knew there and then that I wanted to be a page three girl too. Yes, when I grew up, I would be just like Mum in that photo!

In the summer when I was ten years old, I would dress into my denim shorts and a childish, age-appropriate sailor-style t-shirt that my gran had bought for me. I would hoist the shoulders back to reveal my belly button, fashioning it to look as age-inappropriate as possible! I would then parade around on our street, thinking I looked sexy. I would instruct Louise to stand still on the pavement, whilst I walked away from her as provocatively as I could manage for my age.

"Do I look sexy?"

"Yeah; but I think you need to wiggle your bum a bit more."

I would do it again and again until I felt satisfied that I had perfected this art.

"Yeah, that's it! That's a proper sexy walk!"

And with that, we would go back to playing Tig.[8]

In the evenings after tea, Louise and I would spend our time climbing trees, building dens in the woods from old tyres and wooden pallets, and nicking trolleys from Tesco in town. On the occasions I slept over at her house, I would try to climb into bed with her and cuddle my body up close to hers. Whenever I would go over the road to call for her, to ask her to come out and play, I would greet her with a kiss on the lips. This was hugely inappropriate, and

---

[7] The Sun newspaper's regular team of topless models, who would always appear on the third page.
[8] A childhood game of chase.

she eventually told me politely to knock it off. The rejection stung. But not half as much as Vicky's fingernails, three years before.

Vicky lived up the road from Louise and me. She was a scruffy-looking ten-year-old girl who lived on the estate with her equally scruffy-looking mum. Vicky's mum used to swan around the estate thinking she was the bees knees because she was the manageress at Poundstretcher in town, but she'd recently been sacked for being caught being a bit light fingered with the stock. Subsequently, she had fallen on hard times and no other places would take her on. Everyone on the estate knew that they were poor, and took pity on them, pretending that they didn't know that Vicky's mum used to pocket the money she collected door to door for 'charity'. Vicky used to enjoy playing with her mum's make-up; and her ultra-long, unkempt nails were painted a garish, much-too-old-for-a-kid red. Most parents on our street spent their Friday nights at the local working men's club, but my parents weren't big drinkers, as they couldn't afford to go to the pubs. Thankfully, they were also of the opinion that alcohol caused many a problem in society. Dad said if he wanted a nice cold beer, he'd bloody well have it at home, thank you very much. The price of a pint was extortionate these days, and anyway, you couldn't have a minute's peace with druggies coming in and out every two seconds, trying to sell bags of meat and food processors they'd got from the back of a lorry. I was glad that my parents weren't pub parents, and only really went out on New Year's Eve, when they would have fun creating unique fancy-dress costumes.

Mum had recently taken to hanging around at Vicky's house, putting the world to rights over copious cuppas and millions of cigarettes. One night, Mum and Vicky's mum had a rare night out at the local pubs, and I slept over at their house. The 'babysitters' were the local teenage tearaways, and they took over the house like maggots on a five-day-old carcass. There were loads of them. Even getting to the bathroom was like auditioning for The Krypton Factor[9]. They lined the staircase, fingers and tongues everywhere, covering each other's necks in love bites. Duran Duran's latest album was blaring out from a ghetto blaster, and half-empty bottles of booze were dotted about the floor. It was an intimidating sight for a seven-year-old, I can tell you. Vicky and I were excited as we were allowed to sleep in her mum's double bed. There was a TV in the bedroom and we felt grown-up, watching post-watershed programmes. Vicky lay next to me, wearing a little, girlish cotton nightie.

"Can I tell you a story?" she asked.

Not really paying attention, as I was watching the TV and feeling rather sleepy, I replied, "Yeah, okay."

"Well, one day, I was walking down the snicket (an alleyway near our home) and a man came up to me and asked me if he could show me something."

"Oh?"

"Can I show you what he did next?"

"Yeah."

And with that, she reached over, put her hand under my nightie, and slid a finger into my vagina.

I sucked in my breath in shock. I hadn't been expecting this, and the pain was immense. I could feel the sharp edge of her scraggy nail

---

[9] A shit, yet strangely compelling eighties TV programme, which featured adult contestants in shit tracksuits, clambering over even shitter obstacle courses.

scratching my insides, as pain shot through me. I laid rooted to the spot, willing my body to move, so I could shuffle away from her. I couldn't. She was three years older than me, and I was too scared to tell her to stop. It lasted for a split second and was over before I could register in my young mind what had just happened. Vicky pulled her hand away and sat up beside me.

"Can I lay on top of you?"

"Y… yeah, I suppose."

She quickly pulled her nightie over her head and threw it on the floor. Then she rolled up my nightie from the bottom, so it exposed my naked body, and climbed on top of me. I felt her warm skin against mine, and I felt like I was being crushed under her weight. The breath had been squeezed from my body, and the screams to shout at her to get off me were lodged in my throat. I just lay there, not comprehending what was going on. Vicky wriggled about on top of me for about ten seconds, before climbing off and retrieving her nightie from the floor. She dressed, and lay back down, pulling the duvet back up to her neck. Turning to look at me matter-of-factly, she said, "That's what sex is."

Well, that meant absolutely nothing to me. I was too young to understand. I knew that in the eyes of society, being naked together was wrong, but that was about it. We carried on watching TV for a while and fell asleep. I must have blocked the memory out, because I never thought of it again until decades later.

One morning when I was thirty-three, I awoke to see particles of this memory coursing through my mind. It came in staggered flashes, bit by bit. I relived the memory again and again; for about half an hour; until all the jumbled pieces came together to form one event. My heart raced; I couldn't catch my breath, and my head felt light. I had remembered it all. My first thought as I lay in bed, with this seemingly new information was, *Oh God. This kid was mirroring something that must have happened to her!* I didn't know this to be true, but it made me wonder, and the thought deeply disturbed me. Vicky wasn't a bad kid. She was my friend and wasn't trying to hurt me. She was just showing me something she had learned. Was it something that someone had shown to her prior to this incident?

My second thought was, *Why the Hell did Mum leave me there that night, with all the teenage idiots?* It wasn't the teenagers who had hurt me, though. It was an ordinary, sweet, ten-year-old little girl. Mum couldn't have foreseen that any more than I could have. We weren't two curious children playing at being doctors and nurses – this had felt different. Did it explain why from around that age I had displayed behaviours that were inappropriate and sexualised, towards my unsuspecting pre-pubescent female friends? The mysterious factor was that I hadn't consciously remembered the experience with Vicky until I was in my thirties; but my subconscious had. The brain sure is one complex organ.

CHAPTER 3

Hard-up

Around the same time that I discovered Dad's porn mag stash, I started to draw strange pictures. I would lie in bed, with the pad of coloured art paper that Mum had nicked for me from the offices she cleaned on an evening, carefully drawing with a black felt pen. I would draw pictures of naked women spread-eagled across the page. They would have shackles around their necks, wrists, and ankles; with chains attached. The chains would disappear off each corner of the paper. I would pay attention to details such as pubic hair and nipples; and would admire my work, proudly. Afterward, the realisation of what I had just drawn would hit me, and guilt and self-disgust would overcome me. I would screw the paper into tight balls and hide them at the back of my bedside cupboard. I didn't have a clue why I was doing these things, because I was too young to have sexual feelings, or understand what they were. I guess that made it all the more confusing to me; thus, the guilt. Pleasure, shame, pleasure, shame.

The mattress factory boss had recently made Dad redundant, and so far, he hadn't found a new job. Of course, he blamed this on the small number of Polish immigrants in the area. My parents squandered much of their benefits and Mum's meagre wages on drum kit paraphernalia, hair extensions, and other necessities they needed to keep their too-cool-for-school status. The benefits entitled us to free school meals and uniforms though, so in that sense, we never went without. Now, I can sympathise with what it must have been like in most working-class areas around that time. My parents were barely adults themselves, and this was only just the start of the nineties. Jobs were scarce, and it was bloody tough for them.

Mum took me to the local Town Hall one morning, to pick up some brand-new clothes which a few local boutiques had donated. We stood in a long queue that spilled out down the big stone steps and onto the pavement. Mum clutched her numbered ticket tightly while we waited… and waited. I swear we were there for about seventy-six hours waiting for our turn, in that cold Edwardian building. After an eternity, and before we had reached the front of the queue, a man shouted out, "Bra! There's a spare training bra here! Anyone need a bra?"

Mum waved her ticket in the air frantically, pogo-ing up and down on the spot, and yelled back, "Yeah! Here! Here! My daughter needs one!"

Every head in the queue turned to look at my little crimson face.

Then I died. The end.

Why these freebies didn't extend to PE kits, I'll never know; but I wished they had. I didn't have fashionable branded trainers, as they cost a fortune back then. That, I understood. I'm now a parent and I sometimes have a hard time kitting out my teenage son with all the latest gear too. Mum rectified this little problem by picking me up a pair of white Adidas trainers, with orange stripes down the sides, from our local Help the Aged charity shop. I nearly fainted when I saw them. *Actual Adidas trainers – yes!* They were no longer in the shops, but I could remember the kids in my school year wearing them a couple of years before, and that was good enough for me. I thanked Mum and skipped up the stairs to my room with them. I tried them on, and to my sorrow, realised that they were far too big. "Why so gloomy, kiddo?" you may ask. I was a size four and a half, and these were a bloody seven. They were so long that they curled upward at the toes. Partly because they were second-hand and a bit squashed, and partly because they were the wrong size. I couldn't wear them – I'd be a laughing stock. I looked like Sideshow Bob[10] from The Simpsons. Clown feet. *Gutted.*

To think that once upon a time, I could do jack-shit with balls. How things change, eh? I detested PE; but our teacher, Mr. Johnson – a small, skinny, Scottish man – was lovely. I got the feeling he knew of our money situation, and he took pity on me. He could have been a dick, but he wasn't, for which I'll be eternally grateful. I didn't dare upset Mum by telling her that the trainers were far too big for me, for fear of sounding ungrateful. I knew she sometimes got upset about not being able to provide for us, and I didn't want to worry her about money any more than she already did. I kept it to myself and decided that the solution would be to wear my Tote's Toasties socks instead of trainers. They had only just come out in the shops, and everyone who was anyone had a pair. Mine were black, and had little white teddy bear-shaped grips. The grips were sticky, so I knew that I wouldn't slip on the sports hall floor. At first, Mr. Johnson appeared slightly irritated with me when I declared apologetically that I'd forgotten my trainers. After three consecutive occasions, I think he sensed what was going on, and in pity, he let me do PE forevermore in just my socks. My peers didn't seem to notice, thank goodness. I had escaped unscathed.

I also didn't have the regulation white or blue T-shirt. However, I

---

[10] An amusing character with phenomenally large feet, from the TV programme 'The Simpsons'.

did have a fabulous heat-sensitive Global Hypercolor t-shirt that Gran had bought me for Christmas. The whole t-shirt was one colour; but when it became warm, the colour changed. Mine was sky blue. Not navy blue, the school colour, but it would do. I was pleased to have this t-shirt in my possession. They were dead stylish, and I needed all the help I could get in that department. Mine was a little too small. Well, it was the right size, really; but in those days it was cool to wear t-shirts two sizes too big. Anyway, it was an actual Global Hypercolor T-shirt, which counteracted the sizing issue. I was finally trendy. *Whoopee!* So, as I had no alternative, I thought I would wear it for PE class. I felt great, leaping over the vaulting horse and chucking balls around the echoey sports hall. I was carefree, and I was super-duper fashionable. I could conquer the world!

Not for long.

Out of nowhere, laughter filled the room. I soon realised it was directed at me. A sea of fingers pointed towards my torso. I stood still in the middle of the room and slowly looked down at my top half.

Oh. My. Actual. God. I had big white patches under my arms where I had been sweating. Not only that, but the whole outline of my bra had turned from blue to white! I was only twelve, and shy about my newly developing body, so you can imagine my horror. There goes that old friend of mine again – shame.

Well, after that incident, I didn't dare do PE again. Thankfully, a few girls had started their periods around that time, and I pretended I had too. Mine was a very long period and lasted about six months. God knows what Mr. Johnson must have thought. I've often wondered why he didn't ring the hospital to tell them I was slowly bleeding to death. Since then, I've shied away from competitive sports and now prefer solitary exercise. Work-out DVD, anyone?

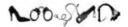

When I was still twelve, Mum and Dad had the crazy notion that we should escape our town and current financially strained lifestyle. They didn't want to carry on living on that estate anyway, they said. It was "full of nonces, crackheads and shirt-lifters, and being run into the ground since the Pakis had started moving in". Dad said that before we knew it, we'd be overrun by the bastards. My parents' answer to these growing societal problems was to up sticks and run away to somewhere in the British Isles. Full of good ideas, those two. Together, they decided that the most sensible thing to do would be to post our door key through the Council office's letterbox, with a note attached, explaining politely that they no longer required the Council's help, because they were ready to move onto pastures new.

Dear Council, go fuck yourselves!

So now we lived in a rented holiday chalet in the arse end of nowhere, with an outside toilet, on a tiny island with about eight houses. I had imagined it to be like the all-inclusive Benidorm holidays that I'd heard some of my more privileged school friends rave about. It was not. The 'fire station' was a cart, on which sat a fire extinguisher and a hose, and was towed along by car. The Post Office was a tiny shop, which was hardly ever manned. It sold stamps and yellowing old postcards, and that was all. We had a telephone box outside the chalet, which was a vintage A and B button one. I had never seen one of those before, and I haven't since. There was no school there. There was no anything there. I had to travel by boat to the boarding school on another island. I shit ye not. I would be away from my family for five days a week, and I didn't want to go.

I got bullied pretty badly at that school because I was from 'down south'. My accent was wrong, my shell suit[11] (which Mum had got from the catalogue and not paid off before we had scarpered) was the wrong colour – anything the girls in my dorm could come up with as an excuse to terrorise me. Mum, true to form, had bought a bin bag full of cheap, second-hand clothes to take with us; courtesy of an advert in the Free-Ads. To the islanders, it must have looked like a time machine had transported us from the past; and we had landed in the future. Mind you, the island itself looked like it had been stuck in a time warp – what with that weird telephone box. Maybe that was it – maybe the telephone box worked in the same way as in the film, Bill and Ted's Excellent Adventure.[12]

I had made one friend called Andy; but the girls used to hide my trainers so I couldn't go across the road to the boys' hostel to see him. Yes, I had progressed to owning trainers which actually fit me. 'Nicks'[13] pleather trainers. *Fail!* Soon Andy made new friends of his own and started similarly treating me – picking on me and making me look stupid in front of the other kids. Eventually, they initiated me, and one girl became my friend. We ended up wreaking havoc in the local area, picking on other people and making them miserable instead. It was kill-or-be-killed, and we relished the killing. I hated that school. We were only there for a few months before we came

[11] Fashionable, yet tasteless nineties tracksuits, made from shiny and highly flammable material. They rustled like a hundred crisp packets as one walked.
[12] Funny family film, starring Keanu Reeves. The telephone box in the film doubled up as a handy time machine.
[13] A cheap brand of PVC training shoes which only two types of parent bought their children – those who were poor and those who wanted to punish their children in the worst possible way.

back to live in our shitty home town, which seemed like paradise in comparison. Mum and Dad went begging to the Council for number 22 back. Can you believe they said yes?

Upon arrival back at home in our familiar old town, we wearily stepped out of the car and all the estate kids greeted us. It pleased them to see us, but I don't think their parents felt the same way. They swarmed around us excitedly, wondering why we were home. Questions were fired at me from all sides, and I felt strangely popular.

So, we were back home; and back to being skint. Friends donated some retro-looking furniture cast-offs, and we made the place look like our house again. We were probably in a worse situation now than before, because the council had removed all of our carpets. Mum and Dad seemed to be able to afford cigarettes, but not our daily milk delivery or the loan money they owed to the local Provident.[14] We were always having to hide behind the chairs in the living room when the milkman or the Provy woman came to collect their money.

When Mum and Dad were a few pence short for their fags, we would have to remove the sofa cushions and hunt for pennies that had fallen down the cracks between them. I would occasionally find a whole pound, which made me feel very rich. With this operation completed, Mum would send me down to the shop at the bottom of the road, with a note to give to the Shop Keeper:

---

[14] A loan company which charged high interest rates, and collected door-to-door. The loan money would last about two weeks if we were lucky, but took months to pay back in small instalments.

10 Regal Kingsize please. Can we owe you the 9p that we are short? Thanks.

Mum's signature would be scribbled underneath. Dad said he "couldn't stand Pakis", but said that the ones down the shop were alright as they never short-changed us. No matter what the race of the shopkeeper, it would have been difficult to shortchange us, as we were always getting stuff on the tick. Mum and Dad loved their ciggies. They were avid collectors of the Focus points cards that you got inside cigarette packets. They kept them in a big Tupperware tub in the kitchen cupboard, and once collected enough to order a brass carriage clock, which they proudly displayed on top of the gas fire in the living room. (The teak framed outset ones with the metal bars on the front, that heated up the room in 0-60 seconds. They go for a small fortune on eBay these days. Who knew?)

We didn't have a washing machine in those days, so Mum would pile my old baby buggy high with black bin bags filled with dirty washing. She would make the half-hour journey down to the launderette in town, with me running alongside her, trying to keep up. The trek back was Hell, as it was all uphill. Pushing a buggy full of wet washing was no mean feat, but Dad couldn't be arsed driving us there and back. We would arrive back home; me with achy legs and Mum dripping with sweat.

Mum loved a bargain, which was a good job because in those days we had to be frugal. She would collect as many Co-op dividend saver stamps as she could throughout the year, and at Christmas our fridge would resemble the fridges on Tom and Jerry cartoons that had wibbly-wobbly jellies inside, super-size joints of ham and perfectly shaped chicken drumsticks balancing precariously on the shelf edges.

Our fridge would be jam-packed with black forest gateau, trifles, vol-au-vents, and food fit for kings. Christmas dinner was like a scene straight out of Benefits Street reality TV series. Mum would serve us a banquet which covered the whole table – plates filled with the food brands that I'd only ever seen on television adverts before, which we wouldn't usually be able to afford.

The rest of the year, Mum would head down to Tesco with me in tow, at just the right time that the reduced items were being priced up. The deli counter there would be the last stop, where Mum would get a cheap bag of various meat trimmings for our beloved pooch, labelled as 'Dog bits'. We would come out of there laden with bags of goodies, which could last us for around four days after the expiry date. Even the dog would know he was in for a treat when he saw us walk through the door – carrier bags brimming with bright yellow labelled packets. He would sit there, wagging his tail in excitement. One day Mum was in the kitchen and I asked her what she was making for tea.

"Mixed meat pie, love."

"What kind of meat?"

"Oh, just a few different kinds."

I thought for a second. "Mum, it's not dog bits by any chance, is it?" Silence… "Mum? It's dog bits, isn't it?"

"No."

"It is though. It's dog bit pie, isn't it?"

"Yeah." And with that, we took one look at each other and burst out laughing. Mum knew she couldn't con a conner. I refused to eat it, but Dad, none the wiser, said it was the best pie he had ever tasted.

CHAPTER 4

Blow jobs and bad boys

At thirteen, I took an even bigger interest in boys. They seemed to be everywhere I went, and it felt like I was a kid in a big, sexy sweet shop. Mucking about in the park, across the road from home, I met a lad called Steve. He was almost seventeen, scruffy-looking and had his floppy jet-black hair parted in the middle. At school, we called this style 'Curtains' and only the coolest lads wore their hair like this. His looked like it hadn't been trimmed for ages, as it was two different lengths because his under-cut was growing out. Steve wore a much-too-big, grubby-looking, creased Adidas football training coat, scuffed trainers, and smelled of stale fag smoke from the roll-ups that were constantly hanging from his lips. He lived on a notorious local Council estate, was a bit of a bad boy, and I fancied him like mad. *Be still my beating heart!*

Steve and I had our first proper kiss in the snicket, whilst he was walking me home one evening. I had to be in for nine-thirty, and we stopped for a quick cuddle on the way. He pulled me towards him, and my heart nearly jumped out of my chest as I felt him slide his hand in the back pocket of my jeans. I stiffened with nerves but soon relaxed when his mouth met mine. *So, this is what all the fuss is about!* I now understood. I didn't care that his tongue tasted like an old man's pipe remnants, because it felt as though there was a party going on in my pants. We kissed and kissed, and before I knew it, nearly half an hour had whizzed by. The next thing I knew, I was being grabbed by the collar and marched home by my dad. *Oh, crap.*

"What the fuck were you doing?"

"J… J… Just kissing, Dad; honest! He's my boyfriend." And with that, I cried.

Mum also wasn't happy. Dad said he was from a gyppo (gypsy) family who were always out on the rob. He was too old for me; he was only after one thing; and besides, I was half an hour late. It was the first time I had ever been home after curfew in my life. They grounded me for a week. It was the longest week of my life. I wanted to obey them, but I couldn't. My teenage body was awash with hormones, and I thought I loved him. I was Steve's Juliet, and he was my Romeo. Nothing would keep us apart. I started to lie about where I was going. It was easy enough – or so I thought.

My first sexual experience was with Steve. I was painfully shy, but curious, and more than willing. I was scared stiff when I first touched his willy.

"Did I just toss you off?" I asked, shyly, as we lay together on my friend's sofa bed.

"Well, kind of. It was more like me shagging your hand." He shrugged nonchalantly.

Right then. That was all I needed to motivate me to do well. *This is a skill I must learn,* I reasoned. He would surely love me then. Steve was happy to assist, and a week later, I was a seasoned pro at mutual masturbation. No flies on me! Wanking was a skill that served me well throughout my life. It became a very useful tool in later years; although I would never have predicted that back then. I'm still a dab hand[15] at it now, if you must know.

Steve and I progressed no further regarding sexual stuff. I was still only thirteen; a hopeless romantic; and I just wasn't ready. I wanted to wait until I was sixteen before I lost my precious virginity. Then would come marriage, and we would live happily ever after. I had it all figured out. Misguided, but I still had a few principles. *No sex until sixteen, end of.*

Steve and I were only together for one month and nine days. I know this because I proudly counted the days, logging them in my diary. I thought of this as a long-term relationship, bless my little heart. He eventually got bored with me being grounded every time Mum and Dad discovered I'd been seeing him. Steve disappeared, back to the murky depths of his estate, never to be seen again. A week later I heard that he had found himself a new girlfriend – one who was older than I, and happy to have sex with him. *So, he didn't love me.* I chastised myself for being so immature and inexperienced. I wanted to be sexy, like Mum, and the women in Dad's magazines. I wanted boys to fight over me, to win my heart. I needed to hone my newfound skills… and hone them I bloody well did.

That year, I gave my first blow job in the six-week holidays from school, and I liked it. Not that the act aroused me, because it didn't at all. The pleasure I felt was from knowing I was good at it.

This was something I could excel at. Art and design, English lit, and BJs – I was top of the class at all three. Heck, if a (blow) job was worth doing, it was worth doing well.

The lad in question, Adam, was sixteen, piss-poor, and he lived up

---

[15] Very efficient and skilled.

the road from us. He was scruffy-looking, claimed that he was allergic to toothpaste, and his bedroom walls were covered in graffiti. Oh, and his widge[16] smelled like a pissy baby's nappy that had been dumped in a skip at the back of a fishmonger's... and left to decay because the refuse company was on a national holiday that week. That putrid smell of ammonia I now know to be none other than smegma. Lovely. I had nothing to go by, being inexperienced and all. I just assumed that all men's bits must be blessed with the same odd odour. It was nothing I couldn't live with. I probably smelled just as bad, seeing as I wore the same pair of tights all week for school.

Mum wasn't inclined to wash the full laundry basket of clothes regularly. It would just be select items we wore the most, and she would leave the rest. I even wore my school tights under my jeans in an evening, because I had no socks. After a quick dab on the gusset with Body Shop Dewberry perfume oil, I'd be good to go. Mum wasn't deliberately neglectful; she just didn't think. On the bright side, I was never cold in the winter. You should try it sometime – tights and jeans. You'll never catch a draught, that's for sure.

I didn't fancy Adam much; and I don't think he fancied me, either. We respected each other, and we got along well. He was a mate, and he was a good lad, with a similar upbringing to mine. His parents would go to the weekly darts and dominoes nights at the WMC, so Adam was left to mind the house, with him being older. This left us plenty of time to experiment with one-another's teenage bodies. There was no love, and no ties. It was the perfect way to learn – no distractions. Well, apart from seeing the following phrase stencilled in red spray-paint on his bedroom wall. It bobbed up and down in front of my eyes, in time with my head:

---

[16] Slang for penis. Short for the childish term, 'Widgey'.

A FRIEND WITH WEED IS A FRIEND INDEED

Yes, he was a massive pot-head, which explained why he couldn't even summon the energy to drag himself towards his toothbrush or the bath once a year. I'd love to reason that he pushed me into it, but he didn't. I did it because I had wanted to. I don't remember how I got into the situation where my head was under his grubby duvet. It just seemed like a natural progression.

The local bail hostel was a bit of a halfway house for those who had either not yet been to court for sentencing, or had completed a sentence and were being integrated back into society. The lads in there were a laugh and not what you'd expect for a bunch of crims. Most were still only teenagers themselves, around eighteen and nineteen years old. I dated a succession of hostel lads, as had probably been predestined. Nothing serious; just a few quick fumbles and stolen kisses before their curfew was up in the evenings. With each one, as soon as they realised I wasn't intending on letting them take my virginity, they would move onto one of my more liberated friends. We all had a fling with a hostel boy at one time or another. They never hurt us, luckily; although I heard on the grapevine that there were usually a few older, convicted paedophiles in there.

That winter I turned my attention to a lad at school, James. He was in the same English class as me, and we had to sit together. The first thing I noticed about him was that he smelled of Daz Automatic washing powder. In contrast to me, who probably smelled of dog piss, sweaty tights and old tab ends. I would sit there, trying to concentrate on Thomas Hardy's boring poetry, whilst slowly inhaling James' clean scent. He was tall, with wavy, auburn hair, hazel eyes, and goofy, almost translucent-looking teeth. Although he wasn't massively attractive, I fancied the pants off him. Unlike anyone else in my English class, he had a sense of humour. We were two mischievous outcasts in a room full of middle-class swots. Our teacher despaired of us, and we were always being thrown out of the room for bursting into fits of giggles. I began to spend a little more time in the mornings lacquering my hair flick so it stood as tall as possible, and slicking on as much clear mascara as my eyelashes would hold. I looked forward to Fridays when we would have English, and eventually, I plucked up the courage to pass James a note under the table.

I have to tell you that I think you smell gorgeous and you're funny, like me.
If you didn't have a girlfriend,
I would ask you out.

(What did I tell you about my manipulation skills?) I had just sealed my fate. James promptly got rid of fat Becky from another class and started going out with me instead. For the next year and a half, we were inseparable. He was a lovely natured lad, and after a month, I knew that I had fallen in love. Not puppy love – actual love. What I knew love to be at that age, anyway. Whoever says kids can't fall in love is so wrong. You will grow to love somebody you spend so much time with, no matter how young you are. James became like family to me, and my parents thought the sun shone out of his arse. He lived on a new-build estate in the same town as me; with his mum, Sandra. Sandra was a normal mum. She wore no make-up, lived in elasticated jeans and knitted, baggy jumpers and had a highlighted, shaggy perm. She had a calming vibe about her, but was nobody's fool. Sometimes I would just nip down to see her for a cup of coffee, one of her Benson and Hedges fags, and a natter.

Things quickly grew serious, and we experienced many firsts together. Sandra would go out on an evening to her Slimming World class at the local community centre, and we would shut ourselves in James' bedroom, still dressed in our school uniforms, playing the latest nineties chart music and snogging our way through every song. We would sit on his bed, facing each other, with my legs wrapped around his waist like a horny little lemur. The kissing gradually progressed into me being braless; then knickerless. After almost three months of dry humping each other half to death, inevitably, we would end up having sex. We discussed it like adults and decided on our plan of attack. We both wanted it to be a memorable and comfortable experience. And it was.

Mum was brilliant. She had always made it her mission to encourage me not to have unprotected sex and not get pregnant at sixteen, as she had with me. I confided in her that the relationship was getting serious and that I had found the boy I wanted to give my virginity to. She took me to the doctor's, and he put me on the contraceptive pill. The pill wouldn't work straight away, so we used condoms for our first time.

Two weeks later, off went Sandra to her weekly weigh-in. We put the 'Dance Zone '93' album on his cassette player, turned off the light, took off our school uniforms and climbed into bed. Soon we were kissing and touching each other and were more than ready. I passed James a packet containing a condom, and he disappeared into the bathroom to figure out how to put it on. Ten seconds later he returned, looking sheepish.

"What's wrong?"

"Erm, sorry, Sinead. I tried to put it on, but I came all over the toilet." *Oops.*

We were both embarrassed but laughed about it. After half an hour, we were ready to try again. This time everything went well, if a little clumsily.

"Erm, Sinead, would you just lie still and stop moving about so much, please?"

How embarrassing. From what I had seen on telly, couples who had sex kind of moved against each other. So, there I was, sort of thrusting away, and we couldn't get a rhythm going. Our hips kept banging against each other instead. James had obviously studied more porn than I had. *Must. Watch. More.* I did as he had asked, and tried to lay still, and hey presto! We were actually having real sex! We lost our virginity to each other, with Urban Cookie Collective – Feels Like Heaven, as our soundtrack. And Heaven, it was. The deed didn't last very long, and afterward, we lay naked in each other's arms; kissing and gazing into one another's eyes, as you do. It felt wonderful. I enjoyed the experience immensely, and I felt as though I had entered a new world – a loved-up super horny dream world. I couldn't wait to tell Louise and my friends at school. The second time was a bit of a letdown, but by the third go, we had mastered the art of novice teenage lovemaking. I still consider myself lucky that I didn't end up losing my virginity to a local dickhead, but to someone who was also a virgin and thought the world of me. I may have broken my promise to myself that I would wait until I was sixteen, but I didn't care. It was the right time – it just felt 'right'.

Sandra soon cottoned on to what was going on whenever she left the house. By day, we watched MTV and played Mario Kart downstairs, and the second Sandra went out, we legged it up to James' bedroom. Well, this one time, she came back early, as her class had been cancelled. Unbeknownst to us, she was pottering about in her bedroom, when James and I had just completed another mini sex marathon. He got out of bed, still with a stonking hard-on, and opened the door to go for a wee. He turned the corner to head to the bathroom, which was visible from Sandra's bedroom. All she saw was James coming around the corner, penis first, and she let out an almighty scream. The sight of her lovely teenage first-born's erect cock had frightened the living daylights out of her. She chased him angrily back into the bedroom, muttering expletives. Now we were in trouble. *Oops!*

"And don't you two think I don't know what's been going on under my roof, either! Anyone'd think you were going for an Oscar, Sinead, with your theatrical moaning!"

Oh, God.

When Sandra had calmed down, she called us downstairs. She passed us each a freshly made cup of coffee, and started giggling uncontrollably.

"You frightened me to bloomin' death, you daft sod!" she said to James, and whacked him playfully on the arm. She was all right, Sandra… for a mum.

I wanted to experience everything I had read about in More! Magazine, and penned a wish list. It went something like this:

Sexual stuff I want to try:

Be licked out

Have sex standing up

Do it doggy style

Me on top of you

Anal sex

I coyly handed my list to James, and we agreed to try out these new things. Mum had lent me a book called The Story of O, and it was very kinky. (It's one of the most sexually explicit, arguably feminist books ever written; and by a woman too.) It was all about sadomasochism and Dom/Sub relationships. Some acts on my list were detailed in the book, and I fancied having a go at them. We set about trying them out, one by one.

"What's the last one on your list?" James asked me, struggling to read my writing.

I grabbed the paper out of his hand and realised that the word 'anal' looked like 'and', because the 'l' was too close to the 'a'.

"What do you think it says?" I replied, irritably.

"Erm… 'And sex'?"

"No, stupid!"

"What then?"

Well, I couldn't bring myself to answer him. My cheeks flushed bright red, and I looked away. It took me ages to admit what it had said. I wondered if it was a bit too weird for him, but I needn't have worried. That weekend, we pitched a tent (in more ways than one) in James' back garden. Sandra wanted to keep an eye on us, and wouldn't let us camp in a nearby field. I can't think why she didn't trust us, can you? We put the tent up, and clambered inside, taking with us a big tub of Vaseline[17] that we'd bought from the local bargain shop. Actually, it wasn't even Vaseline. It was Vaseline knock-off that just said Petroleum Jelly in big, pink lettering on the label, with an orange 50p pricing gun sticker. Classy. I'll leave the rest to your imagination, if you're that way inclined.

During my relationship with James, life at home turned stagnant. Dad spent more and more time in the back room with the door locked from the inside, and Mum had swapped her satin nighties for a fleece onesie that zipped up to the neck. The kisses in the kitchen stopped, and Mum started disappearing to the shops for extended periods. Dad had found part-time work as a courier by this point. When he wasn't shutting himself in the back room, he would be out on jobs.

Nothing to see, here!

---

[17] A long-established, reputable brand of skincare products, best known for their tubs of quality petroleum jelly.

CHAPTER 5

Mucky buggers

Mum and Dad were constantly at each other's throats, and the vibe at home was dismal. Speaking of vibes, there was a massive metaphorical one in the room one night when I arrived home. The elephant in the room was none other than a vibrator. I walked in, to discover my parents having one of their usual heated discussions. I sighed and sat down on the sofa, trying to block out their voices, straining to hear the answers on The Price is Right, the gameshow that was on the television, playing away to itself. No such luck. Dad picked up the remote and switched the telly off, irritably.

"Well, you don't want to have sex with me, do you?" he was saying to Mum. He then turned to me and reiterated, "She doesn't want to have sex with me anymore, Sinead."

I'd like to say that I felt awkward, due to the inappropriate content of the adult discussion that I had inadvertently found myself involved in. I didn't. This was quite a common thing, mediating for my parents when they clashed about personal issues.

"And can you help me understand why there are ten tonnes of plastic in the drawer under her side of the bed?"

Well, I had been reading More! magazine[18] for a few years by then, and not only was the 'Position of the fortnight' informative, but so

---

[18] A popular magazine aimed at over-eighteen-year-old young women, mostly bought by early teens behind their parents' backs.

was the problem page. I knew all about vibrators and dildos; although I didn't own any. I was fifteen and although I had more sexual knowledge than someone my age should have, I hadn't quite reached the sex toy stage yet. Not that I could've afforded one, anyway, with my four quid a week pocket money.

"Well, Dad… dildos kind of touch all the sides, and that's why most of them have so much girth. It's more about the pressure than the size. I'm sure Mum's not using them because she prefers them to you."

Mum nodded in agreement. Dad appeared placated by this explanation. I had impressed myself, realising I knew more than he did, and that I had advised him maturely. I was a fifteen-year-old love doctor. Now *that* was fucked up.

James and I split up that year, just before Christmas. I had snogged his best friend, and he had followed suit and done the same with a girl from the year below. It had been inevitable. We were too young for a serious relationship and I guess we needed to experience the delights of new flesh.

My GCSE exams came and went, and my grades were surprisingly okay. I got Bs and Cs, which was enough for me to get into college. I had expected to achieve As for both English and Art, which I was perfectly capable of. I had been so preoccupied with my break-up with James and the problems at home that I had lost my mojo. Instead of revising and completing my coursework, I had been smoking weed every night with my older friends who lived in a scruffy flat in town. I left school and didn't have a clue what career path I wanted to take. I knew I didn't want to be a nurse, a vet, a teacher or anything that the school careers service had tried to steer me towards. They didn't have any advice for someone who dreamed of being a model.

At sixteen I told Dad that I wanted to be a page-three girl. I wanted to know if I would have his support. Although he would rather that I aspired to be a solicitor or a social worker, he said that he would be happy as long as I was happy. He stipulated that with me being under eighteen, he would insist on accompanying me to shoots so I wouldn't be exploited. Not to be there whilst I was shooting, just as a chaperon and to meet the photographers and crew. Dad knew I was headstrong and would do whatever I wanted, so this was his way of making sure I stayed safe. However, I had no idea where to begin, and felt daunted at the prospect of taking the steps to make this ambition come true. I bummed about at home for a year, giving up on what seemed like a pipe-dream, and instead took up Beauty Therapy. Not because it interested me, but because it was what Louise was doing. I thought it would be fun if we worked together, and for a while it was, until I grew bored.

Just before my seventeenth birthday, I started dating Edward. He had been in a few classes with me at school, and I had never looked twice at him. He was chubby, with waist-length dyed black hair, and not the most attractive guy. He looked a bit girly, in all honesty. He was now, however, in a band; so that gave him a certain amount of kudos. Edward had always been a good school student, and had seemed pretty placid. He had a great sense of humour, and everyone liked him. He was slightly arrogant, perhaps, and a little snobbish, but an alright guy. I took his virginity after three days, and within a month he was a smoker. I was quickly corrupting him, and his mum loathed me for it. She would rifle through his pockets, discover empty cigarette and condom packets, and interrogate him in front of me.

Edward's mum, Liz, was a middle class wannabe who put on a full face of Chanel foundation just to put the bins out. The exact opposite of down-to-earth Sandra, Liz was in her early fifties, with plum coloured, American newsreader-style barrel brushed hair. To complete the image, she boasted an over-exaggerated Queen's English accent, as plummy as her hair colour. Like a cartoon superhero, Liz's physical form was an inverted triangle shape. Her small feet and disproportionately broad shoulders were further accentuated by the shoulder pads sewn into her pink blazer. I would liken her stature to the Honey Monster if she was more friendly looking and not so damned intimidating, but there was nothing cuddly about Liz. She was basically a komodo dragon in a skirt-suit.

Liz was an out-and-out stereotype, driving a top spec Saab, distributing catalogues for Avon, Betterware, and every new pyramid scheme going. She couldn't resist an opportunity to talk about the many teams she had under her, and the thousands in commission she'd earned over the years. A self-confessed sun worshipper, Liz had dehydrated, leathery skin from years of sunbed sessions and the many free holidays to Spain for being a top rep. Queen Liz really believed she was a cut above the rest. She never tired of trying to recruit me. If I wore a longer skirt and presented myself in a more sophisticated manner, my gift of the gab would take me far, she said. I should develop my skill of not knowing when to shut my mouth, by adapting it for working in sales. It might give me better prospects in life than what fate usually awaited girls who hailed from rough estates.

I stood my ground and declined Liz's cult leader coercion tactics. I knew my destiny wasn't to sell lazy-Susans, three in one egg slicers, or any other time saving culinary devices. Later in life, I tried my hand at working with more traditional kitchen implements - although I opted to use them in a more imaginative way than their intended purpose.

Edward's dad was a pale, thin, ginger moustached chap who was a bundle of nerves. I got the impression he did what he was told for a quiet life - a true submissive. As soon as Liz marched sternly and authoritatively through the door from work, he would stand to attention and carry her slippers like a faithful dog.

Speaking of dogs, the family had a senile and blind corgi (only royal breeds would do), called Pearl. She spent her days wandering from room to room with her head down, in a permanent state of confusion. On one of Liz's regular interrogation sessions, Pearl moseyed into the dining room like a fart in a trance. She plodded past Edward and I, walking head first into Liz's ornate vase, knocking a dried pampas grass arrangement on her expensive tapestry rug. Startled, Pearl shook her head, and doddered slowly back out of the room in the same manner in which she had entered.

Having not yet developed a sense of empathy by that age, I found this deeply amusing. As much as I tried to contain it, I couldn't keep my shoulders from shaking with the inward mirth I was nearly bursting with. No wonder Queen Lizzie thought I was "rough as a bear's arse with no decorum". Mid-sentence, she stopped chastising Edward and turned her head like an android. Her steely gaze was now focusing wholly on me. I swear that look could turn teenagers to stone. I half expected red laser beams to shoot from her eyeballs. Folding her arms over her buxom chest, she scowled at me with lips pursed like the hole in the top of a Wet Ones[19] dispenser tub. By this time, I was panicking like I'd just got my finger stuck in one. Liz's

[19] Wet Ones was an eighties brand of wet wipes, contained in a cylindrical tube, with a toothed dispensary hole. To prevent the exposed top wipe from drying out, you had to push it back in through the teeth. The pure panic of getting your finger stuck in the tub's top is unrivalled to this day. The more you pulled, the more the plastic teeth tightened their grip. Pure childhood trauma.

nostrils flared and her cheeks grew redder and redder until they reached an alarming puce colour. I felt a sense of foreboding as I scrunched up my face to prepare for the inevitable eruption.

"You! You've been nothing but trouble since you first showed your face here! Get out of my house, you common whore!"

She shooed me out the door like you would a fly, with Edward still standing behind her, looking on in mortification. With that, I was banished from the palace for a short while.

Edward and I had a lot of fun together, and when I wasn't travelling about with him from gig to gig like a faithful groupie, I would be getting drunk with him on cheap cider and getting up to no good. We were a cool couple, and I loved the attention we got when we were out on the town, dressed in vintage shop sixties clothes. He would pick me up on his scooter, we would go to student nights where Northern Soul and Motown were played, and dance the night away. There was this effeminate side to Edward, though. He was quite vain for someone who wasn't very good looking. Every morning after getting dressed, he would dust his dear mum's Boots No.7[20] bronzing powder all over his face with her old blusher brush which had splayed out bristles and had seen better days. Like magic, he had an enviable tan. Though, if the powder hadn't been so shimmery, it may have looked a lot less obvious.

After dousing himself in a knock-off version of Joop! Chavtershave and dressing in an ill-fitting Ben Sherman shirt, Edward and I would head into town, looking quite the stylish couple. On one such occasion, Edward got a bit carried away with the bronzer, emerging from the bathroom with a perfect set of chiselled, gleaming

---

[20] A popular range of cosmetics for the over-thirties, sold in the British chain of Boots the Chemist's shops.

cheekbones that were likely visible from space. He was impressively ahead of his time, as this was at least twenty years before contouring became a trend. I was too polite to say anything, as I knew it wasn't deliberate and I didn't want to embarrass him. We headed out; me pretending I hadn't noticed and hoping the bronzer may fade a bit.

So, there I was, shuffling awkwardly down the street with my head lowered, hand in hand with Ziggy fucking Stardust. Out of nowhere, we heard the sudden, intimidating sound of a holey exhaust, and turned to see a lad in a souped up Vauxhall Nova driving slowly at the side of us, as though kerb crawling for hookers. He turned his baseball capped head to stare at us, brows knitted, keeping his eleven o'clock gangster grip firmly on the steering wheel. Feeling vulnerable and threatened, Edward and I averted our eyes, stiffened up, and quickened our pace. We clasped our hands tightly together and tried to ignore the unwanted attention. The menacing driver momentarily broke out of his statement backwards lean, to stick his head out of the window and yell at us.

"Fucking lesbians!"

Then he zoomed off as quickly as he had appeared, leaving a cloud of smoke billowing behind him.

Splendid.

Because we both lived at home, it wasn't easy for me and Edward to have sex undetected. We would book cheap, local hotels instead, and take a lot of alcohol with us. One such time, vain as always, Edward was preening himself in the mirror as usual, when he said, "I bet I would look good as a girl, y'know."

I agreed that he probably would. He would make a better woman than he did a man, anyway. And so began the first of many make-up applications on men.

With the same concentration and care that I would tart up my childhood Girl's World styling head, I applied Edward's war-paint. I really went to town on him; feathery false eyelashes, red lipstick - the whole shebang. I tied his long hair into a ponytail and helped to dress him in my lingerie, silver lurex mini-dress and fake leopard fur coat. My strappy sandals were way too small, but Edward somehow squeezed his feet inside. His toes splayed outward, over the edge of the soles. This gave his feet a somewhat deformed appearance, but he was more than happy with the transformation. I studied Edward with my eyes, and a life-sized doll stared back at me. Well, this was certainly different! With an over-accentuated pout, he posed in the full-length mirror.

"God, I actually want to fuck myself."

I wanted to fuck him too. It wasn't because he looked like a woman; it was more to do with the risk factor. It felt deliciously dark; and wrong. The drunker we became, the more we screwed. This was fun!

As with all good things, once you've experienced them a few times, the buzz isn't enough. We just had to push it further, didn't we? I dressed him up a few times, and the last time I did, we ventured out. We must have been a very odd sight, had anyone seen us. We nervously wandered the streets, him wearing my fake fur coat and heels, and me not looking half as glamorous. As it was around half past ten at night on a weekday evening, the streets were practically empty. All of a sudden, we spotted a lad from our old school, staggering out of a pub doorway. He would surely recognise both of us. Dame Edna[21] and I turned on our heels (literally!), and

---

[21] An annoying Australian TV personality who dressed in drag, was embarrassingly un-funny and over-used the word 'possums'.

hot-footed it back home. That experience didn't do it for me, and I wasn't keen to repeat it!

At eighteen, Edward and I moved in together in a neighbouring town. We lived in a tiny back-to-back house meant for university students. We didn't care that we only had two comfy chairs in the living room. We treated ourselves to a rented video player, which cost £7.50 a month, and budgeted £10 a week each for cheap frozen food. We may have been skint, but we were together and in love. Edward was at university now, and I had just started college. I had left the Beauty Therapy training academy and began studying towards English and Sociology A-levels instead. We both had part-time jobs, so we would be able to get by reasonably well. We were two buses away from our parents' houses, and that suited me just fine. Mum cried when I left home, but I was happy to escape the trappings of our estate. Edward missed his mum and her Marks and Spencer's home-cooked dinners, in contrast to our packets of super noodles, micro chips and spaghetti hoops. Also the benefit of her ironing his shirts, in contrast to me, who point-blank refused. At eighteen, I was fiercely independent. Mummy's boy Edward wasn't my husband, and I wouldn't be ironing his bloody shirts. I didn't even iron my own, so sod that for a game of soldiers! Give me an independent, assertive man, any day… but one who submits at the right time.

Edward soon got nasty with me. Although he was arrogant, overconfident and mistakenly thought of himself as a bit of a pretty boy, he was extremely insecure. He never hit me or did anything physically aggressive, but he excelled at dishing out the verbal stuff. He couldn't stand the fact that he had been a virgin when we had met, and I hadn't. Although I had always been loyal and faithful to him, he would call me names, like 'Slag'. Not surprisingly, this label which is used to describe a woman who enjoys casual sex, is now one of my pet hates. My self-esteem gradually dwindled, and I believed that I wasn't good enough for him. In reality, he was a jumped-up little prick, and not good enough for me.

I missed being able to see my old friends in an evening, and we both felt isolated. Edward and I spent our evenings getting blind drunk, wandering to the local shop to rent various porn videos, and having debauched weekends at home. The more controlled and unhappy I became, the more dominant and controlling I grew when we had sex; probably to balance out the dynamics. Edward worked at a local pub as a glass collector, and because he was also good at art he got the job of sign writing the cocktail special offers on the blackboards. He would arrive home with these big, fat chalk pens in his pocket. When we got drunk, I would instruct him to bend over on all fours, and I would violate him with one. He loved this and would ask me to do it again and again.

I suppose one thing led to another. Sometimes I would tie him up and watch him squirm as I subjected him to painful tests, such as dripping hot candle wax onto his naked torso. Then we would have what I considered back then to be mind-blowing sex. I even ordered him to bark like a dog for me on one occasion. He did it, too. It was a power trip for me, as he was often so verbally horrible to me. It was like an act of kinky revenge. Edward thoroughly enjoyed these games. He later progressed to being very, erm, accommodating with that manky old blusher brush of his mum's. I'd have loved to have seen her holier-than-thou, self-righteous face turn pale with shock, had she found out.

After a few big arguments (the last one being when I slammed the door and set off marching down the street to catch my bus to work, with Edward running behind me in just his Y-fronts), we called it a day and moved back to our parents'. Cohabiting had only lasted nine months, and it had been a disaster from start to finish.

Mum was happy to see me, and I felt comforted being back in my bedroom at home. I guess you don't know what you've got 'til it's gone. My parents even bought me a new bed, so I no longer had to sleep on a mattress on the floor. It was good to be back in my home town, but Edward and I didn't get along any better, despite not living in each other's pockets all the time.

FHM magazine had just started publication and was hugely popular with teenage boys and grown men alike. I made no secret about my ambition to model for men's magazines, much to Edward's disapproval. Every month, without fail, He would buy FHM, and would stick the centrefold posters on his bedroom wall. I would fantasise about being one of their poster girls, but Edward said that he didn't want other men seeing his girlfriend half-naked. I just wanted him to look at me in the same way he viewed these beautiful models. I told him about my wanting to be a page-three girl when I had been sixteen. He sneered and said I would have had no chance because my boobs weren't even near perfect enough. I even won a modelling contract with a local agency, after coming second in a beauty contest when we went to Butlins with my parents in the summer holidays. Nothing ever came of it, because Edward threatened to dump me if I accepted the contract. In later years, I appeared in one of the FHM pocket calendars and one of their bonus pull-out booklets. I always did like a challenge.

Edward and I broke up after two and a half years together. He went on a uni trip to Belgium and cheated on me with a classmate whilst he was there. So, it didn't matter how sexy and liberated I was; I concluded that I just hadn't been good enough for him. The split upset me for about a week, and that was all. I had surprised myself, to be honest. I thought I had loved him, and that if we parted company, I would never get over him. I didn't wallow, and I didn't miss him all that much. The reason I didn't give a damn was because a week after our parting, I discovered Ecstasy, and I was, well… ecstatic.

I soon forgot about Effeminate Edward, and my home life now took a back seat. My parents didn't bother me, and I didn't bother them. I was nineteen years old, and I had landed slap-bang in the heart of the back end of the nineties club scene. It was one of the best times of my entire life. I hung around with the down-and-out local outcasts, and I felt loved. We were a group of about twenty, and our ages ranged from fifteen to thirty. We had all had problems, big and small; but came together to form a watertight little family. Ecstasy made me feel pure, inside and out. I was a beautiful spirit, inside a beautiful body, with beautiful friends and a beautiful life. I finally felt like a whole being. A perfect person with no flaws, accepted by all, and rejected by no one. Everyone in the club was peaceful; I witnessed no fighting, as opposed to the alcohol-fuelled fights I had seen in our town centre, on payday night.

Nobody was drunk or disorderly, and everybody was happy and friendly. My insecurities vanished once I was inside our favourite nightclub. The other bonus was that I could dance. I could dance for six hours without stopping, and it felt like I could dance better than anyone on the planet. I was young; I was carefree; and the world was my oyster – until the Sunday come-down, that is. The inevitable down, which followed the up, was just something that had to be dealt with. They went hand in hand. Es were a breeze to come down from;

much less painful than an alcohol-induced hangover. No pounding headache – just tired, fuzzy, floppy lethargy. Our group also took a bit of Speed at the same time to increase our energy on the dancefloor, though. Amphetamine psychosis was a vicious monster. The following day I couldn't eat, I couldn't sleep, and I was full of self-loathing. It helped that all my friends were also feeling the same way; so we were a source of comfort to each other. I would work hard during the week, at my new job in a local newsagent's shop, willing Saturday night to hurry up and arrive. Then I would do it all again. This pattern would repeat for two years. I was the happiest I had ever been. The dance floor was my stage, and I felt invincible.

I had a few short flings and brief encounters with guys from the club, but nothing serious. Everyone just wanted one thing really, and that was to dance. Both sexes respected each other, and it was as though gender differences didn't exist. Boys would kiss boys ("Just for the laugh," of course. Yeah, right), girls would kiss girls, and boys and girls would kiss each other, if the fancy took them. The difference between that situation and normal life, was that nobody felt particularly horny; it was just a way of saying, "You're my friend, and I love you." Kind of like monkeys you see in safari parks, who wank each other off to say hello. It felt like a modern, diluted version of the sixties Free Love movement. It was beauty in its purest form. Same-sex encounters like this were prevalent in the club scene because Ecstasy made people less inhibited and therefore more experimental without the fear of social constraints. I made many lifelong friends from my clubbing days whom I am still in close contact with today. I found the saying to be spot-on that friends who rave together, stay together; because it was a different kind of connection, impossible to experience in real life.

CHAPTER 6

Pills, thrills, and wedding bells

When I was still a regular on the club scene and almost twenty-one, I met the man who was to become my husband. It was midweek and I was at work at the newsagents, when in walked a lad about my age. He had black, cropped hair, and had a moody, sulky look about him. He was about five foot ten and had a pale complexion, which his pink cheeks brightened up. Dressed according to the latest urban sportswear trend, he wore baggy, grey combat pants, a black, long-sleeved Versace Sport top, and funky-looking Acupuncture brand trainers which were the height of edgy fashion. I scanned his bottle of water and packet of chewing gum and eyed him curiously.

Hmm. Water and chewing gum; a clubber's staple diet. He's on something, and he's on his way to a club. He intrigued me. I noticed that he was looking at the floor, in an attempt to appear inconspicuous. Fun fact – clubbers tend to hide their eyes like that; or they wear dark sunglasses so that nobody can see their huge pupils.

I thought nothing more of this mysterious cutie until later that night. I finished work, headed home, then began my going-out ritual. This comprised of enjoying a hot cup of coffee with Speed stirred into it, whilst in the bath. I would dry my hair, get dressed into my white hot-pants, carefully apply my makeup and chuck on a neon orange Adidas tracky top, before heading to the bus stop. Once off the bus and in town, I would walk to the club, pay my entry fee and hook up with my friends inside. We gathered in the toilets and took our Es together, then danced our pants off until two in the morning.

As usual, when the club had closed, I found myself at an after-party at some random person's house, whom I had never met. I went into the kitchen to mingle, and I saw Bottle-of-Water Boy standing in the corner smoking a joint. I threw him the classic line:

"Haven't I seen you somewhere before?"

"Yeah, you work at the newsagents." He smiled, squinting one eye shut to avoid the smoke. I did indeed work at the newsagents.

"Ah, I knew you were a clubber." I winked.

And that was the full extent of the dialogue. I meandered casually over to the other side of the room and carried on chatting with my friends, cool as a cucumber. A few days later when I was at work, in he strolled, clutching a cassette tape. *Snared.*

"This is for you. It's a tape of all the tunes from the club. I'm Tim."

Ah, that was sweet. A mix-tape. I liked him, this Tim. We arranged to meet up the next time we were both at the club.

The weekend arrived as slowly as ever, and Tim and I met up at the club. We chattered away, discovering each other's likes and dislikes – usual dating spiel, and danced together to songs that were on the tape he'd given me. At midnight, we had our first kiss on a balcony that was my usual dancing spot. It had been a great night, and neither of us wanted it to end, so we went back to his parents' place where he lived. After staying up until dawn, learning about each other's lives, we tucked ourselves up in his big, double bed and made love. I say 'made love' because that's exactly what it felt like. That's the thing with recreational uppers – everything is love, love, stupid love; and feelings are accelerated and enhanced. I felt as though Tim and I had forged a strong bond in just one evening, and our sex reflected and cemented this. It seemed like we had a very emotional connection. So much so, that Tim had tears rolling down his cheeks as he climaxed. Yes, really. It sounds like something straight out of a Mills & Boon[22] romance novel, doesn't it? And that's exactly what I thought it was… at first.

Tim was a sweetheart, and he wore his heart firmly on his sleeve. He was a hard worker at a local scrap yard and generous with his money. Intellectually, he wasn't the sharpest tool in the box, but he knew how to communicate the language of love, and that was good enough for me. He had a cracking sense of humour and was playful in a contagious, child-like way. I never noticed back then that he didn't have any friends, apart from nightclub acquaintances. After three days of bonding, we both declared that we were in love. We became like Siamese twins and were never apart. I was crazy about the guy. After two months, Tim proposed whilst we were out shopping in town, and I said, "Yes." I was young, reckless, and caught up in the sheer romance of it all. I just knew that we would last forever. What I didn't realise is that forever is a Hell of a long time, and I had much to learn about this seemingly perfect young man.

Early in our relationship, an old friend of Tim's came into the newsagents where I worked.

"Hi, you're Sinead, aren't you? I heard you were going out with a lad I was at school with; Tim Marshall. I also heard you're a nice lass; so, I think you should know that Tim used to knock his last girlfriend about."

---

[22] A brand of cheesy romance novels, sometimes with quite steamy content. Notoriously popular with the older generation and lonely spinsters with too many cats.

The cheek of it! I thanked him curtly for his warning, served him and bid him goodbye. He obviously had a vendetta against my lovely Tim. Anyway, I wasn't stupid – if any man raised a hand to me, I would be out of that relationship like shit off a shovel. I was no pushover, and I could look after myself, thank you very much! I ignored this well-meaning stranger's warning because I thought I knew better.

Tim and I moved in together after only six months. I thought how fantastic it was that we would always have toilet paper, and I could even choose the brand and the pattern. You haven't lived until you've bought reindeer and snowman printed bog roll. It was so much more luxurious than living with my parents. I kept the house spick-and-span, and took great pride in smoothing down the bedding and dusting the house from top to bottom. It was immaculate.

The trouble started almost immediately. He was a little too flirty with anything in a skirt, and a little too confrontational with anything in trousers. He hated that I had male friends at the club, and he would be rude to them in front of me; which was nothing short of embarrassing.

"Don't be fooled, Sinead. They all just want to get into your knickers. You do know that, don't you? I don't want you to talk to them. You're with me now."

Being the independent little madam that I was, I refused to cut off my friends. Tim was an expert at manipulation though and changed his tack. He decided that we needed to save money for our impending wedding, so we wouldn't be able to go out, anyway. I had to agree; our wedding needed to be our main priority. Before I knew it, I was isolated, with no friends. It happened so gradually that I didn't even notice until it was much too late. He was so controlling with our money that I even became scared to tell him I had bought a skirt that had been reduced to four pounds in the sale at the local market. He would surely be angry and think me irresponsible.

The problem then became my clothing. Not that it was too revealing. Oh no – it was because he didn't like the patterns or the material.

"You shouldn't wear clothes I don't like. I wouldn't wear clothes you didn't like, Sinead. Don't you want me to always think you look nice?"

Again, I was independent, and ignored him. Big mistake. He would take revenge by going out 'til the crack of dawn, spending all our savings on cocaine binges.

Tim acted erratically at home. I would do the dusting, when he would suddenly and irritably snatch the cloth out of my hand.

"That's not how you should do it!" He would re-do the whole house, as I looked on in bewilderment.

We ended up having a quick wedding at a registry office, as we had no savings left. Tim then knew that he had full ownership of me. The bizarre, controlling behaviour and occasional verbal abuse rapidly spiralled into physical violence. If I defied his instructions and refused to obey his word, he would grab me by the neck and pin me against the wall. I would struggle for breath and try to scream, but it would just come out as a panicky sounding gurgle. He would glare at me menacingly, as a warning that I had better behave. Then came the punches. He would be speaking to me normally one minute, and the next I would be flying across our living room from the force of him punching me in the face. I still had my news agency job, and one day I went into work with a purple and yellow-tinged bruise on my jawline.

"Sinead, what on earth has happened to your face?" asked the Manager.

"Eh? I don't know what you're talking about?"

"That bruise on your jaw!"

"I haven't got a bruise."

I was in denial. I didn't want the shame of people knowing that my marriage was failing. I didn't want to go backward in life and end up back with my parents.

At the back of my mind, I still had dreams of being a professional model someday. Like Mum, I had always been a bit of a poser. Being seen as sexy felt important to me, probably because I was so insecure that I thought sex-appeal was the only thing that made me worth anything. When I first married Tim, one of the big tabloids ran a competition called Hunt for a Model. They were looking for contestants to apply. I excitedly sent in two photos that Dad had taken of me, with a posh camera Mum had bought him for Christmas. Tim found the acceptance letter in my handbag. I had been waiting tentatively for the right time to tell him. He went ape-shit, saying that I was a slag and that he forbade it. He didn't want men perving over me, he said. Honour and obey, and all that. My heart sank. That was definitely the end of my modelling dreams, then.

Soon after, I discovered I was pregnant. We were both overjoyed. Tim couldn't wait to tell everyone we knew.

"I can't wait to be a daddy!"

Tim was the perfect husband. He did the housework and cooked our meals, because I found carrying our little one around inside me exhausting. He refused to let me lift anything that he deemed too heavy, and even banned me from popping to the corner shop if it was dark outside, in the event that somebody might pounce on me and hurt the baby. I mistook his possessive behaviour for love. My job was the first thing to go, then my dignity. Tim didn't want me to work anymore. He said it was too tiring for me, and in any case, I was glad really. I was mainly confined to the till area while I was pregnant, because the manager considered many of my usual stockroom and shop floor duties dangerous for the baby. I was lonely there and would enjoy being at home much more.

I didn't. I was even lonelier and felt completely isolated, being unable to drive and having no friends left. I would spend my days cleaning the house, watching a bit of telly and reading magazines, waiting for Tim to arrive home from work each evening. He was my only real connection to the outside world. The abuse worsened, and when he wasn't dragging me around the house by my hair, Tim was thumping me in the face; and even once in my pregnant stomach. As soon as he had done it, he began to cry with remorse, ran into the kitchen and slashed at his arm with a carving knife. I screamed at him to stop, said that I forgave him and urged him to go to the hospital, which he did. That was Tim's pièce de résistance. He used this tactic many times. He would hurt me and then hurt himself so I would pity him. He even phoned The Samaritans helpline once, crying and claiming to the operator that he couldn't stop himself from hitting me. *Cry me a river, you fucking arsehole.*

Tim was a bit of a sexual deviant. I would have labelled his particular style as 'kinky', had it not disturbed me so much. Kink is fun, but this was downright weird. I think the first time I discovered his tastes was when we had visited a sex shop before we moved in together. He wanted to buy a rather long, thin, green jelly butt-plug type contraption. Well, who was I to judge? It wasn't my sort of thing, but we all have our quirks, right? Marker pens, blusher brushes and fingers, yes; but I had yet to encounter butt-plugs. They looked a bit serious for me. I was open-minded and accepting though, as was my nature. That night, Tim and I made our way into the bedroom, and began fooling around, taking sexy Polaroids of each other in various distasteful poses. Suddenly, his eyes kind of glazed over, as though he was in a trance, and he grabbed the butt-plug from its box. In a similar vein to a limpet's instant defence reflex when it's prized from a rock with a penknife, my anus retracted in sympathy. In and out, he shoved and pulled it… with no lube. Well, this masochistic display unfolding before my very eyes astounded me. That wasn't the end, either.

"Take it all, bitch! That's it; fucking take it all!"

What? Take it all, bitch? Well, this was a new one for me! I had humiliated Edward by dominating him for fun and sexual kicks, but never had I witnessed a chap abusing himself; and so aggressively too! I wrote it off as 'just one of those things', and shelved it at the back of my mind, thinking, *Men truly are strange creatures!*

I arrived home from work one day to find Tim in the bedroom. Nothing strange about that, you may think; apart from the fact that he was dressed in my white, satin nightie, crouched on the bed on all fours. Besides that, he was also wearing one of my black leather knee-high boots. I say one, because he wasn't wearing it on his foot, but up his backside. They were my best boots from Barratt's[23] as well! I

---

[23] A posh chain of shoe shops, selling quality footwear (and irresistibly sexy boots, evidently).

was not happy. Like most women, I'm rather attached to my footwear, and there he was, holding the leg of the boot in his hand and fornicating merrily with its five-and-a-half-inch heel. None of the heel base was visible. He took it all, bitch.

Tim and I never really had much of a sex life after that. Perhaps it was because he was so demanding and aggressive whenever we did get jiggy with it. Not only that, but because of the violence, I just didn't have that trust needed to produce the intimacy that kink requires. I must have still had it in me somewhere, but I couldn't find the urge. He just sort of made my skin crawl. I assumed that was part-and-parcel of being married. When he would slide his hand over my crotch in bed, I would freeze, praying, *God, please don't make me have to have sex with him.* It felt as though I was being touched up by a creepy uncle. I would just lay there, make all the right noises and let him get on with it. Little did I know that I had never even experienced an orgasm. Yep; you heard that right! Life was about to get interesting, but it had to get worse before it got better. Much worse.

CHAPTER 7

Money talks

Our beautiful baby son, Morgan, arrived in the hospital, after a gruelling thirty-hour labour, and he was the most perfect little thing I had ever seen. He had a shock of black hair, and his first cry was like music to my ears. As soon as I came around from the epidural, I knew I loved him, and vowed to always keep him safe. Tim doted on him too, and I thought we had turned a corner. He was Nice-Tim again. However, Nice-Tim only lasted two months, before he was back to being Mean-Bastard-Tim. I didn't like that persona one bit. He was impatient, nasty and unhelpful; although he put on his father-of-the-year alter ego when we were around family. One night, I was trying to give Morgan his bedtime bottle in the nursing chair in his bedroom, but he wouldn't feed. There was nothing wrong with him – he was just being overtired and fussy, as babies often are. I tried to calm him, but he cried. Suddenly, Tim burst into Morgan's bedroom, snatched the milk bottle from my hand, and threw it at the door. The bottle burst open, and milk splashed everywhere. I let out a terrified scream, and Morgan cried out in shock. My baby was crying now, like never before.

"What kind of mother are you if you can't even shut your fucking baby up, eh? I'll tell you what kind of mother, a fucking shit one! You stupid, fat fucking bitch!"

He stormed out of the room, leaving me shaking and clutching my tiny baby for dear life. This time Tim had really frightened me. I didn't feel safe in my home anymore. This had to stop, but I didn't know how. I now had a small baby to look after, wasn't working, and I knew that I couldn't afford to live in our home without Tim's wage. It was so daunting for me, at twenty-three. I was just a baby myself, really, and I didn't feel old enough to handle it all. I had no confidence, and my self-esteem was lower than it had ever been.

Around a year later, my confidence was jolted with a massive boost, just at the right time. Tim and I were walking around town, doing a spot of shopping, when a talent scout approached me. I thought it was a joke at first.

"Excuse me? Have you ever modelled? I like your look, and I think others would too. Here's my card. Think about it and call me."

"Oh, no thank you. My husband wouldn't like it." I turned to look at Tim, whom I expected to have a face like thunder. He was grinning like a Cheshire cat, enjoying the attention.

"No, I wouldn't mind at all! Thanks, mate." Tim reached across me and took the business card. The guy introduced himself as Alan.

I thought all my Christmases had come at once, and I wasn't going to wait for Tim to change his mind back again. Within a week I had booked myself on a day's model training course with Alan.

A week later, I went to the studio to shoot a full starter portfolio. Alan put me at ease. He said that I had one of the most beautiful and symmetrical faces for portrait photos that he had ever worked with. Validation, at last. At the end of the shoot, I bagged my first job. It was for one hour, with a photographer who had already been hanging around in the studio that day. The fee was £40. If I could do that for eight hours a day, we would be rich! I was a natural and loved every minute. It was the creativity that I enjoyed the most; and I felt like a film star. What's not to love?

Height-wise, I was vertically challenged, so I couldn't market myself as a fashion model; nor could I get catalogue work unless it was lingerie based. I chose Glamour. Going topless was no problem for me – I was proud of my body. Going full nude was easy too, as long as I could strategically cover my modesty with my hands or a length of material. In modelling terms, this is called Implied Nude. Tim didn't mind one bit, which surprised me. He enjoyed the status that being with a glamour girl gave him. I called myself Olivia, said that I was twenty-one, when I was in fact a young-looking twenty-four, and advertised my portfolio on the internet. Soon offers of work were rolling in. The money was impressive per hour, but it wasn't as lucrative as I had imagined, as shoots only lasted a couple of hours each. The fee structure went something like this:

Clothed: £30 per hour

Lingerie: £35

Topless: £40

Implied nude: £45

I would get offered two or three shoots per week, and the money really helped. I was no longer just a stay-at-home mum. I was a working parent with a job to die for. I decided that if I was going to be serious about this career, I had better get my boobs done. Although they'd always been big, they'd deflated a bit since I'd had Morgan.

I turned to Mum for advice, as her breasts had been surgically enlarged when I was about ten years old. She'd had a few problems with them and had to have them redone twice, but they looked great, and she was still the sexiest woman I knew. I bagged a free operation in Croatia, in exchange for advertising the company that performed the procedure.

Although extremely painful, the op meant I had a week's break from Tim, which was a relief. One of the newspapers flew out one of their photographers to cover my story. It meant that I had another English person to hang out with, so I didn't feel lonely. Although I now believe that as women, we should embrace our bodies in all their natural glory, it's something that I've never regretted. Would I put myself through it if I had that time over again? I'm honestly not sure.

Once home, I discovered that shaving under my arms with EE-cup implants was no mean feat. My boobs felt so solid that I couldn't push them to the side. I had hairy pits for a couple of weeks, but on the upside I could now wear halter-neck tops without a bra!

The glamour industry was full of supportive and friendly people. No stuck-up, cocaine-snorting, tissue-paper-eating London fashion model types – these were curvy, bubbly, pretty girls from up north. I witnessed no bitchiness at all. We were all in the same boat and everybody knew everybody. Most girls were freelance, like me; so, there were no intimidating castings to attend. I worked with whom I wanted, when I wanted; and I worked bloody hard too.

There was a lot more to modelling than standing in front of a camera, looking pretty. It was a full-time business if you were freelance. When I wasn't travelling miles to shoots and posing bikini-clad in front of the cameras in cold studios, I would be at home filing my accounts, and promoting, alongside looking after Morgan and being a housewife. One thing you had to do if you wanted to succeed without a manager, was to be a shameless self-promoter. I was a good salesperson and I knew that if I wanted to get anywhere, I would have to get people to believe the hype, by believing it myself. It was all about acting the part; faking it 'til you make it, if you will. In the days before social media existed, if you were brazen enough to tell people you were an almost famous model, they believed you. Good marketing and a good web presence were essential. I was picked up by a company that managed the sites for the big page-three names and glamour girls. They did a fantastic job of running my online fan club and members' site, and helping me to network.

It would make for juicy reading if I could tell you that glamour modelling is chock full of exploitation, but that wasn't what made me who I became. There were some bad people, like in all lines of work; but mainly good. I knew of girls who had been promised the Earth, taken to America, ended up being plied with drugs and made to do horrendous things on screen; but if you had your wits about you, you would learn to sniff out the rare scumbags and avoid them. I was naïve when I started, so I was very lucky that I didn't end up going that way. I ended up doing many things that I wouldn't dream of doing now, but that wasn't the through the fault of the industry – that was just down to my silly choices, greed and immaturity. I knew many models who stuck to their levels and had the self-respect to not cross them. I crossed mine on more than a few occasions, and sometimes others crossed them too.

CHAPTER 8

Model mother

One of my first shoots was with a guy who called himself Dave Black. He had contacted me online, and said that he worked on a submission basis. This means that a photographer who isn't employed by a magazine will shoot a set of photos and submit them. If the editor likes the photos, they'll publish them. The magazine pays the photographer for the copyright to the images, and the photographer gives the model a cut of the money. It can be quite a lucrative little earner if the photographer is good at what he does. Anyway, Dave reeled off a very impressive résumé – the main buyer of his photos being none other than Cosmopolitan magazine. Well, that sealed the deal for me. *Imagine if I could grace the pages of Cosmo!*

Dave explained that it would be cheaper for him if we shot the pictures at my house. He only wanted an initial unpaid test shoot, to see if I had the look he wanted. I told Tim about it, and he was as excited as me… His parents agreed to mind Morgan for the duration, and Tim and I rushed around, tidying up the house for Dave's arrival. He wasn't at all how I had expected. He was fat and grubby looking, with longish, unkempt, greasy hair and glasses. Each time he moved, I caught a whiff of an overpowering aroma, comprising B.O base notes, with a subtle top note of deep-fat fryer. There was no mistaking the signature scent of Eau de Guy-with-cam (Or G.W.C, the industry nickname for lone pervs posing as photographers). *Oh well, that doesn't make him a bad photographer,* I reasoned. Tim went upstairs and left us to it. I felt uneasy in Dave's company right away. He had a shifty manner about him and kept fidgeting, as though nervous. I offered him a coffee and began to make small talk.

"Sorry Olivia; we have to get on. I'm on a tight schedule today. I've got a few other girls to see after you." He cut me off, irritated with my animated chit-chat.

I removed my bra, and Dave pulled a small digital camera out of his pocket. I was used to being photographed with big, professional cameras. He had brought no portable lighting with him either. I smelled a rat. Those skilled in the art of grooming have a clever way of making you feel stupid if you question them. I was nervous because I had only done a few shoots by then, so I kept quiet.

"Now, if you could just stand over by the fire and bend over so I can see how your breasts hang please."

What? That didn't sound right to me. Surely, he would have already seen my breasts on my profile photos online. I didn't want to offend him, so I did as he asked. I felt so embarrassed, standing there in such a ridiculous, unflattering and very un-sexy pose – bent over with a table-top straight back, straight legs, and boobs dangling southward. I felt like a right pillock[24].

"Okay Olivia, just a few more in similar poses, and we're done. I just need to ask you a few questions now. Have you got any cellulite or stretch marks?"

Well, as soon as he asked that, I knew he was phony. Photographers do not ask such questions. They know that nearly every woman has both. It's what makes us women, and distinguishable from

---

[24] Idiot/stupid person/me.

men. Again, it would have been clear from my photos online whether I had those attributes; and he was standing in front of me, with me being practically naked. Yes, of course, I had the odd bit of cellulite and a few silvery stretch marks. Show me a chick who doesn't. I thought quickly and answered, "Just a minute, Dave... would you mind if I nipped to the loo? I'm busting! I won't be a second."

I legged it upstairs as fast as my stilettos would carry me and whispered to Tim, "Tim, this guy is a fake. Do me a favour and telephone Cosmopolitan magazine. Ask if they know of a Dave Black. Then look out of the window and write his car reg down. Stay there and I'll shout you when he's gone." I tottered back downstairs and went back to posing.

"That's lovely, Olivia. Would you like to do some open leg shots now?"

"Er... no. That's not what we agreed to. I don't do adult work."

"Oh, I know that, but I just wondered if it would be something you'd like to try?"

"No thanks. I feel a bit uncomfortable to be honest, Dave. Can we finish now? I've changed my mind."

"Oh, I see! Well, you've wasted my time then, Olivia. I can't get you in any magazines if I can't see what you look like naked first."

I saw him out, and ran upstairs to Tim.

"Okay Sinead, I've written his reg down, and I rang Cosmo. They've never heard of him. They took it seriously, and said they don't want someone bogus and perhaps dangerous using their good name to mislead and manipulate young models."

We hatched a plan. Tim and I went into the spare room and sat at the computer. I began typing.

Dear Dave,

You have never worked for Cosmopolitan, or any of the other magazines you mentioned to me. You're not even a professional photographer. By five o'clock today, you will post the memory card from your camera through my letterbox, with £100 to compensate me for my time and inconvenience. If you don't, I will post your details online for all to see, to warn everyone in the business about you. If I ever hear your name on the grapevine, I'll report you to the police.

Yours with best wishes,

Olivia

Sure enough, two hours later, £100 and Dave Black's memory card dropped onto my doormat; and I never heard from, or of him again. In retrospect, I wished I had asked for £1,000. Oh, and I reported him anyway for being such a sleaze-ball.

It was a fun and successful year as far as work was concerned. I appeared in national and international mainstream magazines and tabloid newspapers. I did promotional work at car, bike and trade shows. I made personal appearances, signed autographs, did a bit of television work and shot for a couple of album covers. I even worked in Greece for the weekend on one occasion. I was ridiculously excited to be asked to join the panel of judges for one of the regional heats of Miss UK. I had some proud moments and the work was varied and unpredictable. I would go into my local radio station for the odd interview, or they would phone me on occasion, to ask me to comment on the current affairs which I knew very little about, and to join in light-hearted debates. They often liked to wind me up, but it was all harmless banter and they were nice people.

I worked hard, all off my own back and as my own agent. Working for the newspapers was another world. The photographers set almost everything up, hoping to submit shocking, gossip-worthy photos. A few of the more popular glamour girls were signing deals at the time with the tabloids, so they could find fame by recording grainy-looking sex videos. The paper would advertise the videos as being 'leaked', and available to buy. They would then take a cut of the profits and the model would be well on her way to attaining infamy.

I was asked to do a couple of accidentally-being-photographed-getting-out-of-a-car-with-no-knickers-on jobs, which I turned down. I didn't fancy my grandad seeing my blurred out foo-foo whilst flicking through the morning paper, while eating his egg and soldiers. I was also offered the type of job where a model is photographed leaving a nightclub, walking close behind a footballer. I was told by a very pushy London paparazzi photographer it was a sure-fire way to be catapulted into the public eye. The paper could then claim that the footballer was leaving with said model when he had never even met her. I turned down the offer due to the ethics. I definitely didn't want any scary WAGs[25] baying for my blood. I did do some of the less controversial publicity stunt type jobs, though – being an unknown topless partygoer at a public event and cheesy, lighthearted things like that. The editor's assistant phoned me up one day and said, "If it wasn't for Abi Titmuss[26] bagging every front page at the moment, you would've got it at least once this week with your latest stunt,

---

[25] Footballers' wives and girlfriends.

[26] Actress, former glamour model and former nurse, made infamous by the British media when allegedly involved in a sex scandal with another well-known TV personality.

Sinead." *Damn you, Abi Titmuss!* Ah, it was all good fun, and these were fun times, work-wise. Little did I know that my most shocking publicity stunt was yet to happen. In fact, it would end up being one of the biggest regrets of my life.

Journalists, magazine features editors and television production assistants frequently trawled the online modelling community. They would submit adverts, offering money for scandalous stories or seeking girls who would be willing to do crazy, attention-grabbing things to get their fifteen minutes of fame. We would all clamour for the jobs, hastily replying to the adverts and hoping we would be lucky enough to be chosen. That's how most of us without agents got the odd bit of TV and magazine work. You could then advertise on your personal website, 'As seen in such-and-such magazine', and 'as seen on so-and-so TV show'. The more well-known and popular you portrayed yourself to be, the more fans you gained. A bit like how Instagram works nowadays, but harder work, because you only had a website and glamour forums as a base to promote yourself from.

Television still only had five channels back then, unless you were financially flush enough to have a posh Sky package. One of the main channels asked if I would take part in a prime-time reality series that focused on members of the public having unusual cosmetic procedures. They explained that they were looking for someone to be a guinea pig for a new and exciting treatment – having dye injected into thread veins on their legs, to minimise their overall appearance. They knew that if they asked models, there would be more chance of finding someone, because we were the ones willing to do silly things for a TV break. I was told that the procedure would hurt, but not unbearably. I didn't see what harm it could do and reasoned that it would be fabulous exposure, so I agreed.

Well, like the tabloids, if you give television an inch, they take a mile. Everything was carefully set up to boost ratings, and heavy editing took place, to make participants seem a bit scattier than they were in real life. Most models I knew who were freelance were smart cookies, and great business-women. You wouldn't know this from seeing them on TV or reading their magazine interviews, though. The media preferred to portray them as a bit dippy.

A week before the channel had planned to start filming, I had a phone call stating that the thread vein treatment wasn't shocking enough, so the idea had been axed. What they wanted instead was for me to have collagen injected into the balls of my feet, to form a thick, firm cushion under the skin. The theory behind this was that it would make it easier to walk in high heels. I was told that it would be pretty darned painful, but not harmful, and it would keep people at home glued to their screens. Like a dickhead, I agreed, because I was hungry for the work which would keep me in people's minds. Glamour work was competitive, so I didn't like to turn anything down.

I signed all the papers and packed my suitcase with nervous excitement. They were due to start filming live at 9:00p.m. that night. With half an hour to go before I set off for London on the train, I had a last-minute phone call from the production manager. It turned out that the insurance company they used had refused to provide cover for this particular operation, because it was too risky. I was disappointed at the time because one newspaper had already run a small feature about my impending appearance on the programme. I felt that I would be letting people down by not going ahead.

My upset was short-lived because I came to realise that they would have portrayed me as a vain, shallow and intellectually challenged bimbo. Viewers wouldn't have realised that it had been their hair-brained idea and not mine. Plus, they had been willing to let me go through an operation when they had no idea of the outcome or physical risk. All at the cost of my health, just to win a ratings war. I would have probably got a load of stick about it on the internet, too, so thank God it didn't happen.

Everything is smoke and mirrors with the media. Absolutely everything. To really succeed in the glamour world back then, you had to have no childcare commitments, be able to travel to London and back constantly, and be represented by one of the big agents there, to get better known. The further south you worked, the more cut-throat and pretentious the business seemed to be, as that was where most of the big media companies were based. Looking back, I'm glad that I was kept grounded by having a child and having no choice but to stay up north for most of the time. Otherwise my impulsivity (and my occasional stupidity) might have got me into some very regretful situations!

Way back when I was a teenager at school, I had a reputation for being a bit of a wise one in our little friendship group. I was the one anyone came to with a problem, as I gave sound advice where family and romance issues were concerned. Mum and Dad had certainly been good practice! I used to say that my other dream job would be an Agony Aunt for a magazine. It was ironic that one of the tabloids I worked for had a problem page and I ended up featuring on it. A photograph of a pouty and topless me wearing a bright purple G-string took up half of the page, and the other half was supposedly me answering readers' letters. I felt pleased with the spread and I viewed the exposure as quite an achievement as far as glamour work went.

The fabricated answers were cringe-worthy and satirical, but it was all tongue-in-cheek and just a bit of fun. I had made quite a name for myself, and I was very proud. It distracted me from the problems at home; and Tim's temper. He was hugely supportive when involved with my work, though. He even helped to manage my forum, talking to my fans online, revelling in the attention. Somehow, he managed to make my every success all about him.

After a year or so, work inevitably tailed off a bit. Many other models I knew were supplementing their income by working weekends at lap-dancing clubs or escorting. *So sleazy. No, thank you!* Tim and I talked about adult modelling, and he reasoned that it could still be classy, as it was still in the modelling genre. I wasn't sure, but we needed the money because he was spending it as fast as I was earning it. Designer clothes, motorbike gear, anything he wanted really. I didn't care about buying much, but it would be nice if money were no object, wouldn't it? The fee structure went something like this:

Full nude: £40 per hour

UK mag (legs open, basically): £50

US mag (opening the vagina by pulling the labia apart with fingers): £55

Continental (insertion of fingers, toys and other objects): £60

Girl/girl: £65

I spoke to Mum about it and asked what she would do.

"Well, you could try it; and if you find it's not your cup of tea, at least you gave it a shot. There's nothing worse than looking back and wishing you had done something."

Thinking back, I would have done it anyway with Tim's money-hungry influence and my rebellious nature. Everyone likes to have their parents' approval and support though and I was no different. I booked in my first adult shoot. It would be with another female model whom I had heard of, but not met before.

The photographer arrived at the studio with a bunch of flowers and a box of chocolates for me. Nowadays this would be probably classed as a bit inappropriate and along the lines of grooming behaviour. He handled the situation sensitively at first. I told him how I had done nothing like this before; and that I was a bag of nerves. The other model, Natasha, was sweet and girly. She was only nineteen, but had a successful career and could often be seen in the topless sections of the newspapers. I felt star-struck when I first met her, as the popularity she had in the industry was what I aspired to. The photographer told me I needn't worry, as if I didn't like the pictures, he would delete them all. I wouldn't have to do anything that made me feel uncomfortable.

"Right, you lay down on the bed, Tash. Olivia, I want you to climb on top of her and pretend that you're seducing her."

Righty ho. I can do that.

"Okay, now you need to look like you're kissing. It needs to look like a passionate kiss, and I want you to look into each other's eyes. Yep, that's it. Put your hand on her boob, Olivia."

This differed greatly from my usual type of work, but I was quite enjoying it. Because it had been so long since I had kissed a girl, thinking of it afterward felt quite erotic; even though it was only a simulated kiss with no contact. It helped to boost mine and Tim's diminishing sex life for a few weeks afterward.

"Right, now I want you to open your legs, Tash. Olivia put your head down there and stick your tongue out as though you're about to lick her pussy."

Eugh, pussy. Most awkward word in the world, ever. Just awful. *Hmm.* I didn't fancy doing this at all; but it wasn't like I had to touch her vagina with my tongue; so, I did as he had asked.

That was the girl/girl stuff over with. Now it was my turn to work solo. I got changed into some pretty, lacy lingerie, and sat on the satin-quilted double bedspread in the boudoir set of the studio.

"Right then, Olivia, let's get this show on the road! Lay on the bed, please, open your legs, and pull your knickers with your hand, to expose that lovely pussy."

I didn't want to do this.

"I… I'm sorry, but I… I think I've changed my mind."

"Are you kidding me? I've travelled a long way for this, Olivia."

"I'm sorry. I thought I could do it, but I can't."

"I told you I'd delete the images at the end if you wanted me to, but I need you to at least try. Put it this way, love: you either try or you don't get paid for the shoot at all."

My nerves got the better of me, and I cried. The photographer put his arm on my shoulder reassuringly, and half sweet-talked, half threatened me into carrying on. I didn't want to go home with no money. Tim would go mad. I looked at Tash, and she smiled back at me sympathetically.

"It's not so bad, Olivia. Don't think about it. Imagine you're just doing normal modelling. That's what I do. You get used to it. The first time's always hard, but you'll be okay. You did well earlier."

Natasha was a lovely, fresh-faced girl who radiated energy and warmth, and had an infectious giggle. She was tanned, with highlighted caramel hair, a beautiful, natural figure and a big, contagious smile. I found her words reassuring.

"Thanks." I smiled shyly.

So, I got back on to the bed and opened my legs. Another sixty or so photos later, and we were done for the day. The photographer was more than happy with them.

"So, can I keep the photos from today's shoot, Olivia? It's okay, I won't show them anywhere."

I told him he could, and he passed me a paper document, known as a Model Release Form. I read how he owned the copyright, not understanding the magnitude of what that meant, and I signed on the dotted line. He photographed my passport to prove that I was over eighteen and handed me £115 in an envelope. I had worked for two hours, and I had earned what a part-time shop assistant would have earned in two days. I cried when I got home, but it was short-lived. I knew I would do it again. I reasoned that I may as well. I had already done it once, and it hadn't been so bad.

I texted the photographer to ask if he would post me some prints of some photos so I could see the results of my hard work. A month later I received them in the post. They were professional-looking images, with great lighting. I was actually pretty impressed with the quality of the shots. I looked like an all-American girl with a Malibu glow to my skin. Nobody would guess I was a pasty-faced lass from drab old Northern England. There was some wording at the bottom right-hand side of the prints. I squinted to read it:

'Copyright Paul Raymond Publications U.S.A.'

He had only gone and sold them to an American porno magazine. The lying bastard! Not shown anywhere, my arse.

Tash and I became friends and worked together a few times in the following couple of years. Then without warning she disappeared off the scene. I had heard that she'd gone to the US to become an adult actress. Upon searching for her name online a few years later, I discovered that she had enlarged her breasts to ridiculous proportions, had many facial surgery procedures, and had become hooked on cocaine and alcohol. Tash died in her early twenties, whilst working as a high-class escort. The news of her death knocked me for six, because the images I found of her online looked nothing like how I remembered her to be. Her eyes looked soulless as she cavorted on-screen. The comments underneath from so-called fans were sickening to read. Not one of them spoke of what a great person she was. Some even said things like, "Is it wrong that I'm spanking my monkey over a dead chick? Oh well, it's what she would've wanted."

I felt so angry. They didn't know Tash or care that she had been a person with feelings. She was just an object to them, and a means to an orgasmically sticky end. Nobody noticed her smile. She was just a pair of breasts and a vagina to these people she was so popular with. She could have been so much more than the pneumatic hardcore blonde she was famed for being. What a waste of a beautiful young woman. *Rest in peace, Tash.*

CHAPTER 9

Exposure disclosure

Have you ever had one of those nightmares where you're walking down a busy high street, and you look down, only to discover that you're naked? Me too. The only difference between my nightmare and yours is that during mine, I was wide awake.

I received an email enquiry from a couple called Paul and Katalina who ran an adult website but said they had media connections and often did TV work. They had a left a phone number and asked if I could give them a buzz at my earliest convenience. I phoned right away. I didn't want to miss out if it was a rare opportunity. It was Paul who answered. He said that they were doing some syndication work for Bravo TV[27] channel. Bravo had sent out a brief saying that they were doing a special programme focused on female body confidence, and were seeking a model with outstanding bravery, to be filmed walking along the street, fully nude. It would be professionally undertaken, filmed in a classy way, not related to adult modelling, and because nobody else had done anything so daring in the name of feminism before, it would be great publicity. *Yikes.* Of course, I had a few questions.

"Will I be safe?"

"Of course. I will be right behind you the whole time, carrying

---

[27] Bravo TV is an American cable channel. It used to show some eccentric adult content, similar to that of Eurotrash.

your coat and monitoring everything. You'll be filmed close by from the front, so you won't be on your own." I imagined a big film crew with me, full of moral support and giving the entire event a professional edge.

"Okay. Will anyone see me?"

"No, we're planning on shooting on a Sunday morning, so it'll be quiet. It'll be in a quiet area of town, so no need to worry about attracting attention. It'll only be for a short time. We just need to get you for a few minutes, naked and walking."

"Aha. Okay. What's the fee?"

"Well, it'll be nothing up front, but as soon as Bravo air it, we'll receive the fee and we'll split it between us. Half for you and half for us. This is TV, so they pay handsomely. Every time it's shown after that, there'll be royalties."

"So I won't get paid anything at all yet?"

"No, but it should only be a couple of months. We're actually looking for a model for our own site, though. If you fancy doing a few open-leg shots for us while we're out on location, I would pay you a hundred pounds so you at least go home with something on the day."

"On location? You mean while I'm doing the walk?"

"No, this would be totally separate, just for our site. Nothing to do with the Bravo shoot. It would be for our private members' site, so nobody would see it apart from them."

I thought how this would affect Morgan, with it being on international television. Well, it wasn't as if the walk was going to be pornographic at all. It was to promote body confidence and champion the female form. A bit like the odd occasion where I had been a life model for our local colleges and universities. I had found being naked quite empowering. The human body was nothing to be ashamed of, after all. It would probably be superb for my body confidence too. Yes, I was already confident enough to model one-to-one, in carefully thought out poses from various flattering angles, but this would be a different kettle of fish altogether. My wobbly bits would be seen jiggling about from all angles. In real life, I was as self-conscious as the next girl. Time to put my money where my mouth was and practice what I preached – that women should be proud of the miracle that was their bodies.

It's not like anyone I know would see the photos, only Paul and Katalina's members, and they would need a password to get into the online gallery. The photos would be copyrighted, so it wasn't as if anyone could steal them and post them elsewhere. Besides, today's gossip is tomorrow's fish 'n' chip wrapping, isn't it? Morgan was only a toddler, and it would be long forgotten by then. We could do with the money. No one would have to know.

Paul sounded so professional, I had no reason not to trust him. Nothing in his tone roused suspicion in me. The shoot was too much of a big deal to make all that up, wasn't it? Plus, they were a husband and wife team. Women didn't double cross other women, did they?

"Ah, good. Okay, then. Thanks. I'll do it!"

"Great. We'll come and pick you up at 9:30 a.m. on Sunday. Have your passport ID ready so we can do the release forms, and wear something like a coat that you can easily take off and throw back on when we're done."

It was crazy; it was beyond adventurous, it would take nerves of titanium, but if I turned it down, maybe another more gutsy model would agree to it and I would regret it forever. I pictured that famous black-and-white photo of that nude woman hitching a ride with her thumb out. It was controversial, yet classy, and it was timeless. If I could summon the bravery to do this job, that could be me. I imagined the interviews that would follow. I would fly the flag for females all over the world in all my naked glory. For activism to raise a substantial amount of awareness, it needs to shock. This would definitely shock, alright! It would send out the message, "Even if we're naked, we're still not asking for it!"

I felt humbled and flattered that they'd asked little old me. Tim was excited, of course. He loved the idea of the notoriety, and all the new outfits he could buy.

As the week progressed and the day of reckoning loomed closer, I lost my nerve a few times. On more than a couple of occasions, I almost phoned Paul to say I'd had a turnaround and decided against it. But what if Bravo then thought I was a time waster, and it jeopardised my chances of future work? I told myself that I was just being a scaredy-cat and that cold feet were probably natural. If I wanted to be taken seriously in my work, I had to be prepared to step out of my comfort zone sometimes. It goes with the territory.

I had always been adamant that I preferred being freelance rather than having a manager or an agent, but this is where one would have protected me. Unfortunately, I had nobody to shake me and say, "What are you thinking? This is a terrible idea. Absolutely not!"

My intuition had served me well with Dave Black, the Cosmopolitan phony, but not so well this time.

After what seemed like an eternity of "Umming" and "aahing", the morning of the shoot arrived. I chose a black knee-length trench coat, and a pair of beige thigh-length high-heeled boots. I chose the longest boots I had to cover up as much flesh from the bottom part of my body as I could. To cover my top end as much as possible, I wore my long hair down. None of that would physically help, but psychologically it created a bit of a protective barrier, and made me feel a tinsy bit braver.

Half-past nine came around quickly, and Paul and Katalina arrived dead on time. Katalina was a petite, ultra-skinny girl, I guessed of around twenty-six. Her waist-length, dirty blonde, limp hair seemed to drown her sharp-looking unmade-up features. She wore a knee-length, fitted black puffer jacket that looked too big for her slight frame, faded black skinny jeans and scuffed black suede knee-length wedge boots. She had a big smile on her face and greeted me with a hug. I towered above her, which felt strange. She stepped back and grabbed both my hands in hers, looking me in the eye with a sincere expression. She spoke in a thick Polish accent, making her words difficult to wrap my brain around in my hyper-alert state.

"Hi Olivia. It's so good to meet you, finally. I must say, I love your work."

"Pardon? Oh, yes, thanks! Lovely to meet you too. You speak very good English."

Katalina blushed and giggled like a schoolgirl. Morgan toddled over to us, waving his cuddly Teletubby in the air, shouting, "Hello Lady!"

"And who's this handsome little boy, then?"

I scooped Morgan up into my arms and sat him on my hip, getting bashed on the head by Tinky Winky in the process. I chuckled and kissed him on the forehead.

"This is my son, Morgan."

"Hello Morgan. Oh my goodness, you're going to break hearts like your mummy one day, aren't you?"

Morgan broke into a cheeky, wide grin. She seemed nice. She was warm. I liked her.

Paul was a little taller than Katalina, with a messy mop of unbrushed, greying hair, dressed in a shorter black puffer jacket, which made him appear quite rotund. He was older, his skin appearing weathered and leathery. A pair of thick-rimmed glasses were perched on his pink, bulbous-looking nose, and my eyes were immediately drawn towards the open pores. I guessed he must have been a good twenty years older than Katalina. I didn't get the same warm feeling from him. He muscled in front of her and took my hand in a powerful grip, giving it a firm shake.

"Good to meet you, Olivia. We thought we might get the release forms done now before we set off, if that's okay with you?"

"Um, yeah, that's fine."

I signed most release forms after a shoot had taken place. Often when the model and photographer had looked through the shots together. Being asked to sign beforehand should have rung alarm bells for me, but nope, nothing. I just assumed they wanted to save time so they could drop me back at home later, without having to come inside again.

Tim was on his best behaviour, all smiles and charm, as he introduced himself and hurried into the hallway to hunt for a Biro. Paul set the paper down on the coffee table and asked me to sign on the dotted line. He turned to Morgan, who was babbling away to Katalina about the colour of each of the Teletubbies.

"Hello, little man. Are you going to let your mummy sign this paper for me?"

Morgan scowled at him, unimpressed by having his conversation interrupted. I passed Morgan and Tinky Winky to Tim and took the pen from him. I quickly scribbled my signature on each copy, and fumbled about with my passport, opening it up on the page with my photo and date of birth. Katalina snapped a photo on her phone, a closeup of my face, with me holding up the passport next to it. I handed one copy to Paul and kept the other for my records. I was feeling jittery by this point, as I knew it would soon be time to set off. I didn't want to do it, but I did want to do it, but I didn't, but I did, but I...

"Either of you fancy a quick cuppa before you head out?" Tim piped up, breaking my thoughts. I hoped they would say yes, and it would buy me a little more time. I looked out of the window and felt glad that I had worn long boots. It looked bitter out there.

"No thanks. We'd better get going before the streets get busy."

My stomach lurched. Tim gave me a quick peck goodbye, whispering, "Knock 'em dead, babe." He winked at me, I gave him an unconvincing smile, waved 'bye-byes' to Morgan, and closed the front door behind me.

The three of us piled into Paul's Vauxhall Astra Estate, me in the back, and set off on the journey to a town about nine miles from our home. The drive took around half an hour, but felt like all of ten minutes. I was silent the whole way, nerves on tenterhooks. I didn't know what to expect, and the town we were heading for wasn't somewhere I had ventured before, so I wouldn't be aware of the exact location until we arrived. From their perspective, this was probably for the best, because I'm sure they knew without a doubt, if I'd had even an inkling of how the day would pan out, I would have said, "No. Fucking. Way."

We pulled up on a quiet side street on the outskirts of the town centre, and bundled out of the car – Katalina carrying a professional-looking stills camera, and Paul with a huge, heavy canvas video camera bag hanging from his shoulder. Looking around, I noted that all the shops were closed. *Good.*

"Right. Let's get started," Paul said with a smile, as Katalina set up her camera. "We'll just get these shots for the site done quickly, before we start with the walk."

Gulp.

"What do you want me to do?" I asked.

"Just stand against that wall and open your coat. I'll keep a lookout. If anyone walks past, just discreetly pull it closed again."

I propped myself against a shop front, shifted my weight onto my right leg, left knee slightly bent to jut my right hip out, held my coat open and gave Katalina a sultry come-to-bed look while she photographed me. With each click, I would change position and facial expression slightly. Click, click, click. Paul was watching me with concentration, in between looking around like a meerkat on speed.

"Fab, Olivia. Now crouch down and do the same thing, but with your legs open."

I dropped into a squat, eyes darting around, looking for any signs of life nearby. We were still alone. I cautiously opened my legs, so they both had a view of, well, everything. Click. I heard a rustle of a carrier bag and boot soles scraping on the tarmac. I instantly shot up, heart racing, wrapping my coat around me. *Phew. Just a tramp.* We stood silently rooted to the spot for a couple of minutes, to let him pass. He didn't even notice us as he shuffled by in deep conversation with himself, muttering incoherent words while fumbling about in his bag. Katalina glanced over at Paul and uttered something in Polish. Paul wasn't Polish, but he seemed to understand. They both looked concerned, seeing that I was looking antsy and bewildered. Paul nodded in response and turned to me.

"That should do for the site. Let's move on to the next location, shall we?"

Relieved, with nearly-numb fingers, I buttoned up my coat, shuddering as the wind flapped the corners of it about in my hands. It was bloody freezing! I looked up at the sky and felt hopeful when I saw the morning sun was trying its best to break out from behind the clouds. With the same high level of intent as when I would stand in the school dinner queue eyeing up the chocolate sponge cake, attempting to communicate telepathically with the dinner lady so that she'd give me a big corner piece, I willed God to make it sunny. No such luck. The clouds remained, shielding the sun, giving an accurate sense of foreboding. We walked to the bottom of the street, turned onto the main road, and trekked over a zebra crossing which led us further into the centre of town. A couple of people passed us on the way, carrying supermarket bags from the Asda at the other side of town, but it was otherwise quiet. We must have looked a very unlikely threesome – a very casually dressed (and enviably warm) couple with me done up to the nines trotting along behind them, legs bare and a face like a slapped arse. I probably looked like I'd just been trafficked. Katalina would turn and give me a reassuring smile now and then, as though to check that I were still there. I wished I wasn't.

"Are you warm enough?" Paul asked, his voice tone conveying more empathy than his expression gave away.

"Yeah, I'm fine," I managed with a tight-lipped smile.

"Great. Nearly there."

We turned a corner onto another side street. A fast-food restaurant occupied the whole of the corner building. It was closed. Another sigh of sweet relief. The road was silent and there wasn't one person to be seen. Paul and Katalina ground to a halt. I watched with pure angst as Paul unhooked the bag from his shoulder, and pulled out a big, heavy video camera. After fiddling with it for a couple of minutes, he passed it to Katalina, declaring, "We're good."

His attention then turned to me, as I was busy visually scanning the street and straining to hear distant noises, checking that nobody was about to walk around the corner and catch us in the act.

"Olivia, I need your attention now. This is important if we want to get the footage as quickly as possible."

"Okay, I'm listening."

"Katalina is going to be walking in front of you, backwards with the video camera. You'll need to go slowly so she can stay the same distance from you, and not lose her footing, okay?"

"Yep."

"Good. I'm going to walk behind you the whole time, giving you discreet direction; but don't turn to look at me. I want you to keep your head up, walk as though you're just going for a casual stroll, and look into the camera occasionally, if you can."

I gave a little shudder, becoming aware of how cold I was again.

"Okay."

"You can take your coat off now, and hand it to me. I'll carry it for you and give it straight back as soon as the camera stops rolling. I know it's cold, it won't take long."

I stood still, fear now coursing through me. *How the Hell did I end up here?* Paul held out his hand, making an impatient beckoning gesture with his fingers.

"Olivia. Coat."

I fumbled clumsily with my buttons, hands shaking not with cold now, but with nerves. This was it. I glanced over at Katalina, video camera balancing on her shoulder, waiting for me. The camera was much bigger than a domestic camcorder. She looked like she was filming for a documentary. *Get a grip, Winters. Be professional. Don't fuck this up. This is for Bravo, remember. BRAVO.* I looked up, gave Paul a smile, and slowly removed my coat. I was naked. Naked in the fucking street. In October. Instinctively, I covered as much of my exposed chest as I could with one arm, hugging myself as tightly as I could manage, hand clasped under my hot-to-the-touch armpit. I covered the front of my genitalia with the other hand. My mind automatically flashed back to Sadie and our dads' factory. I felt like I'd been here before. What if someone saw me? I'd die with embarrassment. *Bravo, though. Concentrate, Sinead!*

Paul shot Katalina a quick look, nodded once, and whispered from behind me, "Hands away... Go!"

Oh. My. God.

I reluctantly dropped my hands to my sides, and began walking stiffly towards Katalina, who was walking backwards at the same pace as I.

"Slower!" Paul hissed sternly from behind.

I slowed down. My mind sped up and my heart raced in absolute physical and mental incongruence. *Focus.* I remembered to look at the camera, as Paul had instructed. I put on a confident expression, conveying ever-so-slight defiance, and gave a wry smile in line with Katalina's vision.

"Good, Olivia, good. In about five seconds, we turn this corner on your left. Then another ten seconds or so, and we're done. Whatever happens, just keep walking."

Whatever happens?

I kept my eyes fixed on Katalina, who gave a quick glance to her right so she could navigate the corner without banging into anything.

Relief shot through me, then dizziness overcame me for a second. We had nearly finished. I had nearly done it! It hadn't been so bad. Scary, yes; but…

People. Lots of people. Lots of people buzzing about in all directions, clutching shopping bags, food and phones. Families queuing for the mobile burger van, women jostling each other to get to the fruit stall, impatient kids nagging for sweets and throwing tantrums. *This can't be happening.* It was happening, alright. I had just walked into a bustling town centre, butt-naked, apart from my footwear… on Market day – only the busiest day of the sodding week! My entire body jolted as though someone had just jumped out and pranked me. I gasped in shock, eyes wide, like a stag caught in a Land Rover's headlights. Don't doubt me when I say that nothing, and I mean nothing, can take a person from tired to wired in a matter of nanoseconds, like being naked in a town centre with an unforeseen and unsuspecting audience. I literally quaked in my boots, not from cold this time, but from abject terror. I wanted to get this over and done with as soon as was physically possible. Paul interrupted my jumbled up thought process once again.

"Ignore them. Keep walking. Look straight ahead."

What would a confident model do? She would carry on walking with her head held high, that's what. A professional would be brave. I stared straight ahead, so as not to catch anyone's eye, and I walked.

The sea of people parted to let me through, like I was a modern, disrobed Moses. They were as shocked as I was. Astounded onlookers stopped what they were doing to get an eyeful of this evidently mad woman with no clothes on. I could hear gasps coming from all angles, and comments like, "'Ey Shirley, there's a naked woman 'ere!" and, "You'll catch yer death, luv!" With any luck, any second now, the men in white coats would swoop in and rescue me from this crazy, living nightmare. No word of a lie, Tragedy by the Bee Gees was number one in the charts when I was born. It was definitely an omen, because here I was, twenty-odd years later, now a literal walking disaster. I pretended to myself I had clothes on, but I'm sure my expression betrayed me. I must have looked terror stricken. I rounded my shoulders and let my hands fall to the front, dangling them as close to my not-so-private parts as I could.

"Move your hands away!"

Oh, piss off, Paul. My hands twitched nervously. They didn't want to budge. I forced myself to interlink my fingers tightly together behind my back, resisting the overwhelming urge to bring them round to the front again. It's funny what goes through your mind at such unprecedented moments. From a place of unbridled self-consciousness rather than what could be understandably mistaken for vanity, I wondered, *Does my fanny look a weird shape?* I tried to clench my thighs together so my immodesty would be less visible. Even though I'd had breast augmentation, I sometimes I worried that they still had too much droop. *Are my boobs saggy? Is my bum abnormally wobbly? Are my nipples lower than most women's?* Fearing that people might shout cruel comments at me about my body, I consciously pushed my shoulders back. Chest out, chin up.

"You'll take someone's eye out wi' them, lass!"

Whether this was an insult or a compliment was by the by, but I guess it answered my sagginess question. I had just begun to console myself that this was only a few insignificant minutes out of my whole life, when, "Right, Olivia, turn around and do it again, back the way we came."

From the side of my mouth like a bad ventriloquist, I murmured, "What? Again?"

I panicked as it registered what he was asking of me. A desert storm swept through my mouth, drying it out in its wake. I momentarily snapped back into my real self. I was so taken aback, the word didn't want to come out. I spluttered and croaked, "Okay."

I knew he was taking liberties, but I didn't want to waste his and Katalina's time by being a cry-baby and ruining the shoot. I had to appear professional at all costs. After all, this was for Bravo, wasn't it?

Olivia sprang back to life inside me. I put back on my who-gives-a-shit model persona and (for my sins) turned to walk the other way. I heard a stampede of footsteps, and was suddenly framed at either side by a bunch of young lads who couldn't have been any older than twelve.

"Oi! Are you from Playboy?"

I kind of wished I was. At least that would have given me a certain amount of kudos, and to an extent, an excuse for my unnecessary nudist display. I bristled, searching my brain for something smart-arse to retaliate with, but ignored their attempt at conversation.

"Aren't you shown up?"

The little bastard. Weren't they too young to even know what Playboy was? More to the point, where were the parents of these overconfident tearaways, anyway? 'Shown up' was not the phrase I would use to describe the mortification that I felt. At least I no longer had to worry about the cold. I was positively roasting, basting in the white-hot lava-like juices of my burning shame. I did my damnedest to pay no mind to their loud laughs and jeers. The crowd of shoppers had tripled in size by now, some standing still and gossiping into their phones, and some walking by without stopping, rubbernecking on the way past. Most of my dedicated audience were standing like statues, goggle-eyed. If there's one thing I'm thankful for about that day, it's that camera-phones weren't properly a thing yet.

On automatic pilot, I walked back the way I came, with my eyes firmly fixed on our starting point in the not-so-far away distance. I heard someone shout, "The coppers are here!"

Paul and Katalina heard it too. The crowds dispersed, as though they were the guilty ones. Within seconds the camera was back in the bag from whence it came, and my coat was on and buttoned up to the neck. I swear my heart nearly stopped dead the moment I caught sight of two male police officers coming round the corner. In an almost comedic fashion, Paul, Katalina and I stood a couple of feet away from each other, casually and aimlessly looking around like we had never met. We may as well have been whistling with our hands in our pockets too, to complete the guilty-as-sin sketch-show-like scene. My heart quickened and thudded in my chest as the bobbies approached with purpose, and stopped in front of us.

"Excuse us."

We all turned to face them in a surprised 'Who, me?' fashion. Gesturing over my left shoulder, the officer continued, "We've had a report from the charity shop over there, that there's been a naked woman walking about, with a couple with a video camera. It wouldn't be you three, would it?"

I turned and saw the charity shop in question. There was a curtain-twitching kill-joy Mary Whitehouse[28] type, glaring at us from behind the window, her arms folded in victory. I didn't even know bloody charity shops opened on a Sunday.

"No," we all sang at once, looking confused and shaking our heads frantically, like we hadn't a clue what he was talking about. The one who hadn't spoken was also standing with his arms folded, his expression unfathomable and giving off a menacing aura. Mr. Inquisitive started up again, this time directing his questions at Paul.

"We've been told it was you. Let's not mess about here. We want to get this over and done with as much as you do, and we'd rather there wasn't a scene, sir. Can you explain to us what you've been doing here today?"

Paul sounded uncharacteristically friendly. "Nothing really, just been out with the camera."

"Taking photos of a naked woman?"

"No, just urban stuff. Buildings mostly."

The officer looked irritated and unconvinced by Paul's nonchalance.

---

[28] Mary Whitehouse was a famous, conservatively dressed, fuddy-duddy pensioner, appearing regularly in the media with her angry campaigns against liberalism and promiscuity. She is still an object of humour, inspiring the name of the nineties TV sketch show, The Mary Whitehouse Experience.

"Right, sir. We've given you ample opportunity to tell the truth. We know what you've been up to. Can I search your bag, please?"

It wasn't a question, though. The officer pulled the camera kit bag forcefully from Paul's shoulder. Katalina and I looked on, helplessly and scared stiff. The Spanish Inquisition fella handed his misery-guts silent partner the bag, and he rummaged through it. I had to save face. *What can I say that's both cheeky and funny to cut the tension?*

"Would you like a signed poster for your station wall, lads?"

What the Hell, Sinead? Oh my God, I'm SO gonna get arrested! Katalina was making 'eye faces' at me, communicating that she wanted me to shut up immediately.

Bag-Ferret carried on with his ransacking of the camera paraphernalia, while the talkative one looked directly at me, bemused by my audacity.

"Er, no thank you, miss. What have you got on under your coat?"

Wasn't it rude to ask a lady such a question? What made him assume I was the naked one, anyway? Katalina was standing a couple of feet away from me and he hadn't even looked in her direction. The guilt was written all over my done-up-like-a-dog's-dinner face, but I couldn't weaken my resolve now.

"Never you mind! Arrest me, Officer!" I said in my best, breathy, feeble, girly voice, holding my wrists up in mock surrender. Officer Humourless shook his head and rolled his eyes.

"Okay, Joker, I can see I won't get anywhere with you. I think it's best you go on home now, don't you?"

It took the attention off me when the officer with the bag pulled out a little aerosol canister and turned to Paul, who was shifting about uncomfortably, hands in his pockets.

"What's this, then?"

"It's spray mount."

"It's CS gas, and you know it is. This is illegal to possess. Where did you get it?"

"From a car boot sale a few months ago. The guy told me it was spray mount."

"I'll ask you again. Why have you got CS gas in your bag? This is used for crowd control."

"It's not. It's spray mount. I told you."

Realisation crept over me. Crowd control. Paul had planned all along that we would be somewhere busy, and he had brought the gas with him in case things turned nasty and he would have to keep people at bay. The initial quiet street we had used for the shoot had just been a decoy to lull me into a false sense of security. He had known full well that we were about to turn onto a street full of market-goers. It could have potentially been a very dangerous situation. *The sneaky bastard!* Katalina looked at me, worry on her face, and I looked back at her, stunned. I'd been had, and she knew I knew.

"We're going to have to take you with us to the station, sir. I'd like to ask you a few more questions and also inspect your camera and belongings."

And with that, Paul was promptly arrested. They left Katalina and I standing together, looking around like we had got lost. Well, to be fair, we were literally lost. Neither of us knew the area. We had no money, no way of knowing when Paul would get released, and no way of getting either of us back home. To add to the mix, we were freezing.

"Let's just walk and see if we can find somewhere warm until Paul gets in touch," Katalina suggested, unconvincingly cheery.

I had done enough walking to last me a lifetime.

"Okay. We've got no money. What are we gonna do? What if they keep Paul in overnight?"

"No," she chuckled. "He knows how to handle these situations. Don't worry, Olivia. I think I may have some change in my pocket. Let me see."

These situations? So this wasn't a one-off? Katalina stuck her hand in her puffer jacket pocket and pulled out a handful of loose change, mixed with fluff and screwed up balls of chewing gum wrapper foil. She separated the bumf and counted the coins.

"Exactly one pound twenty. We can get a drink to share!" she declared, looking pleased with herself.

I remained expressionless and floppy-faced. *Oh yay. Best day ever.* We traipsed along a few streets until we came to a traditional-looking, run down pub.

"Shall we go in here?"

"Yeah, whatever."

I followed Katalina through the doorway and into the dimly lit room. Cigarette smoke whirled through the stale air, trapped with nowhere to go. Very much like us in this miserable situation. Sitting at a little circular mahogany table, a couple of old blokes in brown trilby hats were quietly immersed in a card game. A small group of middle-aged, beer-bellied guys with shirts straining at the navel were congregated around the bar. One of them broke out in wheezy half cough, half laugh like Muttley from Wacky Races as I walked past, making some smart-alec remark about the resident stripper being here. Little did he know how close he was to the truth, and that I had naff all on under my coat. I obviously stuck out like a sore thumb, even with my coat and boots on. Intimidated, I looked down at the sticky, patterned brown carpet. Glasses clanked irritatingly and constantly, making it hard for me to think straight, and the sickly sweet smell of ale made me feel queasy as I drew breath. Yellowing, nicotine-stained, once-magnolia walls added to the unhygienic aesthetic. I plonked myself down on a threadbare maroon velour-topped stool, and stared blankly at a wonkily positioned framed print, portraying a tasteless scene of dogs playing pool.

Katalina wove her way through the chairs and tables carrying a pint of weak dilute pop.

"I had just enough for some orange cordial. We can share it."

For two hours we sat, engaging in sporadic bouts of awkward small-talk, and taking intermittent, tiny sips from the bitter-tasting glass of witch piss that sat between us. Mostly we just said nothing and stared at the wall like it was a competitive sport. After what felt like a lifetime, Katalina's mobile phone cut the silence with its nineties euro-pop ringtone. She jumped up and took it to the toilet with her while I remained seated, anxiously wondering what fate now had in store for me. She returned, grinning like the cat that got the cream, gushing, "Paul is out without charge! I knew he would be fine. The police wanted to see the footage, but Paul had already removed the memory card and given it to me when he saw the police coming towards us. They have no proof of anything. Quick thinking, huh?"

This at least meant that I wouldn't get arrested for indecent exposure, thank God.

When Paul arrived in his car to pick us up twenty minutes later, on the way out of the pub, we walked back past the bar. I set the empty pint glass down on the bar top, and heard the voice of the landlord mutter, deliberately within earshot of me, "Tight cows. One drink between two for two hours!"

This really was the most rubbish day in all the history of rubbish days.

A smiling, remorseless Paul greeted us both and opened the car door for me to climb inside. I sat stony faced in the back of the car, avoiding his eyes in the rear-view mirror. I swallowed hard, feeling my throat starting to burn. I looked up at the car roof, trying my best to send the well of tears that was filling up my eye sockets, down into my body.

"You okay in the back, Olivia?"

Oh yes, never better. I flicked my model switch to 'on' again and forced my billionth smile of the day.

"Yeah, I'm fine, thanks. Don't you worry about me."

There was no buzz of elation or feeling of accomplishment, like I usually felt at the end of a day's shooting. Just regret, humiliation, and a sense of impending doom.

We pulled up outside my house and Paul handed me my hundred quid in an envelope that I had earned from doing just the photos. Morgan was in bed having a nap when I got back, which was a good job, because as soon as I got inside I ran into Tim's arms, letting out the traumatised sobs I'd been holding back for the past few hours. My body limp and heaving, Tim patted my back, said the obligatory 'there-theres' and gave me the odd affection-less but well-meaning squeeze.

"You'll get over it, babe."

A month and a half passed with no word from Paul or Katalina. I eventually initiated contact by phoning Paul. He sounded surprised to hear from me. Excitedly, I asked him what Bravo had thought about our stunt.

"I'm afraid they didn't accept our submission, Olivia. Never mind, eh? Let's just chalk it down as experience."

"You're kidding? After what we went through?"

"Aha. Sometimes it just happens that way."

"But I thought they knew you were doing the shoot for them? I thought they'd specifically asked you?"

"What? Oh... no, you must have misunderstood me. We were just doing it off our own backs hoping we could submit it and they'd want to use it."

"Oh. So this means I won't be getting paid for my work?"

"I'm afraid not. We haven't been paid for it, so there's nothing to give."

I didn't quite know how to react. Paul seemed to want to get off the phone as quickly as he could, so we exchanged our goodbyes and I hung up. It dawned on me that I had done something for free that most people in their right minds wouldn't do for a million pounds. Had they had made up the whole Bravo TV story from the very beginning, to lure naive girls? Most probably. Had they ever worked for television at all? Most probably not.

Tim was right, though. I got over it, and that was because I conceded that everything happens for a reason. Did I really want thousands of TV viewers witnessing the most nightmarish experience of my entire life, anyway? That's not how I wanted to be remembered. I knew I needed to learn from the experience and thank my lucky stars it hadn't turned out even worse. for starters, I could have been arrested. I was still bitter at Paul and Katalina for how they had staged everything, but it wasn't as though I would ever had to see them again. I told myself to be more wary the next time a job offer came my way.

A few months later, I was looking online for modelling work, when I saw a banner for a porn website. On the moving banner I noticed an image I recognised instantly. It was a photo of me, naked against the shop window. *Shit!* I hadn't even considered that the photos would be promoted anywhere to entice paying members. I clicked on the banner. Paul and Katalina's website flashed up onto my computer screen. There I was, flashing my bits for all to see, with a clickable link over my crotch area, telling viewers to 'Look inside'. The play on words made me feel revolted and embarrassed. I dug out my copy of the release form from the shoot. Sure enough, it mentioned that the copyright holder could use the material for whatever reason they saw fit, including website promotion. I chastised myself for not having gone through the model release with a fine-toothed comb before signing. Would I never learn? If I hadn't been so bloody careless, I would never have got myself into that situation. I licked my wounds and got on with it, with a developing sense of wariness and mistrust.

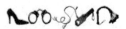

Eight months passed by, and I was online as I always was in the evenings, firing off emails to prospective photographic clients and updating my online portfolios. The tapping of the keyboard was interrupted with a call from Louise.

"Sinead, I don't know how to say this, but the whole video of that walk thingy you did is online."

My stomach did an almighty backflip.

"Oh God. Email me the link, now."

"Okay. I didn't even know about it until one-legged John over the road told me about it. Everyone knows."

"Alright Lou, I'm gonna go now. Just send me the link please."

"Okay, bye."

A minute later, I received an email from Louise. I clicked on the link in the message. Up popped my video, on one of the most popular porn websites in the world. *Please, no.* My heart sank. If I had thought the shoot had been a nightmare, then this was a full-on waking night terror. I needed to think, and fast! I had deleted Paul's phone number and emails a few months after I had last spoken to him. Every time I had seen him on my contacts list, I had felt pissed off, and triggered by awful memories. I had decided to get rid of them, thus pushing the con-artist couple as far to the back of my mind as they would go.

I located the contact form on his and Katalina's website, and typed out a message, imploring them to take the video down. I tried to appeal to their better nature and explained that it wouldn't be half as bad if the video were behind a locked members' area, but putting it up on porn sites for free could ruin my life, and that of my family. I never received a reply. I didn't have a leg to stand on, and they knew it. Whether they had conned me into doing the walk or not, all that mattered legally was that I had signed on that fateful dotted line, giving them permission to do with my shameful footage as they pleased. Also, most of mine and Paul's conversations had been by telephone, so there was no record anywhere of him claiming that the shoot was specifically for Bravo. I knew I would have no choice but to accept that the video would be there to stay, but on a night in bed,

I would lay there, unable to sleep, analysing the whole thing from start to finish. *They must have seen me coming. I bet they thought I was born yesterday.* They would have been right. Yes, my model alter ego, Olivia, put on a good show of being streetwise and switched on, but in actual life, Sinead was about as wet behind the ears as they come.

For years afterwards I felt thoroughly ashamed of myself, always wondering what people thought of me. Did they consider me a slag, like Tim used to say whenever he was in one of his rages? I'd had a bit of stick over the years from people who judged me without knowing me. Those mostly in glass houses who took pleasure in throwing stones my way. But what did I expect? It was my own doing. At first my mental health suffered, but I learned how to develop a thick skin. In later years, when the video was on even more free websites (I had never considered that the internet would grow so huge!), I decided that enough was enough. I had done my time of feeling disgusted with myself, and it was time to fight back. The sites I contacted were understanding when I explained to them what had happened. Many of them have female customer support, so they were empathic and kind. I felt so grateful to them. More than they could ever have imagined. Before they were all taken down, I did download a copy of the video though. I had a feeling that one day when I was old and it no longer mattered, I might want to look back with good humour, and be able to say to myself, "I did that crazy thing. It really happened."

Funnily enough, not so long ago, I was telling a new-ish female friend whom I had grown to trust, about the complete farce. By this time I had grown so desensitised to it, that I was happy to show her the proof on my phone, without coming over all 'I hate myself'. That was tremendous progress for me. As she watched me strutting my stuff down the high street in a state of complete undress, she put her head in her hands and started laughing. I started laughing too. *Wait... no,* she was crying!

"Oh God, what's wrong? Why are you crying?" I was sincerely shocked that she would react that way. I put my arm around her shoulder and pulled her in closer for a hug. "Please don't cry, what's up?"

"I can't watch it, Sinead. It's too real. You were so young and so..."

"No, no, honestly, it was years ago now. I'm totally fine. It was my own daft fault. I chose to do it."

I gave her a smile to reassure her I wasn't lying, that I really was okay.

"But you were so bloody vulnerable. Imagine if you had been arrested and it had been all over the newspapers. People top themselves over stuff like that, y'know." She sounded angry.

What? I certainly had never wanted or expected sympathy. In fact, I had always blamed myself for being attention seeking and downright stupid. My friend obviously saw something other than what I saw as I watched myself on the screen. I saw a young fool who had no fear of consequence. She saw a young woman, exposed, humiliated and exploited. Was she being over dramatic, or was that really me? I didn't know; I had never allowed myself to think of it from an alternative perspective.

CHAPTER 10

Dirty cash

I was washing the dishes one day; when I heard the letterbox clatter. I dried my hands and went to investigate. I picked up a scrap of paper from the mat and read with interest. It was definitely a man's handwriting.

Hello! It's your neighbours here. You would be more than welcome to pop round one evening for coffee.

We're here for a good time, not a long time!

I didn't have a clue what this friendly, yet cryptic message meant. I assumed that it was from our next-door neighbours. We had recently had a small dispute about their dog using our garden as a toilet. I smiled at the olive-branchesque gesture and immediately went around and knocked on their door.

"Oh, hi! I've just popped round to thank you for the lovely note. We'd love to come over at the weekend if that's okay with you?"

Our neighbour, Karen, looked at me in confusion.

"We didn't send it, Sinead."

I felt my cheeks flush as I explained to her what I had received in the mail. I told Tim about it, and he looked as confused as I. I soon forgot about it, and life continued as normal.

Tim wouldn't limit his abuse to the home. Occasionally he would slap me in the middle of the street, or pull me down the road by my hair. Now and again passers-by intervened, and sometimes they turned a blind eye. One evening when he had hurt me and I was feeling desperate, I called the police. I thought if I had him arrested, the abuse would stop.

As the court date loomed, I lost my nerve. It was a catch twenty-two situation. If he had to pay court costs, it would come out of his wage, and that was the only money we had to live on. And what if they sent him to prison? I didn't want Morgan to suffer – we needed to buy nappies, wipes and baby food. What if we ended up homeless? I wrote a letter to the judge who would deal with our case. I lied that it had been an isolated event, and that it had stemmed from financial stress. The judge believed me, and as I stood in the big courtroom listening to the story all over again, I wished the ground would swallow me up. I felt so ashamed.

"Timothy Robert Marshall, I order you to pay sixty pounds in court costs, and you will be bound over to keep the peace for twelve months."

I released my breath in relief. *Thank God for that.* We went home and life resumed with minimal discomfort for a while. Tim, being a magnificent liar, made me doubt my intuition frequently. I believed that I was nothing without him, no matter how much I despised him. I dusted myself off, buried the pain within the walls of my blackened heart, and carried on living the lie that was my marriage.

I was still doing quite a bit of modelling, and because I had upped my levels to Continental, we were never that short of money. Tim and I even did an adult-themed shoot together for a lovers' guide book. We received £700 for the shoot, and Tim enjoyed spending it. I got talking to another model at a studio one day, and she told me about how she used to work at a lap-dancing club to earn some extra money to pay for her wedding.

"Why don't you give it a go?"

Well, I was already showing my wares to the world, so dancing suddenly seemed less sleazy to me than previously. The money would be nice, and at least I wouldn't have to be opening my legs all the time. Maybe if I started dancing, I could stop the adult modelling. I didn't mind modelling topless and upwards, but I didn't exactly like it. I preferred the creative editorial stuff. The adult work was just a means to an end, and I would rather not have had to do it.

Of course, I didn't really have to do it. It wasn't like anyone was holding a gun to my head or anything. The reason I say 'had to' is that once your adult images are published, editorial photographers won't touch you with a barge pole. You're tarnished with the adult model label, and a lot of mainstream photographers lose the respect they once had for you. You're only good for two things – tits and arse. Plus, you get used to the money, so you feel that you have to do the jobs to support yourself to the same standard. And what kind of real-life employer would touch you with a history of pornographic work? Therefore, so many girls get stuck in the industry with no other prospects or way of progressing out of it. They have no real-world qualifications – only modelling. Trying to move from that kind of work to something different can be a daunting prospect, so it's a better-the-devil-you-know situation.

On one non-adult, fully clothed shoot, the photographer tried to grope me whilst I was posing. He had seen on my profile that I did sometimes offer work of an adult nature, and he assumed that my body was public property. He thought it was acceptable to push my boundaries and touch me. I fled from the shoot scene, shaken up and in tears. The photographer couldn't understand my reaction at all. My boundaries were quickly becoming blurred, without me even noticing.

It thrilled Tim that I was thinking of going dancing. I was blissfully unaware of the real reason he wanted me out of the house. I was ridiculously nervous on the first night. A club in a big city close to where we lived hired me on a trial basis. Whether they kept me on depended on if I got through the audition; and how much I earned on my first night.

The club was dimly lit and had wall-to-wall red velvet-covered seating. The walls were decorated with leopard-print wallpaper and sconces which held fake flickering candles. A skinny, blonde girl led me down a narrow staircase to the changing room. It was kitted out with Formica work surfaces like you'd find in an old-fashioned kitchen; and lots of mirrors. About ten scantily clad girls were busy getting dressed, fake tanning each other's backs, applying thick make-up, smoking and gossiping. Nobody turned to see the unfamiliar face who was being shown around their lair. They had far more important things to be getting on with. Money was the only thing that mattered to anyone there, and nobody wanted to work any longer than they had to.

I was told to get changed into a long gown and wear it until midnight, which was when we girls were to take off the dresses and wear something more revealing. I had brought with me a red, floor-length stretch lace dress. I put on a pair of matching seven-inch platform shoes, checked that my hair and make-up were just right, and went back upstairs.

The audition was nothing like I expected. The boss was a fat, miserable-looking Lithuanian guy called Sam, and he reminded me of Baron Greenback[29] from the children's cartoon TV series, Danger Mouse. He seemed disinterested in me as I politely introduced myself, as though I was taking up his precious time. Pretty rude really, but I guess us girls were just a commodity to him. Sam beckoned a curvy, small-breasted, bottom-heavy, Brazilian-looking girl over, and told her she was to show me the ropes.

"Hi, I'm Isabella. Follow me."

Isabella ushered me through a long, dark, narrow corridor. On either side of the corridor, running to the end, were little booths. Some had a velvet curtain drawn across, which only came halfway down so that just the dancer's legs were visible. That was so that the bouncers could check that the girls weren't doing anything they shouldn't be. (The rule was that at least one foot must be visible on the ground, but nobody stuck to it.) A few booths were empty with the curtains open, and I was able to see inside. They were like tiny little rooms, just big enough for one person to sit down on the seat. The wall opposite the seat had a full-length mirror hung on it, and that was all that was in there. At the top right-hand corner of each ceiling was a piece of string connected to what looked like a light-pull. This was the cord that should be pulled if a customer tried to touch or became abusive. Good idea, you would think... except that the cords had all been cut so short that no girl could reach them. They were just there because the law said they had to be. The law also said that the club had to be advertised

---

[29] A repulsive looking villain, who resembled a big, green, ugly toad in a suit, and was also a bit of a twat to Danger Mouse.

as a 'Bar and Diner' on the outside signage; but inside there were no menus, no food and certainly no chef. The only thing being dished up in that place was lust, and the only stirring taking place was in the loins of the customers.

We reached what Isabella called a 'group booth'. It was ten times the size of the small booths, with wall-to-wall seating and mirrors. I followed her inside.

"It's okay; I'm not gonna make you audition. That would be just embarrassing for you. Just watch me and copy what I do when someone asks you for a dance. A dance lasts around four minutes, which is generally the length of a song. You always take the customer's money first, then you take the money to the bar and exchange it for dance tokens. Don't let the customers touch you and always try to entice them into booking another dance before they leave the booth. The fee is £10 per dance, of which you get £7 in dance tokens. At the end of the night, you cash the tokens in with Sam in exchange for money. That's what you get to take home. That's basically it. Just remember all that; tell Sam I watched you dance, and that I said you were a natural. Good luck!"

After watching Isabella slither and slide all over the seats, I was in awe. *I'll never be able to do that,* I thought. Oh well, it was too late to back out now. For someone with low self-worth, I was certainly a brave little madam.

I went back into the bar area and waited for the customers to start to rolling. To say that I was shitting myself is an understatement. I sat next to a quiet girl called Destiny (they all had exotic names like that) and watched what she did when a customer approached her.

"Hi, I'm Destiny. Would you like a dance?" she purred, snaking her arm around the guy's waist. Then she led him by the hand to a booth.

Right… here goes nothing. I looked around the room as though stalking my prey and settled upon a short, fat, balding man wearing glasses who was standing on his own. I sauntered up to him, swaying my hips seductively.

"Hi, I'm Olivia. Fancy a dance? It's only ten pounds, and I promise to make it worth your while."

He gulped and nodded. I took him by the hand and led him up the little corridor.

"Sit down, please. Hands by your sides. There's no touching. Now sit back and enjoy!"

Right on cue, Christina Aguilera's 'Dirrty' started playing. Luckily, it was a song that I knew well and had danced to in nightclubs plenty of times. I swayed in time to the music, pulling my best porno-face, and wiggling my hips as I slowly and teasingly shimmied free of my clothing. My dress fell to the floor to reveal my almost naked form. This was going well, and I was enjoying it. I felt empowered as the man looked on me with wonder. He hadn't noticed my stretch marks or cellulite. Either that, or he just didn't give a shit. It was now or never, so I nervously slipped off my knickers, being careful not to bend over so far that he could see my dinner. The guy's eyes nearly popped out of his head, and I had to stifle a giggle. The dance was over all too quickly, and I couldn't wait to do it again. It was like the adrenaline rush from getting your first tattoo or doing karaoke for the first time.

That night I did forty dances and went home with £280, minus the floor fee of £20 that all dancers had to pay to work there. *Easy money!* I returned the following Saturday on my own, and every week thereafter for the next eight months. Dancing taught me that the naked female form is a beautiful thing. There were girls at the club who were fat, thin, short, tall – all shapes and sizes; and every one of them was desirable to someone who entered the bar.

I no longer strove for physical perfection. I was beautiful and sexy enough just how I was. I learned that when it comes to the basics of sexual desire, most men don't give a shit what a girl looks like. The girls were great, and I forged some lasting friendships. They weren't brainless bimbos either. One of my friends there was studying to be a doctor, and dancing helped to pay for her medical degree. Girl power!

CHAPTER 11

Hustlin'

Tim and I enjoyed the money from my dancing job, but I found many of the men to be pervy and started to dread asking guys for dances. After the initial empowerment, the nights became long, and I felt exploited and disempowered. I would text Tim at around 1:00 a.m. and say I'd had enough for the night.

<Hi Tim, done 36 dances and tired. Can I come home?>

His reply was always the same.

<Just do 20 more. We need the money. If U could stay 'til about 3 that would B good.>

So, I would do as he asked. I grew physically fitter; the cellulite disappeared, and my bum lifted. I had never looked so good, but I felt crap about myself. I was bored, and I wanted my old life back. I was bored with the stripping but loved the camaraderie at the club. I had opened up to my friends there about my unhappy marriage.

One night at the club, a big group of Sam's Lithuanian friends came in. They were rude, obnoxious and disrespectful to the girls. I was reluctantly dancing for one of them, when he reached out and grabbed me around the waist, pulling me toward him. I pulled away instantly and told him he must sit on his hands or I wouldn't continue. He tried it again, and I stormed angrily out of the booth and down the corridor. I marched up to Sam's desk and told him what his friend had done. I complained that I couldn't even pull the panic cord because it had been cut too short for me to reach. His reaction shocked me.

"What do you fucking expect, you silly bitch? You're a fucking lap dancer. Now get your arse back in there and fucking dance!"

So, I did. I went back in there and fucking danced. I felt that I didn't have much of a choice; but from that moment on, I *really* hated my job. I realised just how little Sam cared about the girls who were helping to line his pockets. We were nothing to him. When he looked at us, he saw nothing more than pound signs. I vowed to myself there and then that I would do whatever it took to make sure my dancing days were numbered.

Life carried on as normally as could be expected in the circumstances. I couldn't put my finger on it, but Tim appeared to have a bit of a spring in his step lately. The house was always tidy when I arrived home at 5:00 a.m. after a twelve-hour dancing shift, and he had even changed the bedding so I didn't have to do it during the week. However, now when he was in the occasional rage, he would hiss at me, "Just you wait until this twelve months of keeping the peace is over, you bitch. You're fucking dead."

He would drag his finger across his neck, simulating slitting my throat. It terrified me. It was only a matter of time until his court order expired. I was a dead woman walking. He had never hurt me in front of Morgan, but I realised that he could, and if I didn't claw my way out of this destructive marriage soon, he most certainly would. I was so down in the dumps that I went to my doctor.

"I just feel like a black cloud is hanging over me all the time."

He raised one eyebrow at me, looking unconvinced; so, I added, "My husband is hitting me."

That did the trick. He promptly wrote me out a prescription for anti-depressants. Taking them soon made me feel numb, like it was someone else experiencing my life. I wasn't happy though, and I knew that I had to leave Tim, somehow. I needed a plan.

If I was going to leave, I decided that I needed to learn how to drive. I still can't believe that Tim allowed me to, but he did. He was probably just thinking how great it would be if I could chauffeur him about on his regular clothes-shopping trips. It took me a year to pass my test, but I felt determined. Now I just needed some money. When Tim gave me his wage so I could pay the bills, I would stash away the odd twenty-pound note. He never noticed, and soon I had six hundred pounds in a secret account. I knew that I would be financially stable without him, because I was still dancing. After one particular incident when Tim had pushed me to my limit, I decided that it was time.

He had been working away all week and had arrived home for the weekend. I had been juggling caring for Morgan with trying to get the clothes washing done in time for his return. An hour before he was due to walk through the door, I realised that I had run out of washing powder. Tim was furious with me.

"A good wife would make sure we're always stocked up on groceries and cleaning products. What have you been doing all week, you lazy cow? Watching telly on your fat arse, I bet."

Morgan began to cry.

"And you can shut that fucking kid up too. He knows exactly what he's doing – the little shit!"

Well, that was it. That 'little shit' was our child. I realised that as

Morgan grew older, Tim's anger and violence would end up being directed at him too. *Over my dead body.* I was old enough to manage the abuse Tim inflicted upon me, but Morgan was a helpless toddler. I turned to him and said calmly, "Tim... Morgan is not a little shit. We haven't been getting along now for a long time. I think it's time that we went our separate ways, don't you?"

The anger faded from his face, and he began to cry. I spoke softly. "Come on, Tim; you know it's for the best. Maybe just a trial separation so that we can get our heads sorted? I can help you find a flat, and we can get back together when we've had a bit of space from each other."

Tim couldn't argue – it was definitely for the best. If I could just get him to leave the house willingly, thinking it was only a temporary separation, I would be halfway there.

"Okay," he said, looking defeated.

And that was how simple it was. Needless to say, Tim never got his precious washing powder. Dirty clothes for a dirty little man with an even dirtier little mind.

It took about a month to source an affordable apartment for Tim to rent. As he worked away from home quite a bit, sleeping alone became easier. If it hadn't been for the girls at the club, and the confidence and support they gave me, I wouldn't have had the courage to end my marriage.

In the final week of our cohabiting, just before Tim was due to move into his new place, I invited Louise up for a cuppa. We had a good old catch-up natter and a few coffees, then she asked me if she could use my computer to check her emails. She brought up the

Hotmail home page and clicked the cursor on the log-in box. A saved email address popped up – SexyTim25@Hotmail.co.uk. Louise looked at me, and I looked at her, then we both looked at the screen together. We didn't need to say anything; we both knew what we had found – Tim's secret email address. He wasn't the brightest guy in the world, so I could guess his password easily. Morgan2002.

What I saw next nearly made me fall off my swivel chair in shock. There were lots of emails from a local swinging website, and various dating sites. Curiosity got the better of me, and I clicked on the most recent one. Up popped Tim's profile. He was looking for local couples and single women to come around to our house to have sex with. *Oh, sweet Jesus!* After changing his profile picture to an unflattering one, his penis size from average to small and sexual orientation to homosexual, I changed his password so he couldn't get in to alter the info I had entered. I clicked onto a few of the many conversations he had been engaging in. He had been chatting to a lady who looked like an angry sumo wrestler, wearing a studded leather collar, telling her, "You look gorgeous! Fancy hooking up for some no strings fun tonight?"

She had replied to his polite and courteous message, and their conversation went something like this:

"Yeah, why not? My place or yours?"

"My place. My wife works nights. Lucky me, eh? You can meet me in the pub across the road from mine. I have a two-year-old son, but he never wakes up. I can just leave him asleep and come to meet you."

"I'm sorry, but I don't think that's a sensible idea. I wouldn't feel comfortable knowing that you had left your son alone in the house. I wouldn't feel at ease having sex at your house with him there either. Sorry."

Thank God she had used her better judgement. I knew Tim was a selfish bastard, but I couldn't quite believe how low he would stoop just to ejaculate. *The spineless creep.* I thought back to the strange note I had received in the post a few months earlier. It all made sense now. It had been from a local swinging couple. I do often wonder when I'm walking to the corner shop and back if I've ever passed them and exchanged pleasantries, not realising who they are.

There were more emails too – most of them from men dressed as women, with Transvestic Fetishism[30], whom he had already met. This was getting crazier by the minute. I noticed that on his profile he had been given feedback, written by a woman who was one half of a male/female couple.

"Really enjoyed meeting Tim. He was friendly and genuine, and my husband and I had a great time with him. I particularly enjoyed watching."

She what? She enjoyed watching what? Tim with her fucking husband? In our fucking bed, when I was stripping for cash and he was asking me to work later and later? *Oh, my God.* My heart raced, and I felt faint. I ran downstairs and lit a cigarette outside. What if he hadn't used a condom? What if he had passed an STD onto me, on one of the rare occasions that we had engaged in sex? My whole body was trembling with shock.

I have no idea how I kept this discovery to myself until Tim arrived home for the weekend, but somehow, I did. When I heard the key in the lock that Saturday afternoon, my heart raced once again in that all-too-familiar way. I was waiting for Don Juan in the living room, and I had practised my lines to perfection.

---

[30] A sexual fetish (commonly thought of as a disorder) for wearing the clothes of the opposite gender. Not to be confused with Transgenderism.

"Welcome home, Sexy Tim twenty-five! I enjoyed reading about all your little secret rendezvous. I've printed everything out for the divorce courts. Forget waiting until your move-in date. I think you'd better pack your things right now, don't you?"

He just stood there, speechless.

"Just tell me one thing, Tim. Please, please tell me you used a condom and didn't put me at risk."

He looked me dead in the eyes, raised one eyebrow slowly, as a smirk crossed his lips.

"What do you expect, living with a bitch like you?" And with that, he turned and went upstairs to pack, leaving me standing there, dumbfounded.

In the weeks that followed, I began my transition into an independent, single mother. I did the sensible thing and went for a sexual health check, which to my relief came back clear. I changed my first light bulb and put the dustbins out for collection for the first time. It shocked me to realise how dependent on Tim I had been. It was a strange time, because I mourned the death of my marriage, but I also felt excited at the prospect of entering a new phase in my life. It took a while for the paranoia to leave me that he may return and hurt me, but leave me it did. Tim's parents stepped in and made sure that he paid me regular child support money, and they looked after Morgan on the days I had to work.

I had my home, my car, a beautiful little boy, and I had reclaimed control over my life. I felt a surge of pride and empowerment. I filed for a quickie online divorce, which Tim and I dealt with ourselves. It only cost us around £100 and took a few weeks to complete. Tim admitted to 'adultery with an unknown person/persons'. We had been married for five years, and it was over, just like that. He was no longer listed in my phone contacts as 'Tim', but was now 'Take it all Tim'. I got a lot of mileage from that, because for years later, the mental imagery associated with this nickname made me smile whenever he called. *Checkmate, douche bag.*

I did my last adult modelling shoot shortly after leaving Tim. It was for a well-known top-shelf magazine, and the shoot was on the outskirts of Manchester. The day started badly, so I should have guessed it would continue in the same fashion. I had nasty period pains all the way there, and just as I pulled up in the car, I felt a familiar gush of blood soak my underwear. *Great.* I arrived late after getting lost, because of my ancient sat nav telling me to swing a sharp left, which led me to a dead end. *Nightmare.*

When I finally arrived, I did a double-take. I did most commercial shoots in units on industrial estates. This was an almost derelict-looking, run-down detached house at the side of the main road. The sort with black bricks from the constant traffic fumes and smoke coating them over the years. The wooden window frames were rotting and shabby. It reminded me of one of those haunted houses in American theme parks, where actors jump out on unsuspecting victims. I knocked on the filthy, green, flaky door. A short, stocky, wide-eyed guy in his thirties answered it. He looked like he fancied himself a bit. You know the sort – a diamond stud in each ear, fitted pinstripe shirt with cufflinks, slicked back hair, designer stubble, sweat patches under his arms and too much aftershave. He gave me a flirty smile, and greeted me in a cockney accent:

"Alright, darlin'. Olivia, ain't it? I'm Anton. Come wiv me, sweetheart."

I waddled up the stairs after him, like I'd shat my pants, because my gusset was wet from the blood. I had to say something, as this was an adult shoot and I couldn't exactly open my legs in this state. *How embarrassing.*

"Erm, I've just come on my period and I don't have any money on me for any tampons or anything."

He didn't bat an eyelid. He was obviously used to this happening. He passed me a scrunched up five-pound note.

"S'alright love. Take this and get yourself some Tampax from the shop up the road. You can cut the string so we won't see it in your pussy when we're shooting."

Crikey. I couldn't help blushing with embarrassment. I did as I was told and hurried back to the so-called studio, to get changed as fast as I could. I had been told to dress like a secretary. I quickly pulled on a black pencil skirt and a white blouse and tied my hair into a loose bun. I rushed out into the main room, which I guessed would probably have been a living room in the past. It had been set up to look like a bedroom, and four other women were standing about, dressed in various uniforms, waiting to be photographed. Three of them were animatedly chattering and gesticulating with their hands. *Definitely coked up.*

One girl was lying on the bed, her legs as wide apart as was physically possible, with a massive dildo looking like it was trying to escape from her vagina. She held it in place with one hand whilst the other hand pushed one of her breasts upwards so she could reach the nipple with her tongue. Her eyes looked upwards, towards the camera as it flashed. Anton must have been shattered. He was up and down, up and down. One minute he was standing on a stepladder taking the photos, and the next he was lying on the floor doing the same. He looked like he took his work seriously, and was sweating so much with bouncing about that he had to remove his shirt. His dimpled, hairy beer belly protruded over his gold buckled belt. The sight of his sweat-saturated wanker's 'tache[31] made me want to look the other way.

My turn. I had to pose in another part of the room, which had been set up to look like an office. It was the usual rigmarole – sitting on the chair with a pen hanging provocatively from my mouth, legs wide open, and that kind of thing. I think Anton could tell that I was a little uncomfortable, and that I differed from the other girls.

"What you so uptight for, darlin'? Here, have a line of this. That should loosen you up a bit!" He jabbed me playfully on the arm, and laughed. He racked up some lines of cocaine on the top of an old magazine that was lying on the desk.

"Oh no, no, I'm fine thanks. I don't touch the stuff."

"What? You're kidding me, right? No wonder you're so boring!"

"I'm not boring! I just don't like to drink or take drugs when I'm on shoots. I've got a kid to look after when I get home."

"Whatever. Girls, come here! That's a wrap 'til after lunch. Come and get some of this!"

The other models promptly rushed into the office setting and greedily snorted their lines. Then one of them disappeared into the bedroom set with Anton, where they stayed for the whole duration of lunch. It was obvious she was giving him sexual favours, from the wheezy-sounding grunts emitting from under the door.

The whole day seemed very surreal to me. The adult modelling industry was on a different level from glamour. It felt like another world, and I was ill at ease with being a participant. I didn't want to

---

[31] Unsightly line of hair heading from the navel to the genitals.

socialise with the models, who were crass when they spoke. I mean, I was as common as muck in the company of my friends, but I knew how to adapt when in a professional setting. Work-me was a lot different to home-me. I didn't want their dirty drugs, and I certainly didn't want to shag the photographer. I just wanted to do an honest day's work without feeling pressured or uncomfortable, and to go back to being a mum and a housewife afterward. I didn't care if I would be short of cash anymore. I just didn't want to feel like I had to open my legs for money ever again.

One of my images made the centre-fold poster a couple of months later, by which time I had forgotten all about my unease. I proudly showed Mum the magazine. She was super-happy for me and bought herself a copy, telling me, "Ooh, I'm gonna put the poster on the back of the door in my spare room!"

Right on, Mum. My fadge on your door. How proud you must be. She was, though. Say what you want about my mum, but she attempted to support me with whatever she thought made me happy. It might not have been an ideal career, but she let me get on with it and make my own mistakes. Had she advised me against it, I would've just gone out and done it anyway, because that's what kids do. Especially twenty-five-year-old kids who still thought they had something to prove! Show me a wet paint sign and I can't help but touch and get my fingers dirty.

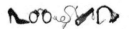

Lo and behold, not long after I had made my decision to keep my legs closed and to go back to only working up to implied nude level, I was asked to cast for Playboy's online members' site, Cybergirls, where the more risqué, non-magazine-friendly images were showcased. It was sod's law because the main ambition of every glamour model was to be able to say they'd worked for Playboy. It had massively helped some of my friends' careers. I thought long and hard about the proposal, but turned it down a few days later. I suspected that I may regret it in the future, but I had vowed to keep within my boundaries.

As if by a twist of fate, soon after, Hustler, Playboy's biggest rival magazine, contacted me. They wanted to interview me and set up a shoot, using one of their UK photographers. I couldn't believe this was happening, all at the wrong time. The features editor guy on the phone was called Robbie and had an accent so American, it hurt. It was a full-on Texan drawl like I'd only ever heard on the telly. I was quite taken with the novelty factor of being called 'ma'am'. He was so polite to say he worked for a jazz mag!

With a heavy heart, I explained that I only worked up to implied nude these days. He thought for a moment and answered, "Ma'am, I respect what you're saying, but I think our readers would like your look and it would be a shame to not work with you at all. I'm trying to think of a way we can still feature you. We did want open leg, ideally; but maybe you could just send us some of your own images? They would still have to be nude, ma'am, but not open leg."

Excitedly, I agreed. We chatted for the next half hour, laughing at each other's accents and chatting about the modelling and magazine businesses. The interview part would be easy because I had to send the answers to his questions by email. Robbie said he would send me a load of freebies through the post, which I thought was a nice gesture. Before we ended our conversation, he joked, "You can tell your friends now that you're the only girl in Hustler to not have opened her legs! Who needs Playboy, ma'am?"

A month or two later, I received the magazine in the post. The spread they had done of me was artistic and respectful, so I was pleased. A few days later, a big box of freebies followed, as promised. The content was enough to make a nun blush – a collection of Hustler's own brand porn DVDs, a red Hustler logo vest, and several glossy, very American-looking magazines. In them were pregnant women, amputees, women dressed up as giant fluffy animal characters, dwarves and giantesses. Mum and I had a good laugh poring over them whilst drinking coffee. It was eye-opening, discovering fascinating fetishes on those pages that we never knew existed. It's amazing what goes on behind closed doors.

CHAPTER 12

Telephone manners

There was one exception to my 'no agents' rule. One night I was looking for work online, when I saw an advertisement on one of the modelling forums, asking for candidates to present the promo links on an adult chat TV station. Promo links are the advertising breaks between one programme and another, where an attractive-looking model would say what was up next and try to entice viewers into calling a phone number which would connect them to a girl. The rate was two hundred and fifty pounds just to film a few different versions at various intervals in the night when the station had airplay. The application was via an agent, so I sent them some portfolio images and a short video of me introducing myself. I was thrilled to bits when the agent emailed me a few days later to say that I had got the job. I had always come alive in front of a video camera, and I figured that it would be easy work. They sent me a contract that same day, so I quickly signed it and sent it back.

A few days later, I set off on the four-hour-long journey down south. I considered anything regarding television fantastic exposure, so I was very excited at the prospect of adding this to my ever-expanding modelling résumé. Mum was living with her new (and much more suited to her) husband, Matt, by then. I told them about the job and they said they'd keep flicking over the telly to try and catch a glimpse of me. I felt lucky that I could do this job wearing a dress and not have to strip down to my underwear like the girls who were working live on the phones. Because I knew that nobody would see my undies, I shoved on a pair of big comfy knickers and slipped on a barely-there tight, black, halter neck mini-dress with a pair of silver stripper shoes with see-through Perspex platforms and heels. I coiffed my hair, so it was big and bouncy, and spent ages on my makeup, making sure that it would show up on the screen. The look I was going for was your stereotypical American model style – big, light pink lips lined with a light brown pencil, blended to make my pout look extra kissable, and long, black fluttery eyelashes, complete with a bronze tan. The long-distance lorry drivers who passed me on the motorway that afternoon must have caught a right eyeful! What a sight I must have looked, driving along the M1 in that get-up.

It was late evening, and the sky was dark by the time I arrived at the huge studio building on an industrial estate. I was about half an hour late because of the slow traffic, so I got out of my car and half tottered, half ran across the car park, carrying my little pink suitcase towards the double glass doors. The reception area was very plush and corporate looking. You wouldn't think you were in an adult television studio. An official-looking woman in her late twenties was already waiting for me, holding a clipboard. Think 'sexy secretary' and you've got a good idea of what she looked like – black pencil skirt, low-cut blouse, patent black stiletto heels and highlighted blonde hair up in a tight French pleat, glasses resting on her nose to complete the image.

"Hiiiiiiii! I'm Amy, you must be Olivia." She greeted me with a warm smile and shook my hand. "Come this way."

She marched authoritatively through a door and down a succession of dimly lit winding corridors, with me doing a little jog behind her in my massive shoes, doing my best to keep up. There were what seemed like hundreds of doors along every corridor, which I assumed led into separate studio rooms. It felt like we had walked miles by the time we reached the end of the hall. Amy gestured towards a small flight of steps, with a little grey door at the top.

"That's the girls' area up there. Drop your suitcase off, freshen up your makeup, give my mobile a call and I'll meet you back down here. Try not to be too long, as we're on the air in ten minutes." And with that, she rushed off, clickety-clicking back down the hallway.

I yanked my suitcase up the stairs and opened the door. Inside were about ten scantily clad girls in a room set out similarly to the lap-dancing club – Formica work surfaces lined the walls, with continuous mirroring above them that ran the circumference of the room. Some girls were doing their makeup in the mirrors, some were sharing gossip and gesticulating with their hands, engrossed in conversation. Some were carefully racking up lines of cocaine with their bank cards and passing round a cut-up plastic straw for snorting purposes. Sharing was caring, it seemed. The girls all had the same aura about them, with wide, cold-looking eyes, like there was no soul or emotion behind them. Loud dance music blared out from a portable CD player on the floor in the room's corner. Just like in the club, nobody turned to look at me as I entered. I thought about saying hello, but didn't fancy my chances of being greeted back.

Amy met me at the bottom of the stairs, as promised, and led me back down the long corridor. She pointed towards a door to the right of us as we hurried past.

"That's the phone room, where the girls chat to people who phone in. Just chat; no filming in there."

As we got a little further down the corridor, Amy stopped and opened another door to our left.

"I'll just show you what's in here, quickly. These are the bunks where the girls sleep between shows. Sometimes if anyone phones in sick, other girls will cover but will have to work twenty-four or more hours. This is where they sleep when they manage to get a break. This is where you'll be sleeping when you come down again."

Weird, I thought. They had only booked me to do a few promo links. Nobody had mentioned me coming for a second time, let alone staying for so long and sleeping here. I definitely didn't want to have to sleep here.

I peered inside to see what looked like a very glamourous prisoner of war camp. It was about the size of a small living room, with individual booths, one on top of the other and side by side, running along two walls with a narrow walkway down the middle. The beds themselves were skinny, like what you would get on a budget ferry to Amsterdam. Inside the bunks were girls still dressed in their glitzy little costumes, getting in their forty winks, uncovered. I heard several pitches of snoring noises coming from random beds. It amazed me how the girls could sleep so deeply with the ceiling light glaring like it was. I definitely wouldn't be able to sleep in there if my life depended on it. I liked my sleeping space to resemble a womb – dark, cosy and quiet.

Amy closed the door behind us and set off down the corridor again, with me trotting alongside her. Eventually, we reached a set of grey double doors with a sign stating, 'Quiet! Filming in progress'. She opened the door and ushered me inside, whispering, "Right, here you go. You're on in three minutes. Have fun and I'll see you later."

And with that, she was gone. I was in a big, dark room, with a table filled with production equipment. A young, good-looking guy in his mid-twenties with short, black hair was standing behind the table, wearing headphones, a scruffy-looking t-shirt and jeans. He had love bites all over his neck. When I say 'all over', that's exactly how it was. He had that many red and purple marks on his neck, from the collar of his t-shirt, right up to his ears, that they all merged into one. I've still never seen love bites to that scale, since and I recoiled in disgust.

In front of us, at the opposite side of the room, lit mega-brightly with a few tall key-lights, were two double mattresses, covered with cerise pink silk sheets. The bed to the left of the room was empty. A Thai-looking girl occupied the bed in the right-hand corner. She had ultra-long, silky black hair and too much pale foundation, dressed in a red PVC bra and G-string. She was talking seductively into a telephone receiver, although I couldn't make out what she was saying.

Upon noticing me in the room, the producer guy removed his headphones, set them down on the table with all the equipment on it, and quickly dashed over to me.

"Olivia, right? I'm Mickey. You're on in one minute if you want to take your place on the bed."

Surely, he's not suggesting that I'll be taking calls on live television?

"B-but I'm just here for presenting the promo links." My heart was going ten to the dozen now. Pure panic.

"No time to explain. The bosses changed their minds. You're too good looking for that. They want you to do the live chat because they know you'll make the channel money. You've got sixty seconds, quick, get on the bed!"

"No way, I can't do that. I've had no training; I don't know what to say! Can I speak to my agent?"

"Look, you'll have to discuss that with him later. There's no time, just go along with whatever the caller says. Copy what she does."

He gestured over at the Thai girl on the other bed. She lay on her front, humping the bed whilst talking into the telephone receiver.

"I can't do *that!*" I felt paralysed by fear. I would die if anyone I knew flicked over the telly at home to see me gyrating on a bed. It was one thing doing it one on one into a video camera, for a photographer; but live on telly? *Please, God, no.*

"You'll be fine, go!" Mickey gave me a little nudge forward. Feeling that I had no other choice, I hurried over to the mattress, climbed on and tried to find a comfortable position to sit in. I knelt up, stuck my legs out to the right and plonked my bum down. I pulled my dress down self-consciously as far towards my knees as it would stretch and shuffled about awkwardly on the spot. I looked over at Little Miss Humpy. She was now on her back, legs akimbo, thrusting her pelvis wildly into thin air, phone to her ear; and I could now hear what she was saying, because she was shouting so loudly in a strong Thai accent, "Ah yeah! Fock meh, fock meh!"

Distracting, much? I looked over at Mickey and saw him mouthing to me, "Four, three, two, one..."

I wanted the mattress to swallow me whole. A green light on a little black box in front of the bed set-up flashed. I had my first caller. *Fucksticks!* I reluctantly picked up the receiver and the voice at the end of the line said in a teenage-sounding cockney accent, "I fink your legs are lovely. They look so long. I love tall gals."

No way was I going to play this game.

"I'm quite short actually, I'm only five foot three, sorry," I answered flatly.

Beep. The line went dead. Straight away, the green light flashed again. *Shit!* Another voice on the line. This time it was an older, gruff-sounding Geordie bloke.

"You're lush. I've been dying to talk to you. I love natural boobs, like."

"Sorry, they're fake," I replied defiantly.

Beep. Another dead line. The bloody green light flashed again. This was like a bad dream. Another Londoner by the sound of it.

"What d'ya wanna talk abaat then?"

"Nothing, if I'm honest. I'm not in the mood for a chat right now. I have bad PMT, soz."

Beep. Dead line. If the object would have been to have had the shortest call time, I would've won, hands down. I felt pleased and privately congratulated myself on my tactical diversions. I looked across to my left at Little Miss Hump-a-lot. She was an agile so and so, now balancing on all fours whilst gyrating her hips around and around in hypnotic circles. Well, she was actually on all threes, as her right hand was holding the phone to her ear as she shouted into it, "Yeah, baybee. Just like that; mek meh comm baybee!"

My bastard of a green light flashed up again within seconds. Let no one tell you that having a half-decent face makes life easier. It's a lie. At that moment, I wished hard that God would temporarily give me repulsive, deformed features to make these callers bugger off. I rolled my eyes and picked up the phone.

"Sinead, it's me, Mum! Hello! Me and Matt are watching you on the telly. We're recording it!" She was giggling excitedly. *Sweet relief.*

"Mum, Matt, hello!" I waved excitedly into the camera pointing at me from a tripod in front of the mattress. I could hear Mum and Matt laughing and I started laughing too. I clocked Mickey, looking over at me with a furrowed brow and a not-so-happy look on his face. I lowered my voice to a whisper.

"Mum, thank God. Listen, I've not got long. I don't think they're very happy with me. They've tricked me into coming here under false pretences. I want to go home, but they're holding me against my will and won't let me talk to my agent. I told them I didn't want to do the chat, but they made me."

"Oh my God, love. I'm so sorry. We had no idea. Can't you just say you want a break?"

"Not really, they're bloody filming."

"Yes, you can. Ask for a b—"

At that moment, Amy was back in the room next to the production desk, microphone in hand.

"Olivia, you can't take personal calls. We know you're talking to your mum. End the call now please and put down the phone!"

Shit, they had rumbled me. I whispered a very hurried goodbye to Mum and did as Amy said.

"Right girls, watershed time!" Amy shouted over the mic. "You can go topless if you want."

I did *not* want. I instinctively pulled down my dress to my knees again and yanked up the halter-neck straps so they covered my boobs as much as the sparse material could manage. I folded my arms in defiance in front of my chest and scowled. Amy's voice rang out once again, sounding impatient.

"You need to pull your dress down now, Olivia. It's ten o'clock."

"I will not!" I replied with a sulky glare in her direction. *Bollocks to this*, I thought. There was no way I was getting my tits out on live TV. Not a fucking chance. I still felt mentally scarred from the naked walk. Both Amy and Mickey could see that there was no reasoning with me. I watched Mickey snatch the microphone from Amy's hand.

"Right, girls. We're going into an early break. You've got fifteen minutes while the ads are on."

Thank fuck for that. I clambered off the bed mock-up and walked, as dignified as I could (with pins and needles after sitting in the same position for so long), over to Amy. Mickey was now otherwise engaged with Princess Humptastic, who was slobbering and sucking on his neck. He was good looking; but not that good looking. Amy looked at me, perplexed.

"What on Earth was all that about, Olivia?" she asked, concerned.

"I want to talk to my agent. This is not what he booked me for. Can you get him on the phone, please?"

"Well, not right now. We've only got fifteen minutes before we're back on the air."

"I want to talk to him now," I demanded.

I stood my ground. Amy found my contract, dialled the number and passed the phone to me. I realised I didn't even know my agent's name. As soon as I heard him speak, I blurted out, "I've come down here all this way to do the promo and they've put me on TV bloody chat! I want to go home; this is not what I agreed to."

After a pause, the voice said in a calm, charismatic, no-nonsense manner, "Look, leaving right now isn't an option. For a start, you won't get paid, and if you leave, they'll have to shut the channel down because there are no other girls available for the shift. My advice to you right now would be to take a minute to cool off, then get back on set and stick it out just for the last couple of hours. I'll speak to you in the morning."

I handed the phone back to Amy and left the room, saying I would get a drink of water, go to the toilet, and be back on set in ten minutes.

I don't think so. As soon as I was out of Amy's sight, I legged it to the changing room as fast as my Perspex-heeled feet would carry me. I quickly grabbed my little suitcase and ran down the corridor, not daring to look behind me. *Where the Hell is the way out?* I panicked. I ran along the corridors, car keys jangling in my hand, stopping to try every grey door that I came to. They were all locked. I managed to open one of them and accidentally ran into a room full of girls on crash mats, all talking into headsets. It was the room that Amy had told me about on my way into this formidable place. It looked like a cattle market.

I uttered an apology to the sound guy, who looked at me in annoyance, and I quietly shut the door behind me. I now realised whereabouts in the building I was, and ran breathlessly through the door to reception, back through the double glass doors and to my car. I threw my suitcase in, buckled up as fast as I could and sped out of the car park, tyres screeching. I don't think I've ever felt so relieved in my life. They must have been so angry with me. I drove for five minutes, then stopped at the side of the road to ring Mum.

"Sinead, you are so funny. You looked so grumpy on the telly when you were pulling your top up. Oh my God, me and Matt were in stitches when you were being all dramatic, like you were being held hostage. You'll never guess what? They had to take the channel off the air when you left."

"No way?"

"Way. Come over tomorrow and you can watch it. We recorded it for you to see." *Mum, you legend.*

The next day, I drove over to Mum and Matt's house and we all huddled on the sofa to watch me being a proper diva. It was so funny. We were all rolling about laughing at my angry faces and smug looks whenever the phones went dead. The sound was muted, but you didn't need sound to tell the gist of what I was saying. The last thing we saw before the screen went black was that part where I was pulling my dress up to my neck, saying, "I will not!" followed by a fifteen-minute promo link, then the words:

Sorry for any inconvenience. This channel will be off the air until further notice.

From that day forward, my family has always referred to my little adventure as 'The day Sinead shut down a whole TV station'. The channel went bust not long after. The tale never fails to impress at family parties.

Not long after my TV ordeal, one of my connections at one of the local newspapers asked if I would like to attend a small film premiere that would showcase the work of an upcoming local film-maker. They were looking for what they called 'local celebrities' to attend, which would give the event a newsworthy article in the local rag the next day. I thought it all sounded very upmarket and dazzling, and I accepted their offer instantaneously. I was so excited in the run-up to the event, but I knew I would have to schmooze with the members of a famous football club, plus a load of well-known local personalities. These would be people who earned amounts of money that I could only dream of, and that intimidated me. I worried about potentially showing myself up in front of my betters. The scruffy kid from my childhood haunted me. I wanted to feel as worthy as these important people.

The day before, I hurriedly dragged Mum around the indoor

market, while I tried on various outfits on the sale rails. I was skint as always, so I knew it would be a difficult task sourcing something which looked classy and expensive, but that cost no more than twenty-five quid. I finally settled on a black corset-style top with a matching floaty knee-length skirt. I would still look every inch the glamour girl, but not tarty. On the night I paired this well thought-out ensemble with my sparkliest pair of shoes that could probably pass as Manolos from a distance, and a fake Louis Vuitton bag that I'd bought in Turkey on mine and Tim's honeymoon.

I can't remember what the film was about now because I was too busy at the time looking around and feeling utterly star-struck at seeing people I had only seen on TV before. In real life, they all looked so, so… short! I entered by walking up the red carpet, thinking, *Well this is fucking nuts!* A photographer stopped me on the way in and asked me to pose. Me being photographed on the red carpet. *Just wow.* They had asked me to attend because I was a well-known local personality. Yes; well known for providing the important public service of getting my boobs out in the papers, to make tradesmen's days pass with at least one smile. The mind boggles.

The next day there was a substantial amount of coverage in several local papers, and they'd mentioned my name on a list of all the guests. The newsagent's shop where I used to work had put a poster with a headline about me being there, on one of those wooden boards with the strong metal mesh that holds the paper in tightly. I walked past it that day, blushing with pride… and back again at eleven at night, to nick it. You can take the girl out of the council estate, but you definitely can't take the council estate out of the girl! I still have it to this day, in my memory box. One day when I'm six feet under and my kids are clearing out my dusty loft, they'll find this treasure trove of craziness, and think, "Bloody Hell, Mum was a right dark horse. What a tinker she was!"

The film premier had enabled me to play at being a celeb for a day, which I had enjoyed immensely. It felt a bit like playing princess dress-up as a little girl. A very glossy commemorative program was published a few days later.

I was sent a copy, and flicked through the new-smelling pages with excitement. On page fifteen, there I was; captured in time, immortalised forever on that red carpet. I, with my fake persona, fake nails, fake tan, fake breasts, and fake chocolate brown hairpiece; complete with my fake Louis Vuitton bag... Held the wrong way around, the printed bronze-coloured monogram upside-fucking-down, giving away my true social status, and practically screaming, "Only a tenner from Turkey." I may as well have carried a placard saying 'Imposter!' with a big arrow pointing downward. *Way to go, Winters, you knob! Ho-hum; back to being a pumpkin then..*

A few weeks later, the local newspaper asked if I would fancy attending a charity luncheon with most of the same people who had attended the film premiere. They had a novel idea, which was for the guests to pay for their meals, and the restaurant would donate all the takings to a well-known children's charity. I didn't want to attend on my own, as I knew I would have to sit around a big table with all these pretentious toffs at either side of me. It worried me that I wouldn't have anything interesting or intelligent enough to contribute regarding conversation. My fear of embarrassing myself caused me to have a bit of a last-minute wobble, so I asked for permission to bring Mum and Matt along too.

"Of course, Sinead. The more the merrier. The more funds raised for the charity, the better," was the reply. *Excellent.*

Nothing could go wrong.

The scene in the evening was exactly as I had expected – a load of well-known folk who hailed from the local area, sitting at the longest table I'd ever seen, wearing fancy designer clothes and chattering loudly, competing with one another with tales of their past histories of charitable work. I had Mum at one side, and Matt at the other, acting as human shields so I only had to talk to them. I felt relieved that nobody would rumble me as being an air-head. The meals were incredibly expensive and looked just like restaurant meals looked on TV; one tiny morsel placed on an oversized plate, with some unheard-of sauce drizzled over the top in a swirly pattern. To add a bit of pizazz, a solitary mint leaf had been strategically placed on top of the creation.

Matt was quite a big guy and was notorious for being a foodie with an impossibly big appetite, and it was obvious from the look on his face he was less than impressed with the food they had served us. I heard someone remark about what good value the meals were, and how beautifully presented they were. Matt, who had been pretty quiet until that point, piped up, "Doesn't anyone else think the portions are a bit on the small side, considering the extortionate pricing here?"

The Mayor's wife sitting opposite us replied, "Well, perhaps, yes; but I'm sure that none of us are going to quibble about portion sizes when we're raising money for the children."

Matt looked at her with a bemused expression, and his words seemed to come out in slow motion. In his even stronger-sounding-than-usual South London accent, he expressed that he didn't quite agree with Mrs. Mayor.

"Fack the kids, I'm starving! I thought it would be an all-you-can-eat buffet!"

I felt like diving on him to cover his mouth with my hands, whilst shouting, "Noooooooooooooooooooooo!"

Eyes widened in unison down the whole length of the table. An awkward silence swept across the room as imaginary tumbleweed blew past us. Mum froze like a statue with her silver-plated fork held to her mouth, mid-bite, only moving her eyeballs to look sideways at me, searching my face to determine what I was thinking. All I could do was shuffle uncomfortably in my seat and let out a little ice-breaking, polite-sounding squeak. I realised by the expressions of those around me that they considered my nervous laugh highly inappropriate. *Oh, shit.* I made a mental note there and then never to invite family to another work event. Ever. Chuffin' Nesbits[32], my lot are. Can't take 'em anywhere, honestly.

---

[32] A common, uncouth Glaswegian family who were characters in a comedy sitcom.

CHAPTER 13

Slippery when wet

I didn't experience 'The big O' until I was twenty-six years of age. How on earth does someone who began their sexual exploration at such a young age bypass the joys of orgasm completely? Even I don't know the answer to this question. It's truly baffling. I think it must have been partly to do with my ignorance and partly because of the lack of experience of the men in my life up to that point. At an early age, I had learned the science of orgasms and how they worked, thanks to 'Just Seventeen' and 'More!' magazines. I also knew that they were a wonderful thing and supposed to feel fabulous. I can't remember what I age I began masturbating, but it never became a regular thing because I didn't find it all that enjoyable. I could go years without touching my lady bits.

I had been with my ex-husband for six years; and married for five of them. I had never really enjoyed sex to its full potential with him. I had always assumed that the reason for that was because he was a bully, but I think the fact that I derived no serious physical pleasure from it must have been a big factor. Before Tim, I had only ever been with teenage boys, so maybe that explained a lot. Also, I can't remember anyone who had concentrated on my clitoris for over three seconds at a time; so, I wasn't aware that it functioned at all. I didn't even know that I hadn't been experiencing orgasms – I thought the tingly feeling I got before I stopped a masturbation session was, in fact, an orgasm. I thought maybe I just didn't enjoy them as much as most people.

Since the age of fifteen, I had watched a heck of a lot of pornography; but the problem was that it was all very theatrical, Americanised and directed solely from a male perspective. You know the sort – male porn stars doing that awful looking, painful flicky tongue thing. Oh, and loud, screaming fake orgasms; from loud, fake-looking, pumped up mouths.

Regarding vibrators, I had owned one, but I had rarely used it. Again, I blame porn and the fact that anything remotely phallic-looking was usually being used for insertion – in and out and out and in, at high speed and with often with quite a bit of vigour. When I attempted to imitate this action, the feeling of the initial insertion was nice enough, but after that, I gained little or no pleasure, eventually losing interest. I had tried masturbating with my fingers, but again, I would just mimic what I had seen on porn films, which again, was insertion or some bloke flicking away clumsily with his fingers until the lady in question looked 'wet' enough for full-on sex.

I had no knowledge of the function of the clitoral hood, and that it should be pulled back sufficiently enough to expose the clitoris, rather than blindly attacking the poor thing. I also hadn't figured out that to make the clitoris swell, the surrounding area of the vulva needed stimulation beforehand. On porn films, I had only ever witnessed a female having an orgasm via penetration with a penis. That had never happened to me either. On my own, I could get to a point where it felt great, then I would become too sensitive. It would end up being painful, and I would have to stop. I didn't know of a way around this, but it was probably for lack of lube, besides my poor technique. In short, I knew bugger all. Sad times!

So, back to my life after Tim's exit… this was around the time when I saw amateur porn for the first time. The video was of a woman masturbating, and there was no man with her, for a change. She looked like an ordinary woman – familiar curves, pretty, with naturally blonde, bobbed hair. She was kind of sitting upright but leaning back on a sofa. The sofa looked ordinary, too. It wasn't a velvet chaise lounge scattered with leopard-print cushions. Everything about this was real. She took a bottle of lubricant and squirted it onto her palm, rubbing it between her hands to warm it up, before smearing it over her vulva. As I watched, I felt quite aroused, and this was because I was viewing it from a woman's perspective – as though I was that woman. I watched with interest at what she was doing with her fingers and saw that it differed greatly from what I had seen before, or practised on myself. She seemed to reach that all too familiar stage where the sensitivity took over, but instead of stopping as I did, she carried on regardless.

As she climaxed, the camera zoomed in on her vagina and I noticed that it was pulsating rhythmically, and secreting a small amount of creamy-coloured, almost translucent liquid. I had never in my life seen that happen in the porn films I was used to. There was no screaming or thrashing about, just breathless moans and the woman tensing her whole body, then relaxing. Then it hit me – what this woman was experiencing looked a little like what happened to me when I was asleep sometimes. (My body probably needed to regulate itself, due to the lack of orgasms, and wet dreams were a manifestation of their absence.) So I recognised that pulsating action, and the mysterious, jelly-like substance that I had discovered between my thighs upon waking. I wanted to experience what she had, and I decided there and then to make it my mission.

That night, whilst in bed, I decided that it was now or never. I made myself comfortable, grabbed a dusty bottle of lube from the back of the wardrobe, and got busy. It's funny – nowadays I don't take notice of all the physical changes that happen during orgasm, but that night I noticed everything. Everything was amplified – the tingly feelings creeping up from my toes to my thighs, the little twitches in my eyelids and the racing of my heart. No magazine had ever described these things. This was life-changing shit! I felt enlightened, and I felt excited about my discovery. I had experienced my first orgasm at twenty-six, and I had a lot of catching up to do.

I later discovered that on average, around seventy-five percent of women have never orgasmed through penetration alone, and fifteen percent have never experienced an orgasm at all. I felt cheated for never having being taught about female pleasure in sex education class at school.

Finding out how my nether region should be operated at such a ripe old age had a strange effect on me. I reacted like a fourteen-year-old boy would. I wanted to do it again and again, and I wondered what it would feel like to be brought to orgasm by a man. I was officially on heat, and had two options - I could either masturbate myself into an early grave, or make it my mission to find out.

The dancing was getting to be too much for me and the clients were getting too creepy, so I left without warning. I worried about how I would live on around £800 per month after taking such a huge drop in my wage, but I figured that it was worth being skint, rather than lose my dignity. I was still modelling, so I reasoned that I would just have to try harder to find shoots. I quickly spiralled into debt but kept it to myself as much as I could. I didn't want anyone to think I was irresponsible or not as independent as everyone thought. I just wasn't used to handling finances after being with Tim for so long. Before I knew it, one credit card had turned into five. I thought that balance transfers onto cards with 0% interest were the way forward, but the interest-free periods only lasted so long, then I was back to square one.

I had to buy Tim out of the house and I took on the mortgage on my own. The debts and bills continued to pile up, and I started to pay the mortgage with a credit card. My parents had always been very traditional, and kept their finances very private when I was younger. I had never been taught how to budget or prioritise, so I was terrible at money management; just like they had been. The lowest point financially for me was on Christmas Eve when I had five telephone calls from various debt collectors. After a year of carrying on like this, I was desperate. The messier my financial situation got, the more extreme things I considered – webcam work, going back to adult modelling; and for a split second – even escorting.

Thankfully, I realised that it was a stupid idea; and anyway, escorting would be sure to mess up my head. I'm a sensitive person and an old romantic. I've always had trouble detaching sex from love. I've never been into one-night stands either, so I knew I wouldn't last long if I went down that road. I would view it as selling my soul. I decided that I would go back to the lap dancing club, just for a night. The angel sitting on my shoulder told me I had moved on and shouldn't go backward. The little devil on the other shoulder was telling me that not being able to feed and clothe Morgan would be going backward. It would only be for one night, and the money I made in that one night would support us for two whole weeks if I budgeted well. That would be going forward, surely?

I turned up at the club without asking Sam if I could go back. He didn't even recognise me and thought I was a new dancer. I explained that I just wanted to work for one night, and he agreed that I could, providing that I worked hard and brought enough money in for the club. I gave him my word that I would. I couldn't believe how much the business had changed in just under three years. Most of the dancers were now of Eastern European origin, and they were much flirtier and more tactile with the men than the girls I used to know. As I walked up the dark corridor with my first customer, I saw girls dancing in the booths, bending right over so the customers could see everything. If it had been a style of modelling, it would have fallen into the 'US mag' category. I stuck to my previous levels and had a steady stream of customers. At around midnight, a guy booked me for a double dance with my old friend, Destiny. She had offered me a thin line of cocaine earlier, as I was so nervous about being back. I had never done coke before, as I didn't like how my friends' personalities changed when they were on it. In fact, I hadn't taken any drugs since my clubbing days, seven years before.

I don't know why that night was any different, but I have always been impulsive. The second the fine white powder had entered my brain via a rolled-up twenty-pound note, I felt fantastic and was brimming of confidence almost to the point of being cocky. We took the customer into a double booth, which was twice the size of the usual booths, and began to strip. Destiny climbed on top of the customer and straddled him, rubbing the crotch of his jeans with her hand. I whispered to her, "You never used to do owt like that!"

"Yeah; but it's all changed, Olivia. We go that bit further now to match Sam's new Eastern European girls, or we don't get any dances."

As I was wiggling my hips at the side of her and not making much physical contact with the guy, I could see the outline of his erect penis through his jeans. He was closing his eyes, and his breathing had become fast and shallow as Destiny rubbed harder and faster. He looked like he was just about to come, when at the crucial moment, Destiny pulled away. The guy looked frustrated and disappointed; and very, very horny!

"If you want more of where that came from, another dance is only a tenner," she said to him, then turned to wink at me.

The man was that desperate for an orgasm by that point, that he would have paid the Earth. He handed over his ten pounds, and the dance started up again. This time, by the time Destiny's dance was over, so was he. I didn't know where to put myself. Fancy coming in your pants in a lap dancing booth, and having to get back home in that state.

Destiny told me that there was now a private room on the upper floor where the girls would take the guys for V.I.P. treatment. It would cost £150 for an hour of the company of a dancer; on a one-to-one basis; away from the prying eyes of the staff. Sam knew all about it, of course. Well, although it hadn't been confirmed, it was obvious that the room was so that the girls could prostitute themselves whilst earning the club a nice little bonus. I felt disillusioned, collected my money and went home with the £240 I had earned. I never went back again. If I had ever thought that lap dancing was sleazy, now I knew that beyond a shadow of a doubt, it was.

A year later, I was booked by one of the tabloids to do a short tour of personal appearances at a few gentlemen's clubs. I would be working with three of their other contracted models, who were friends of mine. The first club was special because it had a bar wide enough that you could dance on it; like in the film, Coyote Ugly. A limousine picked us up, and the driver gave us a bottle of Bollinger to share for the journey. It was such a laugh, all of us drinking and giggling together in this posh car, feeling like celebs. The newspaper had sent one of their photographers along to accompany us, and even a bodyguard. The club had booked another couple of photographers who were there, waiting for us when we arrived. They were poised, ready to snap images of us as we climbed out of the limo and entered the club.

Once inside, our bodyguard ushered us through the crowds of men who were swarming around us and trying to get close, shouting our names. None of us girls were what you would call famous, but we had a good male fan-base thanks to the newspapers, and our online fan clubs and forums. Some of our fans had made it their hobby to follow us around on our tours as we made personal appearances. On this occasion, more guys than I could count had come to get a look at us, as the promoters had done a fantastic job of advertising the event. Seeing this huge place packed wall to wall with oestrogen-hungry, testosterone and alcohol-fuelled guys was nothing short of overwhelming. We were nervous and very, very excited. *This is the life!*

We were led towards the bar area and our big, scary-looking, but soft as a pussycat bodyguard lifted each one of us, so we could stand on top of it. The crowd gathered around the bar as the sexy R&B music played throughout the whole building. The girls and I were wearing matching outfits – tiny black vests with the newspaper's logo emblazoned on the front, and the smallest bright pink hot pants you can imagine, completed with shiny black fuck-me boots. The crowd burst into raucous cheers and hand-clapping as we strutted about on the bar-top, sashaying and grinding our hips in time with the music.

Every so often we would hear one of our names being called out, our eyes catching the glare of a camera flash. The men looked on with awe and the dancers who worked there watched with admiration, not realising one of us was one of them not long ago. It was one of many surreal experiences that the modelling industry had gifted me with, and another one I'll never forget – for all the right reasons. I was on a natural high with my girlies, feeling gorgeous and confident, and having fun with my clothing firmly on, for a change.

When our gig had finished, we had photos taken with the clientele. We sat on their laps and smiled for the cameras. Afterward, we were led through the crowd by a glamourous-looking mixed-race woman in a red floor-length Jessica Rabbit-esque sequin gown. We followed her down a hall and through another door, which led us up a stairwell to a swanky penthouse suite. The suite was complete with a lush, cream carpet, gigantic flat-screen television, huge cream leather sofa, and fancy lighting. *Wow. This place must generate some right money. How the other half live!*

Once inside, Miss Rabbit instructed us to treat it as our own. Now we were out of the dimly lit club, I instantly recognised our chaperon. She used to lap-dance at the old club I used to work at, and used to call herself Lenora. She had seen so many girls come and go since I'd left, that she hadn't recognised me. I introduced myself and we chatted briefly about the old days there. Lenora told me she had worked her way up in the business and now managed promotions at this new club. They had put her in charge of looking after the 'special' clients. They allowed only the special clients to use the penthouse, she said. As I looked around the room, I could imagine the kind of parties and interactions that likely happened between these four walls. It reminded me of the secret apartment at the club I used to work at, which only certain dancers could ever see; and of the rumours that used to circulate among the girls and bar staff who were in-the-know. Lenora passed us a glass of champagne each and chatted with us while we got changed into our jeans and real-life clothing. Two of us had young children to get up for in the morning, so, unfortunately, we couldn't stay and enjoy the luxuries of the apartment. Now, most of the customers had left the club, a taxi was ordered to take us home. The limousine earlier was just for show, to give the right image for us and the club. Now it was back to roughing it when the cameras had gone. Ah well, it had been fun while it had lasted.

The next morning, I opened the newspaper to discover that we had a full centre-page spread dedicated to our special event. *Another one for my Modelling Memory Box,* I thought. I just couldn't believe that the confident and glamourous-looking person in those photos was me. I felt blessed that I was so lucky to be living my teenage dream. To some readers we may have just been four Z-list, brainless bimbos putting on a very unfeminist display at a strip joint; but to me it was the recognition I had always wanted, and a stark contrast to the days when I had worked twelve-hour shifts lap dancing in the booths, being treated as currency by the owner. I felt grateful; I felt empowered, and I actually felt proud.

CHAPTER 14

The hunt

When I had healed from my broken marriage and Tim's violence, I realised how much I had also craved intimacy. It was like a radar had suddenly switched on inside me, and there were men everywhere. Men here, men there; men, men, everywhere! I noticed every bloke that I drove or walked past, and every last one of them seemed to ooze testosterone. I had a couple of half-hearted flings, but they didn't last long. The bodies of other men felt unfamiliar and wrong. I even joined a dating site, and paid the £40 fee, only to cancel it three days later. I just wasn't ready for another guy.

I pulled quite a few girls when I was out on the town though. Girls were safe and expected nothing more than a few drunken snogs. I had never been a girl who copped off[33] with other girls to get the sexual attention of male onlookers. I had always done it because I had wanted to. I enjoyed the feeling of their soft, warm lips on mine, the narrowness of their waists and the smell of their hair. The trouble with this was that I looked like a dolly-bird; and very straight. That meant that no like-minded girl would come on to me. I would have to approach them; which could be a scary task. I'm surprised that I never got punched in the face, to be honest. I had never really walked around during the day, looked at a woman, and fancied her. I loved

---

[33] Slang for a casual romantic encounter, referring to any sexual contact from kissing upwards, but not quite as far as sex.

men, and I felt physically attracted to men, but now and again I would feel that I instinctively needed to intimately bond with a woman. I couldn't explain why – it was just how it was. I didn't have the slightest clue what to do with a vagina at that point in my life. My drunken girl clinches just entailed a lot of kissing and stroking, but that was usually over the top of clothing.

Because it was looking like I might be single for quite some time, I came off the contraceptive pill to give my body a rest. I wasn't prepared for the impact at all. It was like my body was awash with hormones and I had an almost constant, crazy urge for male contact. I had fallen into a bit of a pattern where I would meet a nice guy, be really into them, sleep with them, and then grow bored. I stopped trusting my instincts, as I couldn't understand how I could suddenly go right off a guy after feeling so mad about them a few weeks earlier. I did a lot of self-analysing and decided that the next time I met a desirable man, I would tread carefully and make him work for me.

I had occasionally been attending a local rugby club with Louise. Her fiancé played there, so we would take Morgan and Louise's three kids, and have a nice afternoon out. I was always on the lookout for eligible bachelors, but they were all stereotypical meat-heads with massive necks and thighs, and cauliflower ears. I prefer a neater, prettier kind of guy, with a big smile, soulful eyes, and strong, chunky shoulders. I had quite a lot of free time in those days, because Morgan was with his dad all weekend. I appreciated some time to myself, but with all my friends being coupled up, it was hard to fill the time. As a result, I spent quite a lot of time online, catching up on gossip via Facebook, which was still quite new but quickly growing in popularity. One such evening, I was browsing through the friends list of the rugby club Facebook group, and I stopped dead on the profile photo of a member. All I could see was a side profile image of his head, and it was a head that I liked! Short, bright blond hair with a strong hairline, the most striking green eyes I had ever seen, and masculine, well-proportioned facial features. Something about this guy stood out – his pose looked thoughtful and somewhat serious, as though he had a purpose. All I could see of his details were that his name was Jack, he was twenty-seven years old and that he lived about half an hour's drive from me. This stranger intrigued me, so I clicked the friend request button. My plan – well, my hope – was that he would see the request, have a nosy at my profile photo, fancy me and chase me, without realising that I had made the first move. I had confused confidence with arrogance, and I had adopted the role of huntress when I was emotionally ill-equipped for such dangerous games. I thought it would mean that I was in control if everything followed a plan. I figured that no man could hurt me if I was one step ahead, but I had just made the first move in a self-constructed cat-and-mouse game, with someone who was already a well-practised player.

I had been reading a book on the art of seduction, with great interest, and was enjoying testing out my newly acquired knowledge on every man I met. I would make Jack think he had snared me, when in truth it would be I who had been the engineer. Mum used to tell me to stop reading such nonsense, as it would only bring misery. How right she was. Time had passed quickly and I had been single for almost four years by the time I discovered Jack. I had the world at my feet, and a handful of male acquaintances eating out of the palm of my hand, but until then, never letting them get too close. Oh, how clever I thought I was.

I received a notification telling me that Jack had accepted my friendship, and he had sent me a message. Bam! He had fallen straight into my pretty little trap. I felt like a smug little psychological ninja.

"Now then, I'm trying to think… I don't even play the lottery, so my numbers never came up on Saturday… yet I get home on a Sunday night and see a friend request from you. I'm pretty sure I never bought a ticket for 'Make Sinead your mate'. I'm either a very lucky lad, or it was a terrible typo on your part. Anyway, how are you?"

Suave! I liked how he typed – playful, slightly flirty; and well thought out. He didn't sound like a him-bo, anyway. I looked through every one of Jack's photos and studied his physical appearance. He was around six foot three inches tall and built like a brick shit-house. Not broad and solid like the other players – he was quite lean with it. He wasn't quite ripped, but a lot more muscular than what I'd normally have gone for. He had a good-looking face, but a bit of a squashed nose; probably from being bashed in it so many times on the rugby field. Still, it didn't detract from his overall gorgeousness. He had big lips and large, wide-set eyes, a subtle tan (courtesy of the sunbeds in the gym) and was adorned with various tattoos on his back and upper arms. He reminded me of a silverback gorilla; the way he was built, but with a pretty face. Jack's style was pretty much a cargo-pants-and-distressed-shirt-and-trainers combo in all of his photos. He looked trendy, and I liked that too. I had to have him.

Jack and I emailed back and forth for the next week, then progressed to chatting via MSN instant messenger. He mentioned he had recently started bodybuilding, but still had a lot to learn. I asked him what his main ambition in life was, to which he replied, "To find the true love of a woman, and to watch my own child being born."

Well, what better thing to say to a woman who was ready to find a man to love? I fell for it hook, line and sinker.

CHAPTER 15

Alpha-attraction

I asked Jack if he would like to meet me in town at the weekend for a few drinks.

"I would, but I'm quite shy. How about a DVD and a few drinks at my place? I have a spare room if you'd like to stay. I know you won't be able to drink if you have to drive home."

We decided on the following Saturday night, and I spent two hours getting ready. I dressed to kill, wearing a pair of skin-tight blue jeans with a white studded belt, black patent stilettos, and a pretty black, strappy Karen Millen vest top (chazza shop treasure, obvs!). I piled my hair elegantly on top of my head, in a big, messy bun, and did a smoky eye/neutral lips make-up combo. The whole way there I recited a mantra to myself, "God, please give me the strength not to shag Jack's brains out."

In the seduction book I was reading, the male author suggests that making a man wait for sex is the greatest weapon that a woman can possess. Not only that, but when the situation does finally arise, the thing that makes a man want to stick around is 'sexual mastery'. I was confident that I already had that. I swotted up on my male psychology books before I set off to Jack's house and made a mental note that I had to act like a 'cool girl' so he would look upon me as being rare. I don't think I trusted my judgement anymore because I had been shat on so many times and had a habit of picking the wrong ones. I was addicted to these books and tried to follow their lessons to a 'T'. Maybe if I had a guide to refer to, I could have a lasting, fulfilling relationship? Maybe Jack would be the guy to give me the affection that I craved. I had high hopes and had already invested my emotions before we had even met for the first time.

For the whole of the half-hour drive to Jack's house that evening after dropping Morgan at his dad's, I was a bundle of nervous excitement. I finally pulled up at Jack's home, which was on a posh new-build housing estate. It had four bedrooms, an integral garage, and a shiny, new-looking Mazda MX5 sports car parked on the driveway. *Jeez! This guy must have some money!* I felt rather inadequate, even though I had my own house, my own car, and coped on my own as a single mother. I made a mental note to hide my embarrassing, battered old mobile phone. Jack answered the door with a big smile, looking as pleasing to the eye as ever, and wrapped me up in a big bear hug. He smelled wonderful. Pheromones and aftershave; what an intoxicating combination.

"Great to see you! You should've just walked in."

He poured me a big glass of cider and we sat on the big, plush, brown leather sofa in his very modern beige and cream living room. We never got around to watching a DVD, of course. We chatted about anything and everything and got to know each other better. I cautiously told Jack about my unusual job, thinking he would be unimpressed. I had been doing a lot of private bondage and spanking themed shoots lately, as they paid more than typical glamour. They were all unpublished and shot for personal use (wank fodder, basically). I had already decided that no man would ever come between me and my job. It may have been an unconventional occupation, but it sure beat being stuck in an office, watching the clock. I was determined to beat the recession in my own unique way, and I'd been modelling for so long that it was a part of me.

"Sinead, I think you're awesome. You just don't care about what anyone thinks apart from those you love, do you? I like that about you."

We got steadily drunk and time whizzed by. Before I knew it, it was 3:00 a.m. and we were still talking. My no sex rule went out of the window. I stood up, intending to head to Jack's back door for a cigarette, but changed my mind en route. Thinking, *Fuck it,* I turned back, staggered drunkenly over to where Jack was sitting, and straddled him right there. He looked surprised but hungrily reciprocated. How could he resist? He carried me upstairs in a fireman's lift, and we had passionate sex in his bedroom, in every position imaginable. Not only did he have the body of a racehorse, but he also had the thrust of a stallion and was hung like a Shire (which made my specialty deep-throating a no-go area).

The only thing I had an issue with was that Jack had practically shaved all his pubic hair off. I don't know about you, but I like a man to look like a man. He had also removed his chest, armpit and leg hair. Never mind back, sack and crack; the whole lot had been removed! Jack's body must have been aerodynamic. His entire body felt as smooth as a porn star's pantie hamster. Momentarily, I wondered what the regrowth would be like. Nobody wants stubble rash on their boobies after sex, now, do they? Never mind, I could overlook these minor details because he was so bloody gorgeous.

The sex was aggressively primal, filthy; and fabulous. At 7:00 a.m. we were still bouncing from wall to wall in Jack's bedroom, and got so carried away that at one point, we had sex with me sitting on the windowsill in full view of the neighbours, who were probably on their way to buy their morning papers... or to church, perhaps?

Sinning on the Sabbath day. Tut, tut. In those few hours, we probably covered every position in the Kama Sutra. That poster of my parents' had come in useful, after all. We somehow finished with me masturbating him with my feet, and he came so hard that he shot his load all over his face. This type of kinkiness was new to me, and I relished the novelty. I had met my match sexually, and I was sure I had also ticked the sexual mastery box. I was winning at life!

Afterward, we cuddled up in bed with a tube of Pringles, watching TV and nursing our head-pounding hangovers. Jack told me he had never been so turned on in his life, that he had never met a woman like me before, and how he didn't want me to go home. I jumped straight in the bath when I got back to my house, and discovered that I had cuts on my legs, grazed elbows, bite marks on my bum and fingerprints on my neck, complete with a very sore undercarriage! I received a text message from Jack that night:

<I've just had a shower and I think my willy just fell off from over-use; and went down the plughole! Wow! What a woman!>

He was funny too. *Oh God, I am totally gonna fall for him.*

The next morning, I panicked that I had bedded him too soon, and so, I consulted one of my books. I found the page about having the commitment talk without scaring a guy off, and typed out a strategic text to Jack:

<I would be happy to date you exclusively if you're not seeing anyone else right now; because I don't want to waste my time if you are.>

His reply was equally strategic:

<Well, as we have done the deed already, I would normally close the file. However, I'm still very interested in you; and would love to date you exclusively.>

Close the file? The cheeky so and so! We were both playing the same game here – giving with one hand and taking away with the other. I had not just met my match sexually, but intellectually too.

The second time I visited Jack was a Saturday evening again. A fortnight had passed since our first sex marathon, and I was itching to see him again. Jack told me that he worked long hours doing contracts for a prestigious, worldwide-known electrical company. Because of this, he could only see me at weekends. I dropped Morgan at his dad's and set straight off. The drive seemed to take ages, and all the while my excitement was building. By the time I got to his door, I was craving him like a pregnant woman craves pizza. I walked straight in and found him in the kitchen, lighting the hob. I pulled him towards me, sort of growled at him, and stayed glued to his face for the next couple of minutes. I could feel his huge erection through his jeans, and I needed it inside me immediately.

As if reading my mind, Jack roughly undressed me, then himself. He picked me up with ease. I wrapped my legs around his waist, and we screwed right there. His legs must have got tired after a minute or two, because he carried me, still in the same position, with his cock plugged securely inside me, over to the dining room dresser. He lowered me down on the top, in front of the big mirror he had on the wall, and we carried on. The dresser rocked rhythmically against the wall, and the mirror swung and banged about behind us. The pan of whatever it was bubbled on the cooker top, while lust bubbled in me like lava. We continued there for a couple of minutes before Jack carried me into the living room. He practically threw me onto the sofa, and ordered, "Wait there. I've got to teach you a lesson for being too damned sexy and distracting me from preparing dinner."

I was taken aback. I couldn't imagine what he meant.

Jack left the room and returned a few seconds later, clutching the belt that had been attached to his jeans.

"Now, face the sofa, get on your knees and stick your arms out behind you."

Now, I don't know about you, but it's never been a habit of mine to engage in such debauched practices on a second date. Those things require intimacy and mutual trust, don't they? Plus, I was pretty experienced in all things sexual, but it had always been me doing the tying up before. I didn't know how to react when the roles were reversed. I felt super uncomfortable; and very vulnerable. What if he was intending on tying me up and holding me hostage or something? I had only met him once before, and I knew nothing much about him. Still, he was sexy as Hell; so, I threw caution to the wind and did as I was told.

Jack carefully, but hastily, wrapped the brown leather belt around my arms and buckled it tightly. I lost my balance and fell forward, face-planting the sofa cushion in front of me. Jack sat down next to my head and spanked my buttocks with one of his massive, shovel-like hands. I didn't dare look up as the slaps rained down on my bare skin. I felt humiliated, exposed, and downright shocked. I had told Jack a little about the private spanking photo-shoots I had done, and I think that's why he saw me as someone with whom he could experiment. I wasn't exactly into spanking, but like him, I thought that anything naughty was a bit of fun to spice things up a little. Even so, I wasn't expecting that kind of behaviour from him on my second visit.

I wasn't sure if his dominance excited me or disconcerted me, or both. I had no time to conclude my thoughts, as before I knew it, he was crouching behind me, fucking me doggy-style; hard and fast. My hip bones bumped against the sofa base, and they were beginning to feel a little bruised, when Jack finally gave one last, aggressive thrust and came inside me. He slumped forwards, over my back, and lay there for a minute to catch his breath. Just as my brain was processing what the Hell had just happened, he untied me, flipped me over onto the sofa, parted my thighs and went down on me. I thought I had died and gone to cunnilingus Heaven! Well mannered, great in the sack, affectionate… didn't this man have any flaws? I had never known such an uninhibited fellow before, and all these shenanigans made me want to delve further into his inner psyche.

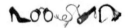

The constant harassment from my creditors continued to chip away at my self-esteem. My car was un-taxed, and every time I had to go to the supermarket or take Morgan to his dad's, I would worry that the police may pull me and chuck my car in the pound. Jack was so motivated with his work and always telling me of his business successes, that I would feel like I was a fraud. He thought I was strong and business-like, but I was secretly struggling. I swallowed my pride and shopped at my local Netto[34] supermarket, but I couldn't even scrape together enough money for what I needed. Instead, I took to going around the supermarkets near closing time on a Sunday, pouncing on the reduced bargains and freezing a load of them for use throughout the week. Mum had taught me well.

If Jack was busy on a weekend, Louise would sometimes pay my nightclub entry and buy me drinks so I wouldn't be at home, alone. She once came to my house armed with bags of groceries for me and

---

[34] A budget supermarket, favoured by the poorest in society. Being seen going into Netto with your mum as a teenager was even worse than being seen going into The British Heart Foundation shop.

Morgan. When I looked inside, it was like glimpsing Heaven – treacle sponge cake, crisps, and chocolate; not just necessities. I was so utterly grateful, but didn't know how I could ever repay her kindness. She struggled to feed her three children and was unable to work, and she had just spent a fortune at the supermarket to feed two families. My self-worth was sinking even lower, and I was afraid that I might never claw my way out of this hole. I had county court judgements coming out of my ears. It was a terrible time for the British economy, and the recession had even hit the modelling industry hard. Photographers couldn't afford to pay for shoots, and as a result, studios were going bankrupt and closing down. The turning point was when I received a letter from the mortgage company, stating that they would repossess my home. *Over my dead body!*

I took on more fetish modelling work of a non-pornographic nature, and couldn't believe the things that aroused some people! I've always speculated on why aggressive hardcore porn is deemed as acceptable by most porn enthusiasts, and society in general, but the very tame non-porno stuff that shows no flesh and harms no-one is looked upon as weird. It's funny how people would rather be caught watching violent and degrading videos, than dare to admit they like something ordinary like watching a woman eat a cream cake or jiggling her bum about in a thong.

Some of the work was a little creepy, I'll admit, such as being videoed pretending to be asleep. The photographer would instruct me to make little movements and subtle snoring noises. Other shoots were an absolute scream, such as when I worked in a studio set that was made to look like a pet shop. The shoot was for a website run by a quirky Swedish couple. They told me excitedly about their ambition to one day have a more authentic looking set in an even bigger studio. Their dream was to have cages stacked one on top of the other, containing a cute human pet in each one.

They trussed me up in a poodle costume, complete with bows around the ears, and my job was to play 'fetch' with the camera-man. The first photo set involved trying to catch a newspaper between my teeth. Sadly, I was unsuccessful, so they thought I may do better at catching a rubber dildo with my 'paws'. I didn't quite get my timing right, and as the tool hurtled toward me, I leapt forward to clasp it. It twirled mid air and smacked me on my right brow bone. I was literally eye to, erm, eye (or head to head if you prefer) with the latest in real-feel cyber-skin technology; complete with a tangled thicket of wiry, artificial pubes and walnut textured silicone testicles. Not my finest moment. You could say I ballsed it up. To disguise the redness of my eye socket, I had a brown patch painted on, which actually looked quite sweet in the weirdest way. The good news is that I finally excelled in my role and beat the highest score of the most marshmallows caught by mouth! Get in!

WAM (Wet and Messy) was a funny old category. The shoots were hilarious, and consisted of models having food fights, or rolling around in runny food, such as gravy, beans and whatever edible substances you could imagine. I had some standards though. I drew the line at savoury slop. Just thinking about the smell of cold, gloopy gravy running down my near-naked person made me gag. If I was to be gunged, I wanted it to be with something sweet... and warm! The first WAM shoot I ever took part in was with a huge bucketful of instant custard. I almost didn't mind the bucket being tipped over my head, because it tasted so good as it dripped down my face, into my mouth. At the end of the shoot I was trembling with cold. It's pretty standard that most studios are a bit on the chilly side. It's just one of those minor inconveniences that you get used to. Although with rapidly cooling custard covering every inch of one's body, the studio temperature was intolerable. Never have I been so relieved to jump into a hot, steaming shower at the end of a shift. Washing the custard out of my hair was a bit of a task, and the smell lingered on my skin a little longer than I'd have liked, but it was a fun shoot and all in a day's work in this unpredictable industry. Boredom was certainly never a factor, that's for sure.

The next day I was on location on Blackpool beach, modelling a new brand of sunglasses for a mail-order catalogue. I was revelling in having the sun on my skin, the wind in my hair, strategically posed on a rock like a goddess statue. I pitied the poor girls who would be stuck in studios on such a glorious day.

"Stunning, Olivia! Give me a bit more bum cheek at this side, and turn your head so I can see the other lens, would you?" shouted the photographer as I turned on another killer pose.

I was really working the sex appeal. It was only the rocks on Blackpool beach, but in my imagination I was on Hollywood hills. I turned my head toward the camera and raised both arms in the air, scooping my windswept hair up with my fingers, behind my neck. *Yeah, baby.* I was on fire today with my poses. I was confident that the images would be sizzling hot.

As I gave the photographer my best 'I'm-so-sexy-and-spiritually-fulfilled-because-of-these-amazing-sunglasses' look, I saw his mouth drop open and his eyes widen. He let out a gasp, like Jaws was behind me or something. I was confused.

"Y-your armpits, Olivia!"

I looked down, and to my horror, I noticed that they were bright yellow. Maybe all my karma had finally caught up with me and God was punishing me by slowly turning me into Big Bird! It took me a few seconds of wondering if armpit jaundice was actually a thing, before I realised that it was the food colouring from the custard on yesterday's shoot. I'm sexy AF[35], me.

Yes, there were some very unique genres of modelling when it came to fetish work. I was often asked to film custom video clips for my fans, which I didn't mind doing. I would charge around thirty pounds for a fifteen-minute video. Sometimes the requests would be pornographic, and sometimes not. The key thing that most people requested was that I mentioned their name throughout the video. It made them feel important, and proved that the video was bona fide custom, rather than duplicated and sent to any old Tom, Dick or Harry. A particularly unique custom video I was asked to film was for a guy called Ian who called himself a Fingernail-Tapping Fetishist. No, I didn't know they existed, either. Maybe he's the only one, who knows?

All Ian wanted was a five-minute one of me sitting at my computer desk, fully clothed, looking directly into the camera, rhythmically drumming my fingernails on the desk and repeating the phrase, "I'm waiting, Ian. I'm feeling very impatient with you right now."

He wanted me to start softly, the tapping growing more frantic and my voice tone becoming firmer as the video progressed.

It remains a mystery why Ian got all hot under the collar from watching fingernail tapping; but the request was nice and easy to fulfil, and what's more, I didn't even have to leave the house to earn the money, because it only took a few minutes of my time.

More times than you would imagine, I was offered what I consider to be repulsive, obscene, highly undignified jobs in a category I found to be the most terrifying. Yep, it was none other than... cue drum roll...

...Tickling.

---

[35] Abbreviation for 'As Fuck', commonly used by teenagers when texting on their mobiles.

I would rather chew my own arm off ten times over and be slapped around the face with the soggy end, than be forcibly tickled on the soles of my feet, whilst having my arms chained to bed posts. Fuck that. I could envisage myself doing a tickling shoot, and I visualised alternating between being absolutely furious, then thrashing about, panic-stricken the whole way through, with a very un-sexy "Just you wait until I'm unchained. I will maim you" expression. What is wrong with these depraved perverts? Do anything that floats your boat with my feet, but tickle them, or any part of my anatomy at your peril. To me there is no worse horror than being tickled. Well, maybe being covered in spiders. There are a lot of sickos inhabiting our planet, and the struggle is very real.

Because I was so desperate for money to pay the bills and my mortgage arrears, I would knowingly put myself in some weak positions. I didn't feel that I had much choice. I undertook a lot of bondage work. Some of the shoots were done by professional photographers for high-end pay-sites. These shoots would often incorporate fancy Japanese Shibari rope work, and the images were tasteful, elegant and very beautiful. However, most bondage shoots were not of this calibre, and would usually involve some guy with a shitty little camera tying me up with scratchy, heavy rope, or worse – locking me in heavy handcuffs. The scenario would always be the same – I would have to appear to be struggling against the restraints, trying to find a way out. My face would have to convey shame, pain, and distress. I hated that type of work, and it was painful.

One bondage shoot is firmly implanted in my memory. I was working at home with an amateur photographer called Martin, whom I had known a while and felt safe with. He was a decent guy, but the work took a lot to be desired. Mainly because it required being gagged. On the more tasteful, high-end shoots, the ball-gag would be loose, so that the ball could be moved about between shots at will. This enabled the model to swallow and to control her own comfort level, sliding it onto her chin if she needed to speak or swallow.

The gag on this occasion was a leather-strapped heavy rubber ball-gag. For authenticity, the gag was buckled tightly behind my head, pulling the ball into my mouth, right behind my teeth. This forced my jaw to open wide around the ball, so I couldn't swallow or speak. That, of course, was the idea. Many of the fetishists who got off on these images went really wild over the humiliation of the model having no control of her swallowing reflex. On shoots like this, the gag would inevitably cause my mouth to fill up with saliva, and I would only be able to breathe through my nose. It feels as horrible and panicky as it sounds, unfortunately. The saliva would build up behind the ball, and start flowing down my chin and onto my chest – thick, slimy and smelly. I would feel angry with the photographer for allowing me to be in such discomfort, but discomfort and humiliation were the whole point of jobs like this; and what's worse is that I had chosen the work knowing that. He wasn't the one at fault. I was the one exploiting myself because the money meant more to me than my pride.

I was in my living room on this shoot, wearing a pretty white lace lingerie set, sitting on a tall four-legged bar stool that I had brought in from the kitchen. Martin said it would be perfect for the scene we needed to create, because it had a back rest to attach the wrist restraints to. My legs were open, with ankles strapped to the two front chair legs, with my toes resting on the metal bar which joined them. My hands were tied behind me, and I had this disinfectant stinking rubber ball-gag contraption in my mouth. The photographer looked very pleased with this scene, and began snapping away in front of me.

"Great! Tighten your eyebrows as though you're grimacing, bare your teeth and lean forward as though you're trying to break free. Yep, stick your chest out like that."

All the while I had bubbles of saliva running over my breasts and landing on my legs. It was revolting. I contorted my body to appear as though I was a hostage desperate to escape, and leaned my upper body forward as much as I could.

I felt the back legs of the chair lift up from the floor. I had leaned too far forward and the chair was about to overbalance. The realisation of what was about to happen hit me, and then the secondary realisation that I couldn't speak to alert Martin. I tried to shout, "Help!"

All that came out was a loud, "Urgh!" from my throat. As I teetered for a moment, balancing on the two chair legs that still had contact with the ground, I widened my eyes to gigantic proportions, to try and catch Martin's eye behind the lens. It was of no use.

My life flashed before me as I began to topple forward. I knew that if I landed on the front of my face, the impact of the thud onto my wood laminate flooring would likely smash my teeth out, as I had no way of protecting them with the ball-gag behind them. As I got closer to the floor, I instinctively turned my face to the right as much as the flexibility in my neck muscles would allow. It all seemed to flow in slow motion, although in reality it would have lasted about five seconds from leaning forward, to hitting the deck. I heard the front feet of the chair scrape, as it slipped from the floor and the whole thing fell forward...

...Splat.

I hit the floor, cheek first, and landed at the photographer's feet in a pool of my own spit. I was unable to utter a sound nor move to relieve the pain in the left side of my face.

"Oh my God!" yelled Martin as he promptly dropped his camera and frantically scrabbled around, clumsily trying to unbuckle me as quickly as he could. It felt like forever. My face was burning hot.

He helped me to my feet, repeating various forms of apology, the words tangling up as he spoke, not making much sense. The poor guy was in as much shock as I was. By this point the whole of the side of my face felt numb. I made my way over to the mirror above my fireplace, to inspect the damage. My cheek was swollen and red, and the beginnings of a bruise was starting to form on my cheekbone. I opened my mouth as wide as I could, to make it click into a more natural position. It ached from being open due to the gag having been there, and felt a little skewiff. Luckily, it was fine, just stiff and sore. Martin gingerly pulled out a hanky from his pocket and handed it to me so I could wipe the disgusting slime of my own making from my face.

I've never seen anyone look as horrified as Martin did that day. He was as white as a sheet, and very, very sorry. He was probably imagining an up-and-coming insurance claim against him, but I reasoned that this kind of mishap was a common risk of the nature of this type of work. I was just thankful that we had chosen to shoot in my living room and not the kitchen, where I had stone tiled flooring. I really would have been a stereotype then; a working- class, northern ruffian with no teeth. The only TV work I would've been good for after that would have been Jeremy Kyle![36]

Trying to explain to parents in the school playground how I came

[36] Mostly working class families airing their dirty laundry on daytime TV. Mostly watched by bored housewives called Sharon, and me in secret when I'm pretending to clean the house.

to have the huge, black bruise on my cheek and purple ring around my eye that transpired later made me feel like a domestic abuse victim all over again, but this time I was telling the truth when I said, "Oh, this? I slipped and landed face-first on the floor. Silly me."

Martin had got an action still shot of me being almost airborne, mid-fall, as I was hurtling towards the ground. I wonder if he used it in his image set for the pay-site he was submitting to. I'll never know because I didn't hear from him after that incident. He was probably too traumatised to pick up a camera ever again! On the more degrading sites, a once-in-a-lifetime photo like that would've likely hit the jackpot. It makes me shudder just to think about it.

If humiliation was the name of the game with bondage work, then I was most certainly winning. First prize goes to Sinead Winters (prize prat, more like!). Mum used to nickname me 'Slaver-Chops' when I was little. I haven't changed a bit.

Whenever the amateur bondage shoots were causing me to feel a bit disempowered, to help me feel better mid-pose, I would kid myself that I was a modern-day Bettie Page[37]. I would return home, feeling even worse about myself, but the jobs paid well. I considered looking for a part-time job to supplement my modelling income, but I couldn't afford childcare; and besides, there was a huge shortage of jobs in the UK and a surge of unemployment. The money I earned was a drop in a very large ocean of arrears, but at least I could keep a roof over mine and Morgan's heads.

Luckily, Jack paid for all of our dates. He would whisk me away for days out walking in the countryside, to the cinema, and for romantic meals. All the while, he would stroke my hand, nuzzle my neck, or whisper sweet nothings in my ear. He would pick me up and

---

[37] Probably the most famous retro fetish model in the world, a true sex symbol.

spin me around in the street, and I thrived on such attentiveness. We were like two teenagers in the first flushes of love. He was a big, gentle giant, and I felt so safe and feminine when he wrapped me in his arms. I trusted him enough to tell him all about my abusive marriage and my dysfunctional childhood. He listened intently and without judgement. It felt wonderful to expose my vulnerable side, assuming that I had found a man who would protect, rather than hurt me.

CHAPTER 16

One-man circus

Jack shared his electrical business with a Silent Partner – a self-made millionaire called George. He told me that George had recently suggested that Jack should join him on an all-expenses-paid, two-week business trip to Monaco. There was a huge trade show being held there, where Jack could weigh up the international competition and gain an insight into how similar companies worked on a global scale. It sounded like a marvellous opportunity. George sounded like a knowledgeable man with many useful connections.

I wasn't looking forward to Jack leaving one bit, but he promised to keep in touch and to send me some photos. True to his word, he did. He emailed me lots of long, detailed messages, with his usual two kisses at the end. He said how he had enjoyed walking around the local landmarks and that seeing such awesome sights had made him feel overcome with emotion. It pleased me to receive a few pictures from him, looking happy and tanned. I had noticed that Jack was alone in every photograph, and I thought it odd. He had been talking about how it would be great if I met George sometime, so I thought he might have had at least one photo taken with him to show me what he looked like.

I went to Mum's for a cup of coffee, logged into my email account there, and showed her the images. I spent most of my time there gushing about how spectacular 'My Jack' was, and the rest of it saying that something about his Monaco trip didn't feel right. I had a hunch that Jack was lying about something, but I put it down to my paranoia from having chosen bad men in the past. I had learned to switch off my inner voice at will. Mum joked that George probably wore a double D cup bra, because his name was probably short for Georgina. *Thanks, Mum!* I laughed it off and forgot about it.

As I was pottering about Jack's kitchen after lunch one day (for 'pottering', read 'noseying'), I discovered some pills in the bread-bin. I recognised the little blue diamond-shaped pills straight away. Viagra. Why on earth would he need that stuff? The man could go like a Duracell bunny! Unless, of course, that was why. Next to the Viagra was a little white bottle, with the word 'Oxymetholone' written on the front. I casually asked Jack what the pills were.

"Oh, they're just hormone tablets."

"Why would you need hormone tablets, and why Viagra?"

"Well, my mate gave me the Viagra as a joke, and the other ones are to keep my hormones balanced. Kind of like how women use evening primrose oil, I guess."

I intuitively felt that he was lying. I knew him well enough by now to know when he was trying to pull a fast one. I said no more about it, and when I got home, I Googled Oxymetholone. *Fucking steroids. Fabulous.* The Viagra then made sense. Steroids make you unable to get it up, and they also cause testicular atrophy (where the balls gradually retract into the body.) His hormones were anything but balanced. I told Jack that I knew his secret, and he cried, telling me all about his poor body image and how he had been bullied at school for being a skinny geek.

Although I had breast implants, it made me feel queasy that Jack's body wasn't real, and that it resulted from his low self-esteem. I could hardly start laying the law down about his steroid usage, though. Jack was an adult and had the right to do whatever he wanted to his body. I thought back over the past few months, and come to think of it, there had been a few occasions where he had cried along to ballads on the radio, and hit the roof about nothing. I had just put it down to him being ultrasensitive. He had the characteristic wheezy breathing too. Why had I never paid attention to any of this? It was all down to the fact that he was a 'roid-boy. I was going out with a friggin' steroid junky. I began to notice the testicular atrophy develop when he was doing a cycle. If I was giving him a quick hand shandy, I would notice that at the point of climax, Jack's testicles would completely disappear. The result was a very empty and saggy-looking scrotum. I would try to ease his testes back down into place with my thumbs, unnoticed so as not to embarrass him. Oh, the wonderful duties of a bodybuilder's girlfriend! Oh well, I can look back now and call him Sad Sac, for my own amusement (which I frequently do). Every cloud…

The bigger Jack grew from the steroids, the worse his moods became. He would accuse me of eyeing up other blokes, interrogate me about past boyfriends and ask me weird questions. One of them was if I had ever been an escort. I felt insulted and couldn't fathom why he would keep asking me this. I told Jack all my secrets, and he would seem to store them up and use them later, as ammunition against me. He would verbally attack me in front of my friends, and after this happened a few times, they refused to socialise with me if he was there.

I dreaded trips to the supermarket because I would always be in tears by the time we got back home. If I picked an item up, he would question why I hadn't chosen a cheaper brand, and would place it back on the shelf. If I didn't put the products on the checkout conveyor belt in the order he preferred, he would insist on packing them into bags by himself. He said he didn't trust that I could do it correctly. I would just stand at the end of the checkout, staring at my feet and looking pathetic, while Jack joked with the assistant about how silly I was for doing it all wrong.

Jack would turn his sensitive, affectionate, Mr. Nice Guy persona back on at will, to confuse me further. The abuse always followed this cycle. There would be a cool-down period where he was a perfect gentleman, then a slow build-up and the abuse would start again. His timing was spot on. He would reserve his aggression for weekends only. He would always cause a scene just before Morgan came home from his dad's, as he knew that I would co-operate out of fear that Morgan would walk in the door any second and see everything. It was around this time that I rediscovered recreational drugs on a larger scale. Or maybe they discovered me.

Mephedrone, street name M-Cat, was a new, groundbreaking legal high. To get past the drug laws, it was labelled: 'plant food – not for human consumption.' It was a research chemical touted as safe, and it was also cheap. I remembered how the old club drugs could promote intimacy and expand one's mind, and I thought if Jack and I took this exciting new drug on a weekend instead of drinking, the violence would completely stop. More fool me. I had had some wonderful, beautiful experiences with people in my clubbing days, and I imagined that Jack and I could connect similarly. We started by putting around a sixth of a teaspoonful of the white granules in a drink about an hour before we went out, and this steadily progressed to taking a bag out with us and snorting it either in lines or from the tip of a Yale key.

I had never really taken to cocaine. I had only tried it a couple of times; and although I liked the initial feeling of confidence it provided me with, the high was short-lived and I didn't like how it made people seem anti-social and cold. In contrast to the complete ego erasure that came as part and parcel of ecstasy usage, coke turned nice people into ego-centric tossers. I liked friendliness, affection, and confidence. M-cat gave me all three. The thing about M-cat was that if you only had a little mixed into a drink, you looked normal, as though you had just had a couple of lagers. It was so easy to get away with taking it on social occasions, no matter how formal or classy the event. Of course, a couple of years later, related deaths were spread all over the newspapers, resulting in it being banned.

The M-cat had the desired effect, and we would spend hours and hours making love in every way imaginable. As soon as the drug started wearing off, we would crave more, so our usage increased. M-cat was like truth serum. We would have intimate conversations full of emotion, about our deepest feelings, fears and insecurities; and we bonded this way. This felt even better than the intense, loved-up feelings which ecstasy pills had given me in the past. And all for a tenner a gram too! Cheap as chips. We got into the habit of setting my video recorder up in the corner of my bedroom, and would record the amazing sex and the deep conversations that we had. The more regular our drug use became, the more bizarre the sex. It would progress from stroking every inch of each other's body, gently whispering words of love to one another, to full-blown physical and psychological fuckery.

I relished my role as the dominant half of our relationship during those times. I was the submissive partner in all aspects of our relationship, during the week when we were drug-free, so it felt good to balance out the dynamics and have Jack under my full control. I would dress up in my fantasy police uniform, and handcuff one of

Jack's wrists with one half of the cuffs. I would lock the other cuff around the base of his balls. I would instruct him to masturbate until he couldn't take the sensitivity anymore. I would only release him if he begged. I would violate him with whatever I had to hand – a long, tapered candle on one memorable occasion. To add further humiliation into the mix, I lit the candle and cackled menacingly. We were videoing this session, and I thought it would be fun to light my cigarette with the flame of the candle. I did so, and sat back, casually smoking my fag, watching the candle burn down – with Jack on all fours, tied to the bed by his neck and arms, unable to move. What a pathetic sight he was, and I got off on the power. It wasn't a clitoris-swelling type of arousal; it was solely psychological. I was the powerful one for a change. To be honest, I just enjoyed making him look a bit of a twat.

Stick that in yer pipe and smoke it.

The old faithful prostate massage never failed to please. Show me a man who doesn't enjoy the occasional finger up his bum, and I'll show you a liar. 'Don't knock it 'til you've tried it' was my motto for most things sexual. Jack even asked me to carve my name into the skin on the right side of his abdomen with a razor blade on one occasion. I hope the bastard still has the scar as a reminder of what he did to me for the two-and-a-half years we were together.

I just loved the fact that Jack was doing disgusting, shocking things at my request. The more taboo, forbidden and demeaning the scenarios, the more exciting and naughtier the feeling. Addictive stuff – sex and drugs, alike. I think Jack enjoyed being submissive as much as I enjoyed being dominant. Much of our time together under the influence of drugs is now a blur, and maybe that's for the best. We left no stone unturned, that's for sure. What a funny old world we live in, eh? Don't try this at home, kids!

CHAPTER 17

Give me a thief, not a liar

We had been together for almost a year when Jack told me about a job interview he was due to attend five miles from his house. I supported him all the way and was thrilled when he was successful. A few weeks later, he told me that the job was actually in Iraq. He said that he wanted a job that gave him more recognition than he got in his current employment. He wanted a bigger house and an even fancier car. Jack was still running his own electrical company but was planning on having a break from it whilst he did the job in Iraq.

I had two options. I could put myself through the heartbreak of leaving him, or I could throw myself into being the perfect long-distance lover. I chose the latter and spent my spare time writing Jack long letters, poetry, and thinking up fun ways to make the time go faster. My old friend, Google, gave me lots of ideas, and I put my heart and soul into every one of them. He was to be away for a hundred and eighty days, so I put on some lipstick and kissed a few sheets of A4 paper one hundred and eighty times. I then laminated the paper and wrote a special memory in permanent marker pen on the back of each one, before cutting the kisses up into squares. I packed them into an envelope for him to open when he arrived at his posh hotel. A kiss a day – who says romance is dead?

Jack had been living in Iraq for almost three months when I began to feel suspicious. I don't know what started it; I just felt that there was something he wasn't telling me. Louise and Mum were up at my house. Louise, a hairdresser as well as my best friend (lucky me!), was cutting and colouring our hair. I was sitting on the sofa, messing about on my laptop and waiting for my turn. I'm a bit of whizz with finding things on computers that I shouldn't, and because Jack had been using my laptop before he had flown out to Iraq, I decided to do a spot of digging. I located an old email address that he had once used for work-related mail. Even though I expected to just find emails from his previous employers, a nagging inner voice (that pesky little devil again!) told me to look inside. His password was already saved, luckily, so Jack's inbox flashed up before me. I read down the list of emails, and saw that most of them were work related; and a few were from George. Being naturally nosy, I had to have a peek.

```
Dear Jack,

I can't wait 'til we can get together again.
I've been missing you. It doesn't matter about
your girlfriend. I know she's just a cover, and
if it means that we will see each other, you can
bring her with you to stay at my place in
Cornwall some time. There's plenty of room and
she would never guess. It's not like we walk
around holding hands, or anything, is it? Email
me when you can,

George xx
```

My heart leapt right out of my body and splattered on the ceiling. Either the dark forces behind every chain letter I had ignored in my life had avenged me in one go, or I was just cursed with horrendous bad luck at random

"Oh my God! Oh my God! Oh, my fucking God!"

Louise and Mum stopped their hair colouring and gossiping, and turned to stare at me in unison.

"You were right, Mum – George is a fucking woman! The name must be short for Georgina!"

She was speechless, but Louise was stifling a giggle with her hand over her mouth.

"It's not funny!"

"It is a bit though, Sinead."

"Shurrup! I'm going to look at the earlier emails. I'll tell you what they say in a minute."

Dear Jack,

It's all on for our trip to Monaco. It will be so good to spend some uninterrupted time together. We can say that I'm taking you to a trade show, and she will never suspect. I've attached a photo of my wife and one of my daughters. It was taken when we were a lot younger, as you can probably tell from my hair! She knows I'm gay, but we still live together for the sake of my two daughters. My wife doesn't want the embarrassment with our social circle being quite respectable and conservative. This arrangement suits us both. I live my life and she lives hers. I can't wait for one of your blow jobs!

Yours with deep love and affection,

George xx

It took a minute to register, as I stared open-mouthed at the screen. George wasn't Georgina. George was a dude. The Silent Partner title was just a cover so they could meet up regularly. I bet he wasn't bloody silent when my boyfriend was sucking him off, the dirty get! The whole story, from their first email together, was right there in front of me.

I checked the whole inbox and found that Jack had met lots of other men for money. There were no emails from women at all. This email address belonged to his alter-ego. I didn't cry. I did my signature shocked-but-calm thing. Mum, Louise, and I laughed and laughed about what a weirdo I had been going out with. I could always rely on Louise to sum up a whole situation in one of her famous one-liners:

"Okay, so your boyfriend's George Michael; but it could be worse."

I needed to take action. I called Jack and told him I knew everything. He tried to deny it all at first until I read out one of the emails to him. He admitted everything and threatened to kill himself. I told him to go ahead, but swore that I wouldn't be attending his funeral, and hung up. Jack rang and rang, and eventually, I answered. He cried and begged me not to tell his family and friends. I calmed down a little and sympathised.

"Look, Jack. You're gay. It doesn't matter. It must have been terrible for you, harbouring such a secret. I get that you've been in denial, but it's over now. I have to leave you."

"No, Sinead, please, please! I love you! It's not what it looks like! George is my silent partner, but he's also gay. I met him on a website where gay men pay for the services of muscular men. The fetish is called muscle worship. They pay me to visit them, and they like to masturbate over my body and ejaculate on my biceps and stuff. I know it sounds weird, but I've been doing it for years. I wanted to tell you. That's why I kept asking if you'd ever escorted before. I thought if you had done something similar, it would have been easier to tell you the truth."

"Er... but you give them blow jobs, Jack. You're in denial."

"I'm not in denial! I'm just liberated. Yeah, I do suck 'em off, but it's only skin. Kinda like shaking hands. How do you think I got my new Xbox? Those things don't come cheap, y'know! Let's just say I'm Tri-Sexual. As in, I'll try anything."

"Oh my God, Jack. How can you even joke about this? Do you look into their eyes while you're doing it?"

"Well, yeah. You kind of have to, don't you? It makes the experience more intimate for them."

"Jesus. Do you bonk them?"

"NO! I'm not into that, Sinead! God, what do you take me for?"

Did I have to answer that?

So, he wasn't gay, but he certainly swung both ways. And not only was he a 'roid boy, but a rent boy too. It was apparent that he preferred long-lasting emotional relationships with women, but needed the occasional man too. I could kind of identify with that, as much as I didn't want to. The difference was that I didn't make gay women fall in love with me under false pretences so I could financially exploit them. Jack said that he preyed on older men because they were easier to manipulate than women. *My God.* I felt sorry for poor George. Jack may have had plenty of money, but morally he was brassic. If me 'getting my tits out for forty quid' was bad, like he had once said to me, then sucking cock for game consoles was off the fucking scale!

Jack flew home the next day. He told his employers that his fiancée was four months pregnant and had lost the baby that day. He told me he had spent the morning researching miscarriages, and before meeting with his boss, he had spent half an hour running from wall to wall in his dormitory. He thought he would seem more convincing if he was breathless and looked like he was breathing erratically due to the shock. He had also researched body language techniques, eye movements, and how to tell lies effectively. I wondered at that point if he was totally devoid of a moral compass. He was the most expert liar I have ever come across, and believe me, I've met a few.

But I loved him. That old chestnut. The same thing you hear from most women in abusive relationships. I felt out of my depth, but with the usual barrage of apologies, flowers, declarations of love and grand gestures, I gave in for the hundredth time. Similar to how Stockholm syndrome works, I bonded with my abuser. I clung to Jack like never before. Instead of leaving him, I rationalised his behaviour by reasoning that as he had now told me everything, there surely couldn't be any more lies or drama. Maybe if I tried to understand him, he may love me and treat me better. I thought maybe the pressure of hiding his sexuality had driven him to be abusive and controlling towards me. Jack now had me right where he wanted.

His abuse changed tack and became frighteningly sadistic. I now got the silent treatment, or he would drive the car like a maniac to scare me when he was in a foul mood. He once went loopy when I mixed the cornflour into milk for the cheese sauce in the wrong order, and refused to eat with me because of this. He would make sexual comments about women on television and on nights out, to make me feel insecure and inadequate. It worked like a charm.

One night, Jack and I had an impromptu night out. His friend came to pick us up in a Rolls Royce he had borrowed from his obscenely rich boss. Jack and his friends were all about image. The whole street stared as the car pulled out of my driveway. That night we danced the night away in the V.I.P. area of a swanky nightclub, and we were in high spirits.

Right on cue, as we were all leaving the venue, Jack caused some ridiculous argument. His friends were looking on as I pulled him away from the door. I wanted to calm him down before things grew any worse, as I knew what he could be capable of. Without warning, he grabbed me in what would have appeared to the several onlookers as a big hug; as though he was making up with me and being drunkenly affectionate. He pinned my arms by my side so I couldn't move, and bent his head down at the side of my neck as though he was kissing and nuzzling me.

In actual fact, he had locked his teeth around the gristly part of the top of my ear, and was biting down hard. I have never in all my life felt pain like it. Childbirth isn't a patch on having your ear bitten. Take my word for it. It was an agonising, unfamiliar pain; so strong and all-encompassing that I couldn't even let out a scream. I felt paralysed and my head felt light. I saw glittery flecks before my eyes, then my body went limp.

Jack let go of my ear but still had my arms pinned by my sides. I sprang to life and tried with all my might to break free, but Jack's strength wasn't the type I could fight against. I wriggled and thrashed as much as I could. The only thing I had left to fight with was my mouth. I lunged forward with my head, frantically trying to bite at Jack's chest so he would let me go. He leaned his upper body right back to make sure that everyone could see my actions. I must have looked like I had escaped from the loony bin. All everybody could see was Jack trying to restrain me in self-defence, because I was trying to attack him with my teeth like one of the angry raptors in Jurassic Park.

He released his grip without warning, and I fell to the floor. My ear was stinging. I reached up to cup it and felt the stickiness of my blood on the cartilage. Luckily, a girl I knew had been leaving the club, and she came running over to pick me up from the floor. Even though my ear was bleeding, she didn't quite believe my version of events. Nobody did. Jack had successfully made me look like an unstable, crazy-making psycho; like the classic psycho ex that so many abusive men seem to say they have.

As he was strutting away, Jack saw that my friend was helping me off the floor.

"Just leave her on the floor. She's a fucking smack-head prostitute. She's been out partying and sucking off every chav in the club, for drug money. Her son is at home, being sexually abused by his dad! Mother of the fucking year, eh?"

Every single person in the taxi queue outside the club turned to look at me in horror at what a terrible person I was. I could see Jack talking to the door staff. He now appeared to be stone-cold sober, and they were sympathising with him. I shouted nothing back. I did nothing. What was the point? Jack had already successfully made everyone think I was mentally unstable. My friend helped me climb into a taxi and I returned home, deflated.

Once at home, my phone relentlessly rang and rang. I refused to answer it, but then the text messages started coming.

<Why don't you just kill yourself, you dumb bitch?>

<You worthless piece of shit. Your son's better off without you. Do everyone a favour.>

<I'm going to ruin your fucking life. I have some very incriminating videos.>

<Your life isn't even worth living, is it? You sad cow.>

<I'm going to make sure Morgan's taken into care. You're an unfit mother.>

<Why don't you just take an overdose? The world would be a far better place without you.>

<You're over. I'm going to make sure your life is wrecked, bitch!>

<Your life isn't gonna be worth living once I'm done with you.>

<Your family is gonna get it too. Their lives are over, as well as yours!>

The messages wouldn't stop coming. I lined up the last of my M-cat on the back of an encyclopaedia, and snorted it all in one go. I needed to forget everything, to feel numbness washing over me. It didn't help. It was about four in the morning and I had already been up for over twenty-four hours with no sleep. Psychosis had begun to set in, and I believed Jack's messages. I was a complete emotional wreck and had never felt so out of my mind before. He had me thinking I was seriously going mad.

I didn't want to kill myself; I knew that. I had Morgan to live for. However, Jack's constant harassing messages were successfully drumming into my brain that Morgan was better off without me. It felt like mental torture, and I think I had a mini-breakdown that night – a total mental collapse. I don't know what I was intending on doing, in all honesty. I was on autopilot as I headed towards the kitchen. Wailing with despair, with quick, raspy breathing, I pulled the biggest, sharpest carving knife from the cutlery drawer. I walked back upstairs, carrying the knife, as though in a trance, and flopped down on the floor at the foot of my bed. I rolled up my left sleeve and dragged the shiny metal blade slowly across my skin. Then I did it again. And again. I watched, vacantly, as the blood trickled from my flesh and dripped onto the carpet. Angry red slash marks covered my arm. I had mutilated my body and had just become a statistic of self-harm. Little did I know back then that I would be reminded of this moment in time, every year when summer came around. I discovered the hard way that scars don't tan.

The next thing I knew, Jack was bursting through my door, shouting garbled apologies. I didn't even look upwards. I was just staring fixedly at my arm, expressionless. Jack got down on his knees beside me, and begged for forgiveness.

"Oh Sinead, I never meant it to get this far. I'm so, so, so, so sorry!"

I stared straight ahead. He threw his arms around me and didn't let go for the next half an hour. We both whimpered like abandoned puppies. After we had both calmed down, and Jack had bandaged up my arm, I laid on the bed with him next to me. I stared at the ceiling, emotionless. After a few hours, I had sobered up and the drug had worn off. I felt like my brain was functioning almost normally again. Daylight filtered through the gaps in the bedroom curtains. I was aware that Jack was babbling beside me and slowly realised the implications of what he was suggesting.

"You need help, Baby-girl. I'll help you get support. Let me call the hospital and I will come with you. You need to talk to someone about what you've done."

What? Am I hearing this right? Suddenly, out of nowhere, I had clarity. Doing this to myself had been the jolt that I so badly needed. I was awake! I knew exactly what had happened, and I had never felt saner than I did at that moment.

Jack had tried his best to encourage me to take an overdose, so he could have me hospitalised, or worse: sectioned as mentally ill. I would have lost Morgan, and I would only have had Jack left to lean on for support. All the way through our relationship, he had been building up to this moment. He wanted nothing more than for me to believe that I needed him; and only him. If I needed him, I could never leave him, and I would be under his complete control. *No fucking way.* I looked him in the eyes and told him firmly and with conviction:

"No, Jack. It's you who needs help. You're the sick one. Now get out of my house before I call the police."

As soon as he saw that he could manipulate me no further, Jack stopped crying and started threatening me again, before leaving my house and slamming the front door almost off its hinges. I quickly ran downstairs and locked the door behind him, before returning to the safety and comfort of my bed. I could hear him, hollering in the street, "But Sinead, you've been self-harming! You need help!"

Naturally, I felt mortified at my neighbours hearing this, but I had gained new strength from somewhere. No man would ever mistreat me again.

Jack didn't let go without a fight. He was like a greyhound with a hare. I received the usual apologetic texts, flowers, and gifts through the post; but they were of no use. His ability to control me had ended. I won't lie, I wallowed and grieved for days, and during this time I did much reflecting. Nightmares plagued me for about a week. In them, Morgan was taken into care because I had been sectioned in a mental hospital. I would wake up screaming and sweating buckets. Even though I knew that I wasn't to blame for all the abuse my previous partners had inflicted upon me, I knew that I was accountable for taking them back time and time again. That decision had always been under my control, and I had waived the right to an abuse-free relationship, because deep down I had felt that I wasn't worth the alternative. The warning signs had always been there, but I had never trusted my inner voice enough to take action. Not until it had been too late, anyway.

I knew that I needed to break this pattern so that Morgan would have a fighting chance of growing into a stable and confident young man with good values. I bought a handful of books on domestic abuse and narcissistic partners, and it all made sense. My upbringing had led me to grow up with poor emotional boundaries where relationships were concerned, due to our family dynamics. As a result, in every adult relationship, I had compromised my values, principles, morals, and beliefs. I did this to adapt to my partners' ever-changing rules and to keep them happy – all the while, renouncing my self-respect.

I had grown up in an environment where sex wasn't taboo but spoken about with ease. While sex could be a beautiful and natural act between two halves of a loving couple, maybe it had been prevalent in too many conversations. Likely because of this, I grew up confused and pretty bloody kinky. As much joy as that kinkiness had brought me, the confusion had royally sucked. The men in my life had gratefully lapped up my open-mindedness but then abused it – either by cheating or pushing my boundaries with sex and anything else they could get their hands on; or dicks into. This had to stop. I had to help myself once and for all.

I booked myself into specialist counselling for victims of domestic abuse, and I felt like I finally had a voice. I told my family and friends what had been going on, and they were supportive. I was no longer alone on the battlefield. I had a long way to go, but I had taken the first steps. My counsellor was called Tracey, and she was awesome. She was ballsy, common as muck, thoroughly unconventional and swore like a trooper. She was probably quite unethical in her approach if I think back, but she showed me how important it is to relate to clients and keep it real. She regaled her personal tales of abuse to me, went 'two's' on cigarettes with me during breaks, and always gave me a big hug at the end of our sessions. She was warm, caring, ever so slightly bonkers, and just what I needed.

I still had a good relationship with the local papers who had featured my latest exploits. I started to sell my own brand of clubwear online, and they were supportive enough to run a feature on it. This little sideline didn't earn much, but it was fun and gave me a bit of pocket money, and I kept it going for five years. I donated a pound from every sale to the domestic abuse charity who had helped me. I felt that it was important to give something back and do my bit after what I'd been through. My heart soared with pride when the charity sent me a letter thanking me for raising money for them over the years. Unfortunately, during this time I received some nasty hate mail via my clothing website's contact form. I had advertised on the site that money from every sale would be donated.

In a memorable email, a fellow female stated that it was because of women in the glamour industry that men felt entitled to be violent towards their wives. She accused me of being a terrible role model and claimed I was enabling abuse by promoting women as objects, because of my glamour work. In her opinion, I was a disgrace to the feminist cause, because people like me betray other women. She said women like me deserve to have violence inflicted upon them by men. I felt crushed by her words. At the time, I was trying to improve my situation by getting out of the industry, and this lady had no idea that I had been in an abusive relationship. Just as my confidence and self-worth were growing, this incident knocked me back down again. These days we call people who send messages like these; 'Trolls', and what nasty pieces of work they are.

Coincidentally, a famous ex glamour model later became an ambassador for the charity, posing with a black eye on their promotional material. It was emotionally evocative and very well executed. How empowering it must have been for her to front such a strong awareness campaign. I hope she never got knocked down or received hate mail from such narrow-minded, judgemental people. If women can't celebrate their sexuality and their bodies for fear of being used as punch-bags, then surely violence and misogyny have won?

What I needed, once again, was to get some money coming in. The slash marks on my arms meant that modelling would be off the cards for quite some time. I wracked my brain for ways to make a quick income, but couldn't think of anything. No way was I going to lose my house – I had an eight-year-old child to think of. I picked up the phone and dialled a familiar number.

"Louise, it's me. Get the kettle on; I'm nipping down."

She always had good ideas; and they do say that two heads are better than one, don't they?

CHAPTER 18

Not from concentrate

I rocked up at Louise's flat, which was on the estate where I used to live with Mum and Dad. Tatty fake Ugg boots adorned my feet; perfectly reflecting how crap I felt about my life at that moment. Rain splattered from the broken guttering onto my forehead as I knocked and walked in, kicking off my leaking boots whilst making my way along the hallway and into the kitchen. Louise was ready for my arrival with a steaming cup of coffee, and passed it to me whilst greeting me with her usual cheesy, high beam grin.

"Y'alright, Sinead? What's the latest goss?"

"I need a job. Shit just got real and I'm proper skint."

I sipped my coffee, and I looked up at her over the top of my cup.

"I've got no real prospects and everyone knows about the glamour work. Nobody would take me on. I need money fast."

"Okaaaaay, what are your skills?"

I looked at her with a cheeky half-smile and chuckled naughtily.

"Sinead! I don't mean those skills. Hang on a minute! Okay, stay with me with this… You can write, yeah? You have a way with words, you can talk 'til the cows come home, you're a computer geek and you're addicted to chatting on MSN. Plus, you're a kinky bugger with no sexual boundaries, not to mention being a good friend. I mean, you're a top listener, like."

Louise was hopping about on the spot, as though she'd just discovered a big secret that she was dying to share.

"Right, but how are those things gonna help me get a decent job where I don't have to wait a month to get paid?"

"Duh! Webcamming! You've got a laptop, a nicely decorated bedroom, loads of crazy modelling clothes, and a whole weekend every week where Morgan goes to Knobhead's house. You can talk the talk, and, er, write the write if whoever's on the other end wants to be anonymous. Nothing shocks you, so you wouldn't be all judgy if your customers were into anything weird. You'd smash it!"

She had a point. This could be something I could excel at. I wanted something more though. I was sick to the back teeth of sexual stuff defining me. I needed something to boost my confidence, to go with my new attitude. I could be so much more than this, I knew I could. Tracey the counsellor had helped me to believe that I could be anything I wanted to be, within reason. The thought hit me like a lightning bolt, and I jumped from my chair onto the floor, making Louise jump simultaneously.

"Shit! That's it! I could be a psychologist! I could help people! Look at all the crap I've been through in my life so far. I could help people like me. Whaddya reckon?"

Louise pondered on my idea for a couple of seconds.

"Now that's a good idea. You would be ace at that. Not gonna get you any quick cash though, is it? Couldn't you do webcamming alongside studying? Summat like psychology takes ages to study. You'd have to go to uni and that."

This was a perfect idea. The more I thought about it, the more I felt that this was the right path to take. I could feel it in my bones.

"Sounds like a plan! Cheers for that. I'll let you know how I get on. Right, I'm offski. See ya soon."

I sipped the last dregs of my cuppa, hugged Louise, pulled on my soggy Uggs, and set off home. *Psychology Student by day, Sex Siren by night.* I reasoned that I wouldn't have to do the cam work for long; then I'd be out of the sleaze machine for good. I didn't realise that webcam work would be my least favourite job of them all so far.

As it happened, I didn't have to use MSN. I asked around, picked the brains of a few of the models I knew, and they told me the basics. They used an online portal that was purpose-built for the job. I uploaded a few sexy photos, typed out a bio to sell myself and set my fee at twenty pounds for ten minutes' viewing time. Customers could remain anonymous or interact. They could either type messages to me and not show their faces, or show their faces and converse with me with audio. The payouts were weekly, and after the website had taken a 30% cut, the remaining money I earned would be wired directly into my bank account.

The following Friday night, I waved Morgan off as he set off for the weekend with his dad. As soon as I saw them both turn the corner of the street, I locked all the doors in the house and set to work dolling myself up. I opted for the fail-safe smoky eyeliner/red lippy combo that had served me so well over the years. I shimmied into a lacy black negligee and patent black stilettos, ruffled my hair for a just-got-out-of-bed appearance, and climbed onto the bed like a newborn fawn trying to walk for the first time. It wasn't easy balancing on all fours whilst trying to look enticing on my rickety mattress! I set the laptop up on a battered little folding wooden table at the foot of my bed, fired up the cam portal, and waited... and waited... and waited. About thirty minutes had passed before I felt like throwing the towel in. Jeez, this was boring! Oh, hang on. A little light had just started flashing next to a guy's name! I can't remember what he was called. I was too busy being saucer-eyed and skittish with nerves.

"Come on Sinead, compose yourself!" I scolded.

Ping!

Fuck! Someone wanted to cam with me! *Oh, my Lord, it's happening!* I had a customer! *Eek!*

I pressed the 'Accept' button and the head and shoulders of a weedy-looking grey-haired fella with a bit of a comb-over appeared screen. He looked about fifty-five years of age, and almost as nervous as I.

"Hiya gorgeous," I purred, seductively blowing him a kiss. "What can I do for you this evening?"

"W… w… well, erm, I'd just like to see you pleasure yourself with a dildo, er, please. Thank you."

What a courteous chap he was. I must admit, I was expecting him to be a bit of a creepoid. Appearances can be deceptive, I guess. A digital clock, like a stopwatch, was counting down in bold red graphics underneath the screen, reminding us both that we were on borrowed time. *I had better crack on, then!*

My first time webcamming was surprisingly easy. It was the same routine I had already done a squillion times in adult modelling shoots, where it had become the thing to film an accompanying video clip. The internet was growing more popular, and photos alone would no longer do. Video clips were a big business, and if you wanted to follow the money, you had to move with the times in this game.

I spent the next ten minutes writhing around on my bed, teasingly removing my clothing bit by bit, gazing Marilyn Monroe style into the little camera clipped to the top of my laptop. After five minutes had passed, I lay on my back, propping myself up with one elbow, and got busy with my trendy baby pink tattoo print vibe. My guy was watching as though mesmerised, transfixed on my bits. I needn't have bothered looking into the camera, in all honesty. His eyes never left my lower half. It didn't matter how pretty I was, he just wanted to look into my... well, my uterus by the looks of it. As I made all the right noises, so did my guy. Yes! He was lapping it up! This was easy. His right arm soon began shaking furiously, so fast that his screen was pixellating. His webcam couldn't keep up with his excitement, bless his cotton socks.

Thirty-two seconds to go...

I inserted the vibrator slowly, one last time for luck, and let out a loud but breathy sigh. Pulling the sex toy out from inside my vagina again, I opened my legs a little wider so he could get a better view, sucking my pelvic floor muscles in and out a few times, to simulate a strong, pulsing climax. (Sorry, mate, if you're reading this. I duped you. I faked it. They all fake it.) I couldn't believe that a few years before, I had experienced my first ever orgasm. Now I was even a dab hand at faking them! Well, seeing this oh so incredible orgasm I was having before his very eyes tipped the poor fella over the edge. I think he died and went to Heaven for a few seconds because he went rigid as though rigor mortis had suddenly set in. Eyes shut tightly, he was looking ever so pained, with what appeared to be a contorted grimace on his face. This bad example of human taxidermy sitting before me suddenly sprang back to life... and let out a loud groan as he came. *Nailed it.*

No sooner had my first guy left the screen, when another customer flashed up. It was like that pretty much all night. I was a newbie and felt popular – fresh meat, I guess. There were periods of waiting around, but they didn't bother me too much that first night. I was sore, but I guessed I would get used to that. Learning the ropes was a bit of a novelty to me that whole weekend. It was mostly all the same stuff – playing with myself in a standard porno manner. I didn't get my first interesting job until the following weekend.

I enrolled at university on the following Monday, choosing a degree course in psychotherapy. The thought of being a mature student was nothing short of terrifying, but those worries were unfounded. Almost everyone in my class was over thirty, and some were even in their fifties. The thing about psychotherapy is that much of it is based on life experience – and I had plenty of that. The best thing about choosing to go back into education in my thirties was that it was expected that the students would have houses to run, kids to take care of and jobs to go to. Because of this, the course was only one day a week, to begin with. I could manage that with no problems, and it meant that I didn't have to go under financially whilst I was working at bettering myself. It would be a hard slog, though. If I wanted to reach my goal of being qualified, it would take around four years. I had already been in the adult industry for eight years, and it had flown by. I had got myself onto this carousel of drama, and it was down to me to get myself off it. One quality I have is that I'm like a dog with a bone when I'm focused on a project. I knew I could do this if I put my all into it. I kept the image of that shiny new degree firmly in my mind. If I could visualise it, then I could surely materialise it.

I found that I had a flair for empathising with others' problems, and counselling came naturally to me. This was something that I was good at, and knowing that gave my self-esteem and inner confidence just the right amount of boost it had needed. The old spark I'd once had for academia and language had been reignited in me. I had always loved writing, and it felt so good to nurture my creativity. My interest in psychology and human behaviour had never gone away, but this time I was putting my knowledge to fantastic use and helping people to understand why they were the way they were. A huge part of the course was devoted to students working through their past traumas. That was difficult, and a few people dropped out because the emotional pain was too much. Everyone on the course had their reasons for being there, and some were more harrowing than you could ever imagine. We all knew about one another's past; but refreshingly, there were no judgements. In the classroom I was just plain old Sinead, and my fellow students respected me for my thoughts and ideas, rather than defining me by my past fuck-ups. I was honest with my tutor, but he assured me that many sex workers became therapists, just like recovering alcoholics and ex-drug addicts often do. My knowledge could be invaluable to others in similar situations. I wanted to help people, and most of all I wanted to make Morgan proud.

In around four years, Morgan would be thirteen. I wanted to raise my lad to be respectful of women, and not to view them as mere sex objects (or punch-bags, as his dad had). I wanted to be a mum he could be proud of, and to do that I knew I would have to lead by example. With the ever-growing rise of the internet, I knew that if I stayed in this job, it would only be a matter of time before Morgan would get to find out about my double life. To me that wasn't a risk worth taking, and no way could I let that happen. You know what teenage lads are like – all hormones and wanking and stuff (a bit like many grown-arsed men too, come to think of it). My worst fear was that one of his future friends at high school would stumble across my images and show him. I winced at the thought of poor Morgan dealing with an onslaught of teenage jokes ending with the punchline, "your mum".

With Morgan at school during the day, I made sure that I crammed in as much camming as I could. I needed to get back into the black with the bank, so I made sure that I took advantage of every spare minute I had. After a few weeks of this, I grew seriously bored with all the waiting around between customers. It was lonely work, too. There's nothing more depressing than spending ages getting ready as though you're going on a night out with the girls, only to spend the rest of the time sitting on your bed at home, waiting around for some guy on a computer screen to show an interest in you. The lack of adult company was a bit pants as well. I was used to travelling up and down the country, chatting away to photographers while I worked with them to create (mostly) beautiful images. When I hadn't been modelling or keeping up with the housework, I had been nattering with Louise over a cuppa. Now I was at home the majority of the time with no company.

I changed my levels on the cam portal, to spark a bit of interest in my potential customers and to try to wheedle out the ones who just wanted sleazy old insertion. I didn't find that kind of work creative, or good for the soul. It was a means to an end, and like being a walking, talking sex doll. Not my cup of tea at all. Those sex toys don't half chafe after so many goes! If I kept going at this rate, it would either result in a prolapse in my later years, or I would end up with a pelvic floor of steel that Jane Fonda[38] would be proud of! The latter fate would have been gratefully received, but I didn't trust the odds to be in my favour. Yep – the dildos had to go.

I changed the photos on my bio to ones that looked more dominant. Chin up rather than down, that kind of thing. With the Fetish box ticked, all I had to do was wait and see what kind of kinky antics would be required of me. I knew a model called Kaley, who loved webcamming and made a heck of a lot of money out of it. She once told me that the trick to being so popular was to tap into the niche markets. Her particular niche of choice was urination – more commonly known as Watersports. Her username was Pee-Slut, and she had a little sleight of hand magic trick. She would have a glass of apple juice placed next to her laptop, just out of view of the customer. Her trademark party trick was to wee into a different glass, held underneath her as she talked teasingly to the guy on the screen. This type of customer would expect her to drink said wee, because that's what got his rocks off. Of course, there was no way in this world she was about to drink her own piss for any money! As the guy was mumbling crude nothings to her, she would distract him by coming up close to the camera and blowing him a kiss, whilst she quickly swapped glasses over. The urine-filled glass was now out of his field of vision, and she would hold the glass of apple juice, which she then drank in front of him. Pee-Slut indeed. I was just gawping at her, open-mouthed when she told me this little gem.

"Well, you've got to be cunning in this game, Sinead, or you don't get anywhere."

She had a point.

---

[38] An American actress who was a huge sex symbol in the seventies and eighties. She was also known for being a fitness fanatic, inspiring women the world over to make poor fashion decisions and dress in brightly coloured, tight, spandex gymwear.

Pee-Slut also had an alter ego, and another genius trick up her sleeve. Enter Scat-Whore, ta-daaa! Scat-Whore would poke chocolate truffles up her bum (the posh Belgian ones with the flaky bits on, for added authenticity). In the presence of her eager customers, she would squeeze them out on camera, as you would when having a dump. Nobody gets hurt or gets nasty bacterial infections, and everyone leaves the conversation happy. Priceless.

It certainly brings another meaning to the old Goonies' phrase, 'truffle shuffle'[39].

Whatever float(er)s your boat.

I thought I would give Kaley's old trick a test run when I bagged my first piss-drinking fetishist. She had quit camming a long time ago, so she kindly agreed to let me benefit from her creativity. All was going well until I reached over to grab the glass containing the apple juice, intending to slyly replace it with the wee-filled one. Picture the scene: me balancing on my knees, atop my bed, with one hand blowing my guy a kiss and the other arm outstretched, clutching the piss-glass. I overbalanced, lurched forward and threw the golden-coloured contents all over the keyboard.

"No!" I yelled in panic as the cloudy liquid made its way between each letter key. Scrabbling around, trying to catch the other glass before the apple juice also became one with technology, I accidentally leaned on a key that cut off my customer. That was probably for the best, upon reflection. I may as well have just squatted over my laptop and pissed on it myself. Not my proudest moment; but at least my

---

[39] An eighties children's film where a fat kid called Chunk exposed his belly and wobbled it in a manner which would put you off your food. He called it 'the truffle shuffle'.

laptop didn't fizzle and blow up. It was like Robocop, that machine – unbreakable, like yours truly.

I've been to a few parties since that fateful day, when people have been tipsy, playing games like Truth or Dare. The following question has often come up many a time:

"What's the most embarrassing thing you've ever done as a Domme?"

This. It's this, hands down.

I soon discovered that there were some very complex fetishes doing the rounds – some of them were bizarre, but innocent and non-pornographic, such as getting off on seeing a young lady pop a balloon by sitting on it, and some of them plain dangerous and downright alarming, such as having one's head submerged in water for sexual kicks. I was enjoying researching and gaining a deeper understanding of the human psyche and had read quite a few books on the subject of fetish and fantasy.

I discovered that fetishes and fantasies hailed from somewhere deep down in us and are related to normal biological, instinctive impulses. One word – Nature. Take rape fantasies that feature so commonly in the female mind, for example. Nobody wants to be raped for real. Rape is one of the most horrific, sexually violent and traumatising crimes that you can think of. In fantasy land it's safe. Nobody gets hurt, and the submissive gets to feel, well, truly submissive. Often, the things that scare us the most and get our blood pumping can also be the most exciting. What a fascinating ability we human beings have! It's like why we watch horror films – sheer morbid curiosity, the adrenaline, and cortisol rush; and because we love being scared half to death. I mean, would you like it in real life if you were being chased through the woods by a machete-wielding killer clown? No, you wouldn't, but it's not real; it's just fantasy-based. It's safe. Now don't pretend you don't have a kink that you wouldn't dare disclose. Go on, I bet you can think of at least one. Nobody has to know…

When I recall my very brief webcamming days, a very memorable fellow called Mr. Swift springs to mind. I had been made familiar with age-play many times in my modelling career. I had also seen many a discussion in online forums, likening it to paedophilia; but paedophilia it most definitely was not. Age-play enthusiasts hated this kind of comparison and would find it extremely hurtful, for obvious reasons. In basic terms, age-play ranged from, say, a wife dressing up in something like a school uniform, and the husband playing a headmaster or something, to full-blown Adult Baby/Infantilism roleplay. I was mature (pun intended) and smart enough to distinguish innocent age-play scenarios from something completely different with creepy and illegal undertones. It was less about the ages depicted in the roleplay, and more about the vulnerability and power balance that the ages represented – the usual Sub/Dom dynamic. From researching into this online, I learned that some people wanted a Mummy and others preferred a Daddy to take control. Some fantasies were based purely on the caring aspect of such a relationship, with no sexual connotations at all, whilst others focused on sexuality. Roleplay was just an extension of people's private fantasies, acted out physically.

Mr. Swift had decided to be anonymous in our session, but he wanted to engage in a conversation in type with me. We agreed that I would speak with audio so I could have my hands free, and he would type out replies as he saw fit. He had privately messaged me beforehand to explain that he was very, very shy and private about his fetish, and implored me to act with sensitivity and kindness, to which I agreed. It seemed that he yearned for understanding and for someone to fulfil his fantasy in a deep and special way. He wanted to feel a connection with his 'Mummy'. Mr. Swift explained that he had cammed with many Mummies before, but they hadn't seemed to understand the psychological dynamics of age-play. I don't know why he thought I would be any different. Maybe I just have one of those faces. I was sure that I could do this well and make it a memorable experience for him. I even did a little online research into the fetish and found that this kink was quite common.

So, Mr. Swift needed a Mummy. His first words to appear in the chat-box on the screen were, "Would you give me a bath, please, Mummy?"

Fuck's sake. How on earth am I going to pull this one off?

I had pushed the boat out in my preparation for this cam-sesh, by dressing in a very 1950s looking circle dress which nipped in at the waist with a wide, black patent belt. I had even tonged my hair, so it looked slightly mumsy, feminine and prissy. A bath though, of all things? These guys were full of surprises!

"Yes, my darling, I will. I know how you love splashing around in the tub."

I had a spur-of-the-moment idea…

"Right, my little love, follow Mummy into the bathroom like a good boy."

I walked into my bathroom, holding the laptop in front of me so Mr. Swift could see where we were heading. I then turned the laptop around so that it was facing me. I slowly bent forward, and lowered the laptop into the bath, as though it were him I was carrying.

"Mummy, I saw your boobies when you put me down in the bath. Hee-hee, they're very big and bouncy. I thought they would fall out of your pretty dress!"

"Ooh, you cheeky little monkey! Nevermind my boobies, let's get you clean. Behind your ears are filthy."

I felt like such a doofus, talking to a laptop… in my bath. Thank Heavens Mr. Swift was the only person who could see this bizarre scene unfolding. *Now, what to do next?* I reached over to the corner of the bath and grabbed a big, round, lilac-coloured sponge.

"Right, come here and let's get you nice and clean, Angel," I said softly as I dragged the dry sponge across the screen.

God's honest truth, that's exactly what I did. There's a fine line between genius and madness, y'know, and have I most definitely danced along that line a few times.

"Mummy, are you going to wash me all over?"

"Yes, I am. I wouldn't be a good mummy otherwise, would I?" I reached behind the laptop, as though I was sponging down the parts of his body that he couldn't see, such as his back and shoulders. I knew what was coming next.

Brace yourself, Sinead.

"Please, not my willy, Mummy. You know what happened the last time, and I was so shy about it."

"Now listen here, you've got to get clean, dear. Don't be shy, it's only me, Mummy."

Oh, God.

I took a deep breath and did what I knew I had to do for the good of my craft.

"There we go, let's give that willy a good wash. See, I'm being gentle, aren't I?"

"Oh Mummy, you're sooooo gentle, yes."

"Is that feeling nice to you, sweetheart?"

"Yes. Yes, it feels veeeery nice, Mummy."

All the while Mr. Swift had a cracking view of my ample cleavage, which was spilling over the top of my sweetheart neckline.

"Right, I think it's time to give you a little treat. What do you think? You've been such a good boy and I'm so proud of you."

"A treat? Wow! Yes, please, Mummy."

I pulled away from the inside of the bath and stood up, lifting one leg and propping my foot up on the side of the tub. What a view he must have had from down there. I could see myself on the screen, and my legs looked awesome in those sheer nude-coloured stockings and cerise suede peep-toe heels. I looked intently down at the camera and rolled up my skirt so it rested on the top of the thigh of the leg that was raised. I opened my leg slightly outwards. I had no knickers on, of course.

"Oh Mummy, what are you doing? I'm a bit nervous," Mr. Swift typed, erm, swiftly.

"I'm showing you something special, love. This is what a lady's bits look like. This is the part that I wash when I'm alone in the bath."

"Oh, I see. How do you wash it, Mummy? Do you use the sponge?"

"Oh no, I don't need the sponge. I just use my fingers."

Fucking Hell, Sinead, how do you think up this stuff?

"Can you show me what you do, Mummy?"

"Yes."

For the next couple of minutes, Mr. Swift was silent. I was glad that I couldn't see his physical reactions if I'm honest. I think they would have been burned into my memory for all eternity. I carefully teased my labia apart and began stroking my vulva, progressing onto sliding my fingers slowly in and out of my vagina. The usual rigmarole; but a very different scenario to what I was used to.

"That looks like it feels nice, Mummy. Does it?"

"Yes, oh yes, it feels very, very nice, Babycakes."

"Oops! My willy has gone all pointy again, Mummy. I'm sorry, Am I a bad boy?"

"Haha, silly; of course you're not a bad boy. You probably think Mummy's private parts look very pretty. Do you think that's why your willy has gone all pointy?"

"Yes, you look so pretty, Mummy."

"Why don't you wash your willy too, darling? It's okay, you can touch it if you like."

"I'm touching it, Mummy, but what should I do?"

Bloody Hell. Do I have to tell him? Okay, deep breath; here goes…

"Just put your hand around it and move it carefully up and down. That's it – just like that."

I spcd up my fingering technique and throwing in a few little moans here and there.

"You won't be cross, Mummy?"

"No, love, I won't be cross. Promise."

I think it's probably fair to say that Mr. Swift shot his biggest load yet all over his computer that afternoon. I'll never know, but I reckon it's a good guess. When I got the feeling that it was all over (the scenario, not the motherload), I bent back down and reached forward, enveloping the laptop in something that resembled a hug.

"Well done, sweetheart. Now, doesn't that feel so much better? You're all nice and clean."

"Thank you, Mummy, I enjoyed that bath. I promise I won't tell."

"That's my good boy."

Session swiftly over.

I did a lot of reflecting on Mr. Swift's session, but it was none of my business why he fantasised about being young. I knew from my research that a lot of time the age people chose to be in their fantasies was the approximate age at which they first became sexually active. I hoped to God that this hadn't been the case for this fellow. I didn't even want to think it may have been a possibility, but I couldn't help but analyse it to death. I felt that I needed to make sense of what I had engaged in. What if Mr. Swift had experienced an unthinkable sexual trauma as a child at someone else's hands? Maybe this was like therapy for him? Maybe this had been the only way that his mind had been able to process, accept and learn to live with such an awful incident? *What if?*

I wrestled in my mind with the details of this session, as it had felt quite uncomfortable for me. It was clearly uncomfortable for him too, with him not wanting me to see his face as most other cammers did. But he had liked it. Not only liked it – he had loved it. I received a private message from him the next day, gushing:

Mistress Olivia,

You were the best Mummy I've ever had in my life. Please don't disappear, I will be so sad if I never get to play with you again. Thank you so much. I don't know how you knew exactly what to do and say, but you did. You were perfect. Everything was just as it has been in my head for so long. Thank you again. I love you, Mummy,

Mr. Swift x

If I had helped him to come to terms with something sinister in his past, or if the case was just that this was a kink which had developed from nowhere, then I resolved that I was okay with either explanation. I reminded myself that he was a grown man who knew what he had wanted. I sensed that the whole thing meant a lot to him on a level beyond sex. I congratulated myself on such fine attention to detail, but I knew I didn't want to do age-play sessions on par with that again. I had a feeling that it would be mentally exhausting and that I would always have conflicting feelings afterward. No, I couldn't be Mr. Swift's Mummy. I hope he found her though, and that he had his happy ending. I realised that none of the work I had ever done was ever only about the money for me. If it had been, I would be a millionaire by now, I'm certain of that.

The money from webcamming was highly appealing, and it helped me out of a sticky situation quickly; but I'm one of those people that if I don't do a job I enjoy, I become miserable, shrivel up and die off. I take my hat off to the ladies who do this kind of work full time. Seriously, I salute them – because I know they'd agree with me when I say that the glamour rating is way below zero. It takes a special and very resilient type of woman to adopt this kind of on-screen persona and be dedicated to it.

I was nearing the end of my tether with webcamming and it had only been around three months. I had barely even started, but I was getting well and truly fed up with dressing up like a dog's dinner almost every day and every weekend, and then sitting around waiting for each customer to pop up. It was mind-numbing. Then the universe came a-knocking with its surprises, as it so frequently does. I logged into the adult portal one evening to see that I had a message from a username I recognised.

Hi Mistress Olivia,

It's me, Lancs-Geezer. My real name is Malcolm. The last time we sessioned, the screen cut out early. Sorry about that. I just wondered if you did private sessions. If so, I would love to book one. I hope to hear from you soon.

Malcolm xxx

It took me a minute to realise who it was. It was none other than apple juice/piss guy. It relieved me that he had thought the camera problem was at his end and not mine. He hadn't realised that I had tricked him and spilled my 'golden nectar' as he had called it. Did I do private sessions? *Do bears shit in the woods?* I replied hastily and said that yes, I would arrange a session with him promptly. I asked him what kind of session he was after, and clarified that I no longer did piss drinking. He said that was fine because he wanted to taste it himself and not waste a drop by sharing it! *Oh, bejesus. The man must be crazy*, I thought. But who was I to judge? He had just given me the best idea ever! I could advertise myself as a Session Mistress and finally get off my knees, off my bed and out of my house. *Cheers, Malcolm!* From that moment on, my fate was sealed. I would be the real-life Mistress Olivia.

CHAPTER 19

Learning the ropes

True to form, I asked Google incessantly about what this new venture would require of me. If Google were a person, it would have found me very irritating. Being a Mistress didn't seem too complicated or expensive, which was a relief. I didn't have the foggiest idea of where to begin and needed all the help I could get. I bought a couple of books on the subject and found them entertaining and informative. I thought it all sounded quite glamorous compared to webcamming.

I didn't yet have a niche market, but I knew I would prefer to convey an image that would set me apart from those offering escorting services. I didn't want to advertise as an Escort, as I didn't want to give the wrong idea. I wouldn't be offering any sexual favours – just titillating fun. Any sexual satisfaction that my customers received would be by their own hand, upon returning to the privacy of their own home, post-session. I settled upon Domination; that way I would feel that I would always be the one calling the shots, and I wouldn't get anyone I considered to be too weird, assuming that they could take advantage. I wanted to make sure I attracted humble, respectful and appreciative clients only. I've always been good at playing up to the camera and putting on an act. I was a bit of a bossy boots at home and had learned natural dominance from my mum and several other strong females in the family. There was a fine line, but using domination as a foundation helped to make being a Mistress seem a world away from what I would have described as an Escort.

First, I needed to advertise my services. This part was easy – I just needed to disable the webcam option and tick the Personal Services check-box, add a few photos of me looking sexy and slightly menacing in a few different outfits with a variety of backgrounds. The law was sketchy regarding the legalities of making money this way and could change at any time, so to be on the safe side most adult workers described their fee as a tribute. It was like a donation, but a set figure. I noticed that most sex-workers and dominatrices had some small print on their introductions, stating that any adult services which take place in the sessions are at the discretion of the two adults in question, would not relate to the tribute, and would take place in their own time. The tribute would simply pay for the company. This was a little loophole which in not so many words meant, "If we shag, I can't get into trouble for it. You're paying for being in my company only; and if we have engaged in any rumpy-pumpy, that's not because you've paid me." Right on. I stated that I would require a deposit of fifty-five pounds in advance, to filter out any uncommitted tyre-kickers and ensure my clients showed up. The deposit would cover me in the event of no shows.

My profile nearly completed, I just had to tick the boxes of the services I was happy to provide. An insight into a whole other world was on the screen in front of me. I never knew there were so many genres and preferences! Each category of service had been abbreviated. I had to look many of them up figure out what on earth they were referring to! The non-exhaustive list went something like this:

OW (Oral With. Oral sex with a condom.)

OWO (Oral Without. Oral sex without a condom.)

RO (Reverse Oral. Basically, the client gives rather than receives.)

CIM (Come in Mouth. Self-explanatory.)

GFE (Girlfriend Experience. The worker acts as though she's in love with the client, with full mouth-to-mouth kisses and affection.)

A-Levels (Anal)

BB (Bareback. Without a condom, in other words.)

CMNF (Clothed Male Naked Female.)

CFNM (Clothed Female Naked Male.)

HR (Hand Relief. In layman's terms this means that the client is masturbated to climax at the end of the session.)

FS (Face-Sitting. Exactly what it says on the tin.)

BJ (Blow Job, of course.)

PSE (Porn-Star Experience. Full on theatrical sexy-time, just like on-screen.)

COT (Come On Tits. The client ejaculates onto the worker's breasts.)

COF (Come On Face. I'm sure I don't need to explain further.)

WS (Water-Sports. Anything involving urine/urination.)

CBT (Cock and Ball Torture. Ouch!)

BDSM (Bondage Domination Submission or Sadism and Masochism. Most services which involve Sub/Dom dynamics no matter how hard or soft, fall into this category.)

CP (Corporal Punishment. Domestic or school-like discipline such as spanking, caning, strapping, etc.)

RP (Role Play. Both client and worker play a part and perhaps dress in costume, to create a fantasy scenario.)

Every day's a school day, eh? Inside information, right there.

I thought I must have seemed like a bit of a prude, only choosing CP and BDSM. I didn't mind that I would be engaging in WS with Malcolm, as I felt that I would be comfortable with him after our cam session. However, I didn't want to advertise that I undertook this kind of work. It was just a one-off for shits and giggles (well, piss and giggles to be accurate). Also, I didn't mind what the clients did to their bodies in the way of self-gratification; but I certainly wasn't going to do it for them. *Eugh, no chance.*

I already had a wardrobe to rival a fancy-dress shop's, and a few implements that I had used as props in both modelling and webcam work, such as canes, straps, handcuffs and the likes. All I needed was somewhere to work from, and I knew the perfect place. I asked Alan, the manager who ran the photography studio where I had done my initial model training all those years ago. We had remained good friends over the years and it was not so long ago that I had been shooting there so much that the place felt like a second home. With all the different sets available, it would be the ideal place to set up shop. Photographers and models could hire out the whole place for twenty pounds per hour, which I thought was a bargain. I was the only Mistress who had come up with the idea of hiring it for this purpose. Thinking outside the box has always been one of my specialties.

If I charged a hundred and twenty pounds for a one-hour session, I would go home with a hundred smackaroonies in my pocket each time. *Kerching!* I also knew that I would be safe there, as Alan would just be through a door and down the hall, working on his image editing. Both uni and this new phase of self-employment gave me a newfound sense of confidence and independence.

Malcolm/Lancs-Geezer and I had arranged a session to take place in a few weeks' time. I had bagged one other session beforehand, with a chap who called himself FishingAddict on the adult services portal. There were some very odd usernames. FishingAddict had specified in his email that he wanted a regular Mistress whom he could serve as a slave. He wanted to do things for me to make me feel 'like a lady' and for me to boss him around and to feel inferior. He had one special request, and that was to bring his butt-plug, which he would insert and remove himself. He also wanted to wank himself off whilst the butt-plug was in place. Fair enough. All I had to do was kick the butt-plug; but not too hard. I could do that. He wanted me to refer to him as 'Slave', which was just as well, because I don't think 'FishingAddict' would have had the same effect. It sounded like a straightforward job, and he sounded like a very respectful and nice enough guy.

The night before the session, I consulted Kaley again on the phone and asked for tips. I knew she regularly worked in dungeons, so she would know what kind of thing to expect. This was my first ever one-to-one session, and I was nervous as Hell.

"Remember not to feel guilty. He's paying you because he loves being treated like shit. Call him all the names under the sun, make him feel like a worthless piece of crap and remember not to break out of the role. Introduce yourself like a Mistress, and exit like a Mistress. Take the money first, and when he leaves, tell him to fuck off. He'll love it, you can't go wrong."

I made a mental note, and excitement took over the nerves. I was really doing it! I was on a power trip before I had even begun.

I let myself into the studio and got to work arranging the set. Alan had asked me to pick up some loo roll for the changing room toilet, but I had forgotten. *Oh well, I can drip dry if I need a wee,* I reasoned, and thought nothing more of it. I used the living room set which had pink and blue flowery wallpaper, a cream sofa and cream-coloured fake sheepskin rug on top of faded mock parquet lino. It looked cosy and domestic, albeit old-fashioned. Perfect for my first session. I dragged the vaulting horse from the schoolroom set in there too, so I could spank Mr. FishingAddict over it. I made myself a coffee to take into the changing room and squeezed myself into a shiny black PVC catsuit and thigh-high, lace-up, patent stiletto-heeled boots. This Cat Woman-esque attire made manoeuvring difficult, but I looked bloody grand! I scraped my hair into a very high ponytail and attached a straight, waist-length hairpiece, so it looked like my ponytail was really long. Yes, I looked quite the Mistress, exactly as I had always imagined a professional dominatrix to look – beautiful, but intimidating. I paced around the studio, creaking as I went, practising my assertive walk whilst I waited for my victim to arrive. The sexy walking that Louise and I had taught ourselves in the school playground all those years ago was finally coming in useful!

My heart leapt when I heard the door buzzer. He was here! I opened the door to a chubby little bald man with no eyebrows, smiling up at me. He wore dark blue straight-legged jeans, pulled right up to his middle, held in place with a brown, shiny buckled belt. On his top half, he wore a baggy white t-shirt. *Tucked in. Cringe.* Not that I had any right to be the fashion police in what I was wearing. He was clutching a scrunched-up Asda carrier bag, containing what I guessed to be the aforementioned butt-plug.

"Hello Mistress, it's wonderful to meet your acquaintance. I've been looking forward to this."

"Hello Slave, it's good to meet you too. I trust you had a good journey? If you'd like to follow me…"

I creaked and squeaked up the hallway towards the studio, with FishingAddict following closely behind me. I let us both into the studio, entered the set and plonked myself down on the sofa.

"Take off your clothes, Slave. All of them!" I barked. My tone sounding uncannily like little Satanic Sadie in her dad's factory, all those years ago.

"Y-yes, Mistress," he replied shakily as he bent down to pull off a sock. Toe first, as men do. Men always do things the most difficult way, don't they? It surprised me to see that he had two pierced nipples with rings in them. To look at him when I met him at the door, you just wouldn't think he would be the type; but he was a slave, I guess.

I gestured with my hand at my new slave to sit down on the floor. He did as he was told and sat crossed legged, with it all hanging out and not caring, gazing up at me adoringly. He reminded me of those chubby, smiling stone Buddhas that they sold in our local garden centre.

"What would you like me to do for you, Mistress?"

Well, I had to stretch this out for an entire hour somehow. I suddenly felt inspired by aspects of Edward's mum's personality. What would Liz do? She would be Queen bitch, of course. Queen bitch it is, then; all the way! Chanelling her domineering presence, I pulled out a perfect, icy 'mum glare' that the old dragon would have been proud of. My trembling slave instantly shrank back in response. Result! In preparation, I had placed some wine-coloured nail varnish on a little side table next to the sofa, beside the carrier bag he had brought along with him.

"You'll paint my toenails with that nail polish over there, you worthless little maggot. Now remove my boots. Chop, chop!" I clapped my hands together twice in front of his face as he blinked profusely in shock. *This is going swimmingly,* I thought as I congratulated myself on my domineering demeanour. FishingAddict did as he was told. He carefully unfastened my boots, pulled them both off and gently placed the heel of one of my feet on his leg. He painted my toenails with careful precision, whilst I sat there looking down at him condescendingly.

"M-may I come and sit next to you please, Mistress?" he asked tentatively when he had finished.

"No, you cannot! How dare you ask such a thing? Your place is on the floor, you cretin!"

FishingAddict appeared dejected and hung his head in disappointment. *This is working like a charm,* I smirked to myself.

I filled the next twenty minutes of our time together by making him crawl around on the floor and complete other humiliating tasks. All the while, I barked orders at him and called him nasty names. Easy-peasy, lemon squeezy, I thought. With fifteen minutes to go, I instructed him to fetch the butt-plug. He scurried over to the little side table and unrolled the carrier bag, dropping the fat, black, shiny latex accessory into the palm of his hand. Jeez, that thing had some girth. Just looking at it made my eyes water.

"Now stick it where the sun don't shine, Slave! Show your Mistress what a disgusting worm you are!"

FishingAddict bent over the vaulting horse and stretched an arm behind him, searching blindly for his bum-hole. He found it and pushed in the butt-plug, dry. *Hard as nails, this one!*

"P-please Mistress, I can't get it in. Would you kindly assist?"

"How dare you? What makes you think I would want to help a shameful creature such as you?" I sneered.

And with that, I lifted my perfectly pedicured foot, and gave the butt-plug a little kick, as he had requested in his pre-session communication.

"Ugh!" he gasped as he lurched forward right over the horse.

Shit, I think I've hurt him, Oh, well, must press on...

I began furiously slapping his bum with my right hand, making sure it didn't land near his stretched-to-the-maximum anus. My hand began to sting.

"Aaaaaaah! Owwwww!" he yelled out in pain.

"Now turn around, lift yourself onto that horse and sit on that disgusting, fat arse of yours," I demanded.

"Y-yes, Mistress."

He did as he was instructed, and winced as he lowered down his backside, forcing the butt-plug in to its full potential.

"Now masturbate for me, Slave. Show me how much you love having that thing in your baggy arsehole. Demonstrate to me how truly pathetic you are."

So, with a pained expression, he did. Wank, wank, wankety wank.

"Look at me!" I yelled in his face threateningly.

FishingAddict's eyes reluctantly met mine as he tugged his todger to a climax, exactly as planned.

"Please, would you pass me the carrier bag, Mistress?"

Strangely, the session hadn't bothered me in the slightest, but seeing him remove the plug made me feel woozy. He turned the carrier bag inside out, put it over his hand like a glove, squatted down in front of me and pushed the blockage out into the bag, wrapping it around the plug like you would a dog poo. Gosh. I had never considered how it would come out. I know I keep saying it, but you really do learn something new every day.

I could smell poo. There was no mistaking that pungent odour. That was definitely poo. *Oh, God.*

"May I use the toilet please, Mistress? I just need to have a little cleanup."

"Erm, yes, yes, certainly," I said as I ushered him to the toilet cubicle inside the changing room. Fucking Hell, he reeked. This was not nice at all. FishingAddict emerged from the bathroom looking uncomfortable and sheepish.

"Right, I shall see you out, Slave. Follow me."

"But I haven't paid you, Mistress."

Shit! He hadn't paid me, and I had completely forgotten to ask him for the tribute at the start of the session. Memory like a bloody sieve, me.

"I'll go to the car and fetch the envelope of money I've got in there for you. Won't be a minute."

I felt scared that he had forgotten deliberately and I worried that if he just got in his car and drove away, that would mean me struggling to pay for Morgan's school meals, the gas, electricity and the rest all week. I couldn't chance it.

"Take off your ring," I ordered.

"W-what? Are you serious, Mistress?"

"Yes, I am. Take off your fucking ring, you degenerate. Give it to me. How do I know I can trust you? You'll get it back when you come back with the cash. Call it insurance."

He looked upset but did as I had ordered. I stood at the studio door, cupping the gold ring in my hand while he headed to the car. Part of me still thought that he might scarper. I guess I just didn't trust men very much in those days.

FishingAddict did come back twenty seconds later. He thrust the envelope into my hand, and I gave him back the ring.

"Mistress, I just wanted to express my thanks for today's session."

I looked at him coldly and sneered, giving a little menacing chuckle.

"Yes, quite," I replied sarcastically. "Now fuck off!" I blurted in his face, in my best Kaley-style mistress tone.

I slammed the door. *Job well done,* I smiled to myself. That wasn't too bad. I wasn't keen on the butt-plug involvement, but it hadn't been that bad for a first session.

I went back into the studio to clear up, re-arrange the furniture I had moved, and went to get changed into my jeans and jumper. I needed a wee. *Damn it! No toilet paper! Oh my God, the poor man.* He went in there stinking of excrement and the poor fella couldn't even wipe his bum. No wonder he had looked sheepish when he had emerged from the cubicle. How on earth he got clean and dry is still a mystery to me. Maybe he didn't. Maybe he had to drive home shuffling about uncomfortably on his seat, marinating in his own faeces; all itchy and burny like when you haven't wiped your backside properly. I felt terrible about it. Oh well, I had only made one mistake, or so I had thought.

CHAPTER 20

Nowt as queer as folk

That whole week was a great success, apart from one small occurrence which shook my confidence a little. Well, maybe it knocked me down a peg or two, which perhaps I needed. My mum always used to say that a person should always remain humble, no matter how respected and successful they become; and I have learned over the years she was right. It's never a good idea to get too cocky, as I was about to learn. I opened my laptop on Monday morning to see that I had received an email from none other than Mr. FishingAddict himself. *He must have written to thank me for our session.*

Dear Mistress,

I arrived back home yesterday feeling very disappointed. I do not know if you really were holding me in such contempt, or if you were in the role, but I will assume that you were in the role. Usually, when I visit a Mistress, she will just be herself and we will chat over a cup of tea before the session and discuss likes and dislikes. I have never been treated so rudely before.

I can tell that you are new to this business because you appeared to look and act like a Hollywood Mistress that people are used to seeing on television. That type of Mistress is more suited to a dungeon, I'm afraid. I would have preferred you in a pair of jeans, being yourself and treating me like a worthwhile person. All I wanted to do was to serve you and be useful. There are different kinds of domination, and it might be a good idea if you become acquainted with them.

Taking my ring from me was the final insult, as it had belonged to my Uncle who died.

I'm sorry if this has come across in the wrong way.

Respectfully,

Slave

God. I felt truly guilt-ridden about it. There I was, thinking I had done an amazing job by treating him like a vile human being, when he just wanted to pamper and worship me, and take control of the part with the butt-plug. I messaged him my sincere apologies and consoled myself that he had omitted the details of my toilet roll faux pas.

With being at uni on a Monday, it meant that with Morgan at school I was available to session between the hours of ten o'clock in the morning and two o'clock in the afternoon from Tuesday to Friday. I would get to the studio for ten, set up and have a cuppa, then read through a printed-out version of my clients' email requests. There were some very specific ones. Fetishists are sticklers for detail. Following that, I would get dressed into whatever the clients required of me, and be ready to receive the first one by half-past. At noon I would host another session, pack up and drive back home. By the end of that week, I had earned around a thousand pounds. It was a tiny amount, though, when I considered that I was horrendously in debt with various credit card companies. I also had an old loan to pay which Tim and I had taken out. I had agreed to take control of it when we divorced, but I also had a massive overdraft to add to all that responsibility. It was a positive start though, and I was hopeful.

I learned from FishingAddict's email complaint that there's a big difference between 'dominant' and 'arsehole', and I didn't want to be an arsehole. I have never been comfortable upsetting people, and to be honest, shouting and name-calling weren't me at all. I concluded that BDSM wasn't the genre that was meant for me. By the end of the week, I had removed BDSM from my list of specialties on the online portal; but I clarified that I still undertook some levels of fetish work, depending on what the clients' preferences were.

The following week, sessions were thinner on the ground, and I only bagged four. I put it down to me being new, and that the initial flurry of bookings had been a fluke. It appeared that I had been right, because over the coming weeks it would plateau at around three sessions per week. Still, that was three hundred quid in my pocket, and it at least covered the household bills and a very frugal food shop. One question which came up again and again in emails was, "How much for a happy ending?"

I reiterated each time that HR (Hand Relief) was not on my list of specialties, and each time I would hear no more from the potential subs who had enquired. There was no way I was going down that road, as I felt it was the only distinctive difference between being a dominatrix and a prostitute... but did I ever mention that I've always been a bit on the fickle side?

Fetish work was so unpredictable, and every booking would differ from the last. This was an appealing aspect because I've always liked to be kept on my toes! With Lancs-Geezer/Malcolm a month later, I felt like I was well versed in what would be expected of me. That was one of the most shocking sessions I've ever done. He wanted nothing more than to sit in the studio's bath, whilst I balanced above him with a foot teetering on each side of the rim, as he held up a champagne glass with which to catch my wee… then drink it. The mind boggles, but he loved it. He resembled someone on holiday, laid on a lilo in a swimming pool, with a cocktail in his hand. Have you ever tried peeing on demand? It's a bloody skill, I can tell you. I thought nothing would come out at first, but then it was a full-on gush-orama! Prior to this, I had only ever tried to direct my wee into a container with the aid of a she-wee, so the accuracy of my aim pleasantly surprised me.

Malcolm was a genuinely lovely guy in his late fifties, with the biggest smile. He just looked overcome with joy at what we were doing. He couldn't stop beaming throughout the whole session! Contrary to the event in which he was partaking, Malcolm had the demeanour of one of the least sleazy guys you could ever meet. I know that sounds difficult to believe, but he really was a gentleman. He taught me about watersports (and not the skiing kind) and what the fetish was all about. There are a few different kinds of watersports enthusiasts – the submissive kind, like Malcolm, who liked to receive the, erm, golden nectar; the dominant ones who liked to do the urinating; the submissive ones who liked the humiliation of peeing in front of someone; and also the dominant ones who liked to see someone else's humiliation at not being able to hold it in.

Malcolm knew it wasn't something I was into, but he didn't mind as he was just so grateful. Apart from the initial nerves, I felt comfortable with him, and we laughed throughout the whole session. We spent nearly the whole hour in stitches. I still don't understand how he found it sexy with us laughing our heads off the whole time. He just seemed relaxed and looked genuinely happy. I don't really get it, but it just goes to show how diverse people's tastes are if we look a little closer.

Inevitably, the time came when the session would soon be over, and it would be time for Malcolm to get himself off, as he put it. I stepped down from the bath and watched as Malcolm started tossing himself off. Nothing was happening. No hard-on transpired, and he looked embarrassed. His penis remained floppy, whilst he continually attempted to revive the poor thing. I didn't know where to look.

"Oh God, I'm so sorry, Olivia. I don't know why it's not working. I think maybe I might be a bit too nervous." The poor fella looked gutted.

I couldn't let him carry on like that. I could just imagine him going home, red-faced, the joy of his session forgotten because he felt that he had messed it up.

"Here, I'll do it for you if you like; but don't tell anyone." Well, why not? It was something I could pull off well, so to speak, and I didn't feel cheap or vulnerable or anything. I felt completely at ease with him, and to be honest, I couldn't have cared less what it may have looked like to an outsider. It was just him and me there, and I reasoned that I wasn't doing anything more than people did on a Friday night with a stranger for free. *Sod it*. Well, Malcolm looked so relieved, bless him.

"Oh, thanks so much. I just don't know what's wrong with me. I'm so embarrassed."

"Don't be," I smiled as I grabbed the bottle of lube from the bathroom cabinet. Alan always had a variety of kinky items in the bathroom set cupboard. God knows what kind of shoots went on in there usually. Maybe they were like this? Who knows? Anyway, I pulled out all the stops and did everything I could think of with my hands to get a rise out of Malcolm's stubborn widge; but it wouldn't budge. It was just flapping quickly from side to side, looking as though it were trying to escape my slippery grasp, while I appeared to be fashioning a work of art on Molly's pottery wheel in Ghost. Still no boner. Nope, not a sausage.

"Nevermind, eh? It was still one of the best sessions I've ever had. Ta for that, Olivia." He was welcome, I hadn't minded one bit. I didn't want to do watersports again, ever, but I now knew what it was all about. I could tick it off my mental list of 'crazy shit I've done in my life'. The nice thing was that Malcolm transferred me an extra fifty pounds into my bank account, even though I hadn't asked for it. My mum also always said that you should never give to receive. See, it pays to be kind sometimes. Mums are always right. I wouldn't have called it a happy ending exactly, but it wasn't a sad one either. Did that count?

I soon settled into my new role and balanced it perfectly with my uni work and home life. It wasn't as lucrative as I had hoped, as I was still skint by the end of the week, but always had at least two sessions a week. My range of outfits and implements grew, and every session was different. You really couldn't make some of the scenarios up with the wildest imagination. It felt good to be treated like a goddess, knowing the men respected me. It was in stark contrast to how the guys in my real life had treated me. There were some very diverse requests, many of which I refused, like Sounding. Sounding is the practice of having something inserted into a chap's wee hole. A guy once emailed to ask if I would chain him to a massage table so he couldn't move and, then slide as many cotton buds as I could fit down his urethra. I didn't have any chains or a massage table in my possession, and the thought of scratchy, dry cotton buds where only a nurse with a medical swab should ever dare to delve, made me feel physically faint.

Ballbusting – that was another one on my 'never do' list. I could just imagine me in that situation – booting some poor bloke in the testicles and then instinctively rushing up to him and fussing, going, "Oh my God, are you alright? Are you hurt? I'm so sorry!"

I don't think what they were seeking was an empathic Mistress, but I can't stand to see anyone in that much pain. I would have been a real disappointment. What if they passed out, and I had to call an ambulance? In fact, couldn't you kill someone that way with the wrong kind of kick? Is there even a right kind of kick? The same with hardcore CBT; I couldn't bring myself to torture anyone's cock and balls in the extreme ways that I'd seen on some BDSM websites. I've fantasised about it when my husband hasn't done his fair share of the cleaning at home, mind you. Men's genitals are delicate things, for goodness' sake. We've all seen how much pain guys look to be in when they're hit in the crotch by a football and they double up, as though winded. Nasty stuff, that.

There were a few things that I tried for a while and then didn't want to do again, such as face-sitting. I knew that many a Mistress did this with no knickers on, but that was way too close contact for my liking. Upon reflection, I was probably quite a prude as dominatrices go, so it's no wonder I didn't make a killing financially. The face-sitting sessions I did were all in thick tights or leggings, with knickers on underneath. With these sessions, the guys would lie down flat on their backs on the floor and I would straddle the bloke in question, putting as much weight as I could on him with my bottom half. There I would stay until the guy would smack the ground with his hands in panic, his whole body convulsing at being deprived of air. I could only imagine the fear they felt, because the thought of them dying bloody terrified me! Again, the potential ambulance issue bothered me with this particular fetish. Not only that, but I had one or two pervs who seemed to think it was okay to stick their tongue out and try to force it through my knickers. They got a slap for that, and I would black-list them from future sessions. People who didn't respect boundaries never got a second chance.

A few men who contacted me had a thing for being what they called 'human ashtrays'. Being a human ashtray ranged from having smoke blown in their faces to cigarettes being put out on their nipples. I have smoked since the age of fourteen, so the blowing smoke in their faces was something that didn't bother me, and there was a certain elegance in the role I played. The smell of burning flesh, however, was something I won't forget in a hurry. Some liked to have ash tapped onto their tongues while they knelt on the floor, and a couple of rare clients wanted to be forced to eat the tab ends. I recall one guy wanting to do that, but he didn't look to be enjoying it as much as his fantasy suggested he would. He left at the end of the session, after going to the toilet, and I found several chewed up, soggy cigarette ends in the bath!

A posh golfer bloke in his late thirties once came to visit. He turned up in a pink, designer, cuff-linked shirt, hair tinted an unnatural black with Just for men dye, and was a bit of a smooth talker. Golf fella had emailed me, asking me to chew up chocolate in my mouth, and spit the melted, saliva mixed goo onto the floor. He requested I push him to the ground and forcibly make him lick it up; although it didn't quite work out that way. He gulped quietly, visibly recoiling; and eyeing it with the same hesitancy as when I considered eating the last cold baked bean on my plate at tea-time.

I threw him the classic mum line, "You'll get what you're given. It's not a bloody hotel!"

Lip quivering, he looked up at me with these scared, childish eyes, on the verge of tears. The ungrateful so-and-so!

"But it looks like baby sick, Mistress. I can't do it. I wanted milk chocolate, and this is white."

I had assumed everybody loved Milkybars. How was I to know? He really ought to have been more specific. *We should leave some desires firmly in fantasy land,* I concluded.

Corporal Punishment was quite a popular theme and usually attracted the older gentlemen who could remember it from their school days. I say 'gentlemen' because they were all exactly that. The CP bunch were a sophisticated breed that had old-fashioned values and treated ladies like ladies. Some of them were quite well-to-do and in high-powered jobs in their real lives and wanted to submit to a powerful woman for a change. The things they asked for ranged from being spanked on the backside with either a hand, a slipper, the back of a hairbrush or a paddle, to brutal lashings with a whip, leather strap or cane. Schoolboy uniforms were commonplace in these kinds of role-playing sessions. As far as being a Domme went, I would say that this was my favourite category of kink, because nobody got undressed and the sexual element was very subtle. Most C.P enthusiasts were also bottom fetishists. I had always believed that having a bum on the large, squishy side was a curse; but in this world of arse-lovers, it was nothing but a blessing. No self-touching or touching of me occurred. These blokes were far too well-mannered and eloquent for any of that.

There was the cross-dressing crew, who would want me to beautify their faces and dress them up all pretty, just as I had done with Edward back in the day. Men love make up and trying on women's clothing at any chance they get. If you don't believe me, wait until New Year's eve and you'll witness a suspicious amount of them voluntarily feminising themselves in the name of fancy dress. I rest my case.

I had quite a few clients who wanted me to force them to wear stockings, suspenders, and corsets and strut around the studio set while I verbally humiliated them. These guys always liked to relieve themselves at the end of a session. Different strokes for different folks.

As with jobs in all walks of life, some clients stood out for me whom I shan't forget, as their requests were quite uncommon. You've heard of the forty-year-old virgin, right? Well, how about the ninety-year-old one?

Colin, a very sweet man in his early nineties, came to see me once at the studio. He had said that he wanted a light spanking with my hand, perhaps progressing onto the cane if he felt like it when the time came. His appearance shocked me at first. I'm not kidding you – he shuffled in, in slow motion with his walking stick, all hunched over and wrinkled, like a three-hundred-year-old tortoise. Imagine the cutest grandad-type figure you can muster up in your imagination and you won't be far off. No matter how hard I tried I just couldn't imagine myself spanking him. He looked like I could knock him down with a feather. This was another situation where I visualised ambulance sirens and a prison sentence looming. It was a minefield, this domination malarkey.

After the usual cuppa and a routine little warm-up chat that I had brought into effect after FishingAddict's complaint, we moved into the bedroom set and I gently helped Colin bend over to place his hands on the bed. I carefully pulled down his trousers, just to the line under his bum cheeks to preserve his modesty, and began the lightest hand spanking I have ever administered. Colin nearly shot up and hit the ceiling. I winced at his reaction, almost feeling the pain myself. A bit like when you hear of someone having nits at school, and the thought of it makes your head itch. There was no way in a month of Sundays that I could cane him if he couldn't take a couple of tiny taps.

"Ooooooh! Owwww!" he shrieked in pain. This was a real pain that he wasn't enjoying and that was enough for me to bring the session to a halt.

"Can we sit and have another drink and just chat until the session finishes, please, Miss?"

"Of course we can, Colin." I smiled sympathetically, pulled up a chair for him and flicked the kettle back on. Colin told me his fascinating and sorrowful tale.

"You see, Miss, I was brought up in a strict and very religious household. My mother and father used to make sure I read the Holy Bible every day. I know the Bible off by heart and I still read it now. I must have read it a thousand times, Miss. My parents brought me up to believe that sex before marriage was a sin, but I never got married, so I'm still a virgin."

I couldn't believe what I was hearing. He was nearing the end of his life, and he had never experienced one of his God's most beautiful gifts.

"The thing is, Miss, I want to experience some kind of physical contact with a female before I die; but it seems that everything according to God is a sin, apart from spanking. I've searched throughout the whole of the Bible more than once to find an answer and nowhere does it insinuate that spanking is a sin of the flesh."

"So, you've found a loophole, you mean?" I asked, sincerely shocked by what Colin was telling me.

"Yes, that's right. I've never even kissed a woman or being naked with one or anything. Even if I were to just be able to know what it feels like to have a proper cuddle and just to know what a kiss feels like, I would die happy."

This was so sad. The restrictions he had imposed on himself so he didn't disappoint God were astounding.

"Colin, that's not something that I could help you with, but there are lots of ladies who would if you felt that you would want to hire one. At this stage in your life, if God loves you, he will want you to be happy. No God wants you to feel lonely or sad. Live your life, Colin; and do what makes you happy."

"That's what I think too, Miss. I've given it a lot of thought, and I don't know why I've accepted these made-up rules all my life. I've only just started to question it all, and I don't know why. I just feel like I've done my bit for God, and now I just want to feel what it's like to be loved. Even if it wouldn't be real love that I was getting from one of these ladies, it would give me an idea of what it felt like, and to have the company at least."

Colin and I chatted until the end of the session, and I gave him a meaningful hug on the way out. I had acted as his therapist for an hour, and I felt honoured to have done so. I felt deeply sad for his situation and angry at how this kind of interpretation of religion had been drummed into him from such an early age. What a waste of a good, kind heart and a working penis. My fast-developing therapy skills were already coming in handy in ways I had never imagined, and it was a lovely change from the usual kind of session. I have often looked back and wondered if I should have just given him a little peck on the lips. It wouldn't have done any harm, but it just didn't feel right at the time. Colin will no longer be alive now and will be with his God. I hope he did finally get his happy ending, in every sense of the phrase.

CHAPTER 21

Cruel to be kind

My ninety-year-old virgin wasn't the only client I had who treated domination as therapy. One guy I saw just the once, Carl, went to a Catholic boarding school as a youngster. He looked to be in his late forties, but the stories he told me that day sounded like something from the Victorian era. One particularly harrowing tale was about when he was ten years old, and a nun had hit him in the face with one of her shoes as a punishment for something minor. He said that the shoes were like clogs, with thick, wooden heels. Hearing this and picturing that poor, lost little boy made me want to cry for him.

A scene that Carl wanted us to replicate together was in the schoolroom set of the studio. I role-played as one of these sadistic nuns, and hit Carl across the face, hard; although thankfully not with a shoe. I also had to cane him across the palms of his hands, which I knew would be terribly painful. It took me a lot of courage to work up to recreating that part of the scene, especially as he kept pulling his hands out of the way as a natural reflex. It took a few attempts until I could cane him successfully, but I felt like I was being cruel. How these evil nuns slept at night, I'll never know. Carl's session was one where I planned extensively and did my best, as I felt it was an important part of his healing process. I've never liked to do things half-arsed, so I even donned an authentic-looking habit and a string of rosary beads. I paced around the room, twiddling the beads menacingly with my fingers. Carl had told me that sessioning was the only way to accept what had happened to him and get it out of his system somehow, by reclaiming control over past events. He had somehow managed to empower himself by turning his fear into his fantasy. If God exists, then he surely works in mysterious ways. I developed quite a dim view of organised religion from hosting sessions such as this.

Speaking of religion, I hosted one session related to the Holy War. The client was an ex-soldier who had post-traumatic stress disorder. The Taliban had held him captive whilst he was serving in the forces. Because of this he was terrified of ropes, confined spaces, and being restrained. Yep, you guessed it – he wanted to be tightly bound and locked in a big box, in the industrial setting of the studio. Very little surprised me in this quirky job of mine, and I found it incredible the lengths that the human brain will go to, to heal the mind from psychological trauma.

I worked with foot and leg worship fetishists a heck of a lot. In this role, I would be asked to wear a pencil skirt with sheer tights or fully fashioned vintage-style stockings, various styles of socks, and usually high-heeled shoes. Rarely was I asked to be barelegged. Sessions usually comprised of me either sitting or standing, while the Sub stroked and admired my legs and feet, sometimes getting a cheeky view of my knickers from their kneeling position on the floor. How honoured they were! Usually, foot and leg worship aspects were just incorporated into a session that was based around a different fetish or fantasy. I rarely got any requests from people only wanting that. Maybe they were just like kids in a sweet shop and wanted to fit in as many kinks into one hour as they could? I can only recall one person who came to me with feet and leg worship as their sole fetish (did you see what I did there?). His name was Graham and I only ever saw him the once. The reason I remember him so well is that he was another client who used my domination services like therapy.

Graham was about fifty years of age and had a grey beard. He appeared to be very nervous, was shaky, and didn't meet my eyes when we were having our little pre-sesh cuppa and chat.

"Are you okay, Graham? You look a little out of sorts, if you don't mind me saying?"

He hung his head and whimpered.

"Oh, Graham! Have I upset you? What's wrong? It's okay if you don't want to go through with it. Please don't cry."

"No, no, that's not it. I just feel so guilty about my wife. I'm so sorry for crying, I'm not a crying person; it's just that I've never done this before. I've fought this fantasy for years. Well, it's more like a need in me that I can't get rid of. I've been so ashamed of it all my life, but I plucked up the courage to tell my wife around ten years ago. We've been married for twenty, so this was a secret I had kept all that time. She accepted it but doesn't understand why I like feet, and it makes her feel uncomfortable. She won't even let me touch hers, and I love every part of her so, so much." He cried even harder. The sound of big, wracking sobs filled the studio as his shoulders and back heaved with the burden of his secret. "I can't go the rest of my life never being able to do this, I just can't. It's too deep in me. This is my last resort. I promised myself I would do this just the once to get it out of my system. I thought it best to contact a dominatrix as opposed to an escort. I don't know why, it just makes it sound better, somehow."

"Graham, I'm so sorry you're feeling so distressed. You don't have to go through with it. You can tell me to stop at any time, you know?"

"I know. I want to do it, but thank you."

Graham didn't want a full hour because he only wanted one simple thing, which was to lay naked on the floor on his back with my bare feet rubbing on his face for a few minutes whilst he pleasured himself. This was a new experience for me and felt slightly out of my comfort zone because of how intimate it seemed. I took my position on the sofa, sitting upright, and lowered my feet gently onto Graham's face. Remaining still for a minute, he inhaled deeply, as though savouring the moment. I rubbed my feet seductively back and forth over Graham's whole face – mouth, nose, cheeks and forehead.

"Please Mistress, may I touch myself?" He was so polite; how could I refuse?

"You may."

Graham had a right stonk on. His penis was one happy chappy by the look of it. He was breathing deeply and I could tell he was turned on by what I was doing to him, and what he was now doing to himself. It didn't take long. I reckon about five minutes in total from the start of the session to the finish.

"Miss, please would you give me permission to come?"

"Yes, I would, Graham. You have my permission."

And with that, he did – all over his hands and stomach. It amazes me sometimes just how much love juice a bloke's body can produce at any one time. That was the last I saw of Graham. I don't like to sound cynical, but getting something out of one's system is never straightforward. Some things are just buried deep in our make-up and never forgotten, whether we want them to be a part of us or not. That's exactly how it was with me and close female contact. I hated that I had it in me, but it wouldn't leave me. There is no getting it out of my system, it will always be there. I guessed that Graham would have tried to suppress his fetish for perhaps a few more years after our encounter; but then, sure enough, he would be back to visit another adult services provider, trying to 'get it out of his system' once again.

I had heard, "My wife doesn't understand my fetish," more times than I could count; and it was always something I felt awkward and conflicted about. I didn't like to think of some poor woman at home, with no idea that their husband was up to no good, but it wasn't my place to judge. Some wives even sent their husbands to me, would you believe? I had gone from being a battered wife to battering other women's husbands for money. You couldn't make it up!

Somehow Graham's situation felt different from most of the other clients I had. Although sexual, it wasn't coming from what I would call a 'pervy' place. He had an ingrained need to feel humble at the feet of a superior female, to feel honoured and humiliated at the same time. Foot worship fetishes are rarely about just feet – it's what the feet represent. Graham's extreme reaction was due to him suppressing the feelings for so long. When that happens, the feelings accumulate until they erupt into a big volcano of desperation, shame and self-loathing. I've learned through the job I do nowadays that it's so important that each of us feels accepted for the unique aspects of our personalities, no matter how strange they may sometimes seem. In psychotherapy, it's called Unconditional Positive Regard/UPR.

There was a client I saw regularly who was in quite a well-known, chart-topping band. He was into the Adult Baby scene and liked me to dress him in specially made adult-sized baby clothes. He would want me to bottle-feed him, change his nappy and tuck him up in a cot. Like I said before about weeing on demand, it's rarely possible. For this reason, when Mummy was conveniently looking the other way, the client would pour a warmed up can of Red Bull down the front of his nappy. This was a non-sexual type of session, with its roots in vulnerability, being free of responsibility and metaphorically shaking off the shackles of adult life. Like most fetish genres, the adult baby fantasists were set into two distinct groups: Subs and Doms. The Doms would be the ones to take care of or punish the 'babies', and the subs would be the ones who liked to feel small and helpless. Almost every category of kink came down to being either Dom or Sub in nature; and although each fetish has distinctive differences from the next, the foundations, key elements and principles are very much the same.

I forged some interesting friendships with some of my clients. Maybe friendship is the wrong word. What I suppose I mean is that we respected one another, and these people became my regulars, so I inevitably got to know some of them on quite a personal level. I think a few of these guys fancied themselves as Sugar Daddies and liked to throw their money around, but some just wanted to show their gratitude for the effort I went to in my sessions. I knew of a few mistresses that did the whole 'Financial Slavery' thing, but I couldn't bring myself to. I respected my clients and didn't feel that it was right to fleece their bank accounts in that way. Occasionally, clients bought me costume jewellery, beautiful theatrical outfits for sessions, flowers, chocolates, clothes for me to wear in real life, shoes and useful implements. One client even sent a calendar from China where he lived. Yes, some travelled that far just for a session! Mostly though, I was just sent dick pics by email from people I had never met. Lots of photos of penises in all colours, shapes, sizes, and states of arousal. How very charming and thoughtful.

One of the most useful and gratefully received gifts was a ten-year-old Mercedes Benz, when my little beat up, rusty Renault Clio eventually conked. It saved my skin as there was no way I could afford to buy another car on my own. Paying for the Merc's insurance, repairs and petrol became an unwelcome struggle, though, so I didn't keep it for long. Sometimes clients whom I felt that I knew well enough asked if they could take me out shopping to buy me some clothes and lunch. I occasionally accepted, and we had some interesting chats and pleasant afternoons out. On one of my birthdays, a regular client said I could choose a gift up to the value of sixty pounds. He didn't have to ask twice. I knew exactly what I wanted.

"A steam mop please!" I blurted out without hesitation. I had seen them advertised on the telly and they were the latest in household time-saving appliances. My Sub couldn't stop laughing. How glamourous was I, eh? I loved that bloody steam mop. It didn't half save me some time with the house-work. Sometimes it's the simple things in life that make a big difference.

A tiny percentage of manipulative clients thought they could buy me and groom me into sessioning at higher levels just for them. They were wrong. I soon realised what they were up to and stopped accepting gifts from them. Flashing the cash to that extent didn't work for me. They could buy my body up to a point, but I wouldn't sell my soul. I had to keep something sacred. I knew it would fuck my head up good and proper and there would be no going back otherwise. I received more than my fair share of time-wasters too.

Initially, I made the mistake of sending long emails in reply, to sell myself well. That was the wrong thing to do because they would just bombard me with more messages, and once they'd got what they wanted in type, I never heard from them again. After I while I could sniff out these little weasels at first contact and I learned to just ignore them. Here are a couple of examples where I lost my patience and took the bait:

Miss Olivia,

I'm looking for an arrangement whereby I need to meet weight loss goals regularly, with penalties for any failures until I meet my final goal.

I would like to be publicly humiliated in a restaurant before being taken back to your place so you can trample me, use me as your ashtray and abuse me to your heart's content. All I ask is that by the time you're through with me, I will be crying my eyes out because of your punishment.

Being met at the station by you and driven to your location would greatly enhance the experience for me. I would love to know what you think. If you could send me an email detailing everything you would like to do to me, that would be great.

Patrick

Jesus, he didn't want much, did he? My reply was concise and to the point:

Dear Fatty,

I'm not sure that a restaurant is the best place for you to be. How did you ever guess that my dream job was to be either a Slimming World Facilitator or a Taxi Driver? I often think I missed my vocation in life by deciding to be a Domme instead. Also, I have Dyscalculia; which would make monitoring your weight stressful for me. The numbers mix up in my head, a bit like how the chips mix up with the cake and Haribo[40] in your stomach.

Mistress Olivia

My disparaging reply had backfired. Patrick got off on the humiliation and like clockwork, he sent me an email on the first of every month, detailing how badly he had failed in his efforts to lose that all-important, stubborn pound, pleading with me to insult him again. I know, I know, it served me right for being exactly what my dad used to say I was – a gobby little git.

To the beautiful Mistress Olivia,

I have had a fetish for vacuum cleaners ever since I was very young. My Aunt Beryl used to chase me around her house with one of those upright carpet cleaners that Hoover made. Thus, began my obsession with different brands of vacuum cleaner. When I grew older, I used to like to take them apart just to see how they worked. I

---

[40] A brand of well-loved children's gummy sweets, famously produced in their factory in Pontefract, a working-class Yorkshire town.

wondered if I could book a session where you let me take your vacuum apart and re-assemble it, as a vacuum cleaner repairman would do. I would then like you to chase me with it until I am backed into a corner where you would then make me masturbate in front of you. I would love you to reply with some of your own vacuum stories.

Yours,

Donal

PS: I know the specifications of most types of vacuum cleaner, so you wouldn't have to worry about me breaking it.

PPS: What brand do you have, exactly?

I thought about Donal's proposal long and hard. Then I pictured my Henry Hoover's little red face, all smiley and innocent. No, I couldn't put Henry through such an ordeal. He was worth so much more. There was only one thing for it – I had to break the news.

Dear Donal,

I have considered your proposal. I must admit that the idea of possibly getting you to vac every inch of my house sounds quite appealing. However, since every room in my house has the finest quality laminate flooring, I only have a steam mop and a dustpan and brush to hand these days. It's funny that you should ask if I have any of my own 'vacuum stories' because I do have one sad tale about the reason I made the tough decision to take my carpet up. It would be lovely if I could tell you it was because men keep spunking on it because of my vacuum cleaner being so darned sexy, and the stains were ruining the look of the pile; but sadly not. The truth is that I couldn't keep up with hoovering it. Do you know why? Because too much of my time was being taken up by tightwads who thought they could get off for free by trying to lure me into email conversations with them instead of booking a session.

I've made my final decision, so you're just going to have to suck it up.

Mistress Olivia

CHAPTER 22

Don't shit on your own doorstep

I had been studying toward my degree for around two years, and it had passed quickly. Morgan was still at primary school, and I was still sessioning. Nothing environmental had changed to the naked eye, but I had changed inside, and that was a growing problem. I was becoming more self-aware by the day and had done a lot of gruelling and sometimes distressing work on my inner self whilst at uni. I had always known that the crazy job I was doing was just a temporary means to an end, but I found it increasingly hard to keep up this constant act as someone thoroughly into the services I was delivering on an almost daily basis. Many professional Dommes are fully immersed in the scene and live their job as a lifestyle choice. They take great joy in what they do, both sexually and mentally. I was not one of these Dommes. My clients all loved to think I was getting off on their fetishes being played out as much as they were, but I had always just been faking it. I was just a very good actor and, to a certain extent, businesswoman. I learned to tell them whatever they wanted to hear. I was a fraud. Maybe not being true to myself that way had taken its toll on my sense of identity.

It was the little things that got to me, like the weird, sickly sweet smell I could detect whenever a guy was nearing climax, then the pungent aroma when they ejaculated. It seemed to seep through their pores and into the surrounding air. I couldn't put my finger on what it was exactly; maybe testosterone-loaded pheromones that didn't match my own chemical makeup? I don't know. All I knew was that it made me feel nauseous every time. I wondered if any other sex workers smelled it too, or if it was just me? I can still remember the whiff now, and the memory of it is so powerful that it still has the same physical effect on me.

I had a couple of embarrassing, near-miss type moments too, which left me feeling ashamed of the path in life I had chosen. Like when the postman delivered a cane to my house one morning. I worked at the studio still, but I had all my mail delivered to my home address. As I opened the door to greet the postman, he handed me what was obviously a punishment cane, wrapped in a bin liner and with Sellotape swirled tightly around it.

"Quite a heavy cane you've got there. Has someone been a naughty boy then, or do you have more than one naughty boy on the go?" he chuckled knowingly.

It mortified me. That was all I needed, the friggin' postie with the biggest gob in the neighbourhood guessing what I did for a living.

The time I had to visit my doctor for tennis elbow felt awkward. It was laughable, as I was so crap at sports in school. Blood sports like caning though; no competition! At school I had always been last picked for sports teams, but now I was first-picked for my super-duper caning technique and big, girly bum. The doctor was less than impressed when I confessed how I had injured myself, and he advised me not to swing so hard for the foreseeable future. I had grown so skilled with the cane; it would bend right back as I swung it. It would cut the air with a terrifying sound, and often break the flesh of the naughty boy's bottom upon impact. This was where my nurturing side came in handy. I would carefully dab Dettol-soaked cotton wool balls on the subs' welts afterward (which probably stung more than the cane) and make them a nice cup of sweet tea to help with the shock. I had nothing to offer the doctor for his shock, unfortunately.

Then there was the time when I sold an original police uniform on eBay that a Sub had once bought for me. It was a complete WPC uniform and even had the little silver letters and number badges, unique to the officer who had previously owned it. It gave an authentic edge to my sessions, but it was getting shabby now and had to go. I listed it for sale and got busy with the housework for the next couple of hours.

So, there I was, minding my own business, giving the floor a quick going over with my trusty steam mop before I had to pick Morgan up from school; when two policemen knocked at my door. Proper plain-clothed police officers who wanted to question me about how I had come to possess the uniform that I was selling. I had to admit that a Sub had sent me it through the post. They didn't find it funny, and neither did I. They probably thought I was a right slapper[41]. I laugh about it now, of course. You've got to laugh, though, haven't you?

I used to model at a studio in Essex once every couple of months for a lingerie catalogue company, and I had been travelling down there for around three years by this point (it's an urban myth that as a model, you get to keep the clothing from catalogue shoots; unless you 'accidentally' rip off the plastic gusset guards, that is). The Studio Manager there was called Jez, and we got on like a house on fire. He was about my age, in his early thirties; slim build, black floppy curly

---

[41] Sexually promiscuous female.

hair, and mixed-race, I think of Afro-Caribbean descent. He wasn't exactly an oil painting, and I wouldn't even go as far as to say I fancied him in a way that I'd like to date him, but we were very comfortable with each other and had a lot of cheeky, flirty banter between us. We would greet each other with, "Looking fit today, mate," and a cheeky wink, but it was an unwritten rule between us that feel-good flirtatiousness was all it was. The attention was nice and made me feel attractive, and when I felt attractive, I worked well. It was refreshing to be around a normal guy my age and not to have to be in a role, as I was most days.

This particular Saturday afternoon at the studio ended up a bit differently from the usual routine. I had just finished a shoot and had got changed back into my pink velour tracksuit (which were all the rage back then), wiped off my thick, waxy layer of stage make-up, and ambled into the office where Jez was doing some Photoshop wizardry. I pulled up a swivel chair next to him and we started chatting over a cuppa, like usual. We always had fascinating chats and shared a bit of gossip about who was doing what and who was shagging who in the modelling industry. This time the conversation turned to various fetishes. Within ten minutes we were both hooting with laughter and clutching our bellies. Jez suddenly stopped laughing, turned to me with a serious expression and said, "Y'know mate, it would be hilarious if my fetish wasn't so fucking weird; but it is."

"Eh? What fetish?" I had seen them all. Nothing shocked me. It couldn't be that bad, surely?

"Okay, I trust that I can tell you this, but if I so much as see the corners of your mouth turn up, mate, I swear I'm falling out wiv ya."

"Shurrup, knob-head, as if I'd laugh at you!" We were always laughing together, yes; but I knew when it would be inappropriate, I wasn't heartless.

"Alright. Okay. Alright. Erm, okay, well I like to have my cock abused. Like, really abused, y'know?"

"Okaaaay, that's CBT then, innit? Loads of folk are into that. You're not weird or anything, Jez."

"Yeah; but it's not like I'm into all that stuff with restraints and having my balls squeezed off or anyfink. None of that acceptable stuff you see online. I mean, I like to lay there and abuse my cock, sometimes to the point of bleeding."

"You do it to yourself?" I tried my best not to sound so surprised, but I genuinely was. I had known Jez for ages and he was one of the most normal, typically trendy and stereotypical Essex lads I had ever met. You really wouldn't think he had any skeletons of the kink variety in his designer closet. It was true that everybody had something, after all.

"Yeah man, it's like I have to injure myself to get off properly, y'know? Don't laugh, mate, but I like to use anything I can get my hands on that I know will leave a mark. Anyfink I can find around the house, like metal whisks an' stuff."

"Fuck me, Jez! That must kill!"

"Yeah, exactly, mate; exactly. The more painful the better, like. It's like I have to push myself to see how much my cock can take; and when it's cut to ribbons, only then do I deserve to come."

Cut to ribbons? Jesus. This was hardcore shit I was hearing.

"Don't worry, I'm not gonna say owt. What do the lasses in your life think about this?"

"That's the problem, I daren't say anyfink. The last one I told ran a mile. Thought I was weird, like. I feel frustrated that I can't be myself with anyone like that. It's fuckin' lonely, mate."

I gave him a sympathetic look and carried on sipping my coffee. Jez looked thoughtful for a moment.

"Would you consider taking me on, like? Y'know, as a Sub or whatever you call 'em?"

"Aaw, you're kidding aren't you, Jez? You know what we're like, we'd probably laugh the whole way through!"

"We wouldn't. This ain't a joke to me. This is something I feel that I need. You don't get it. I knew you wouldn't get it."

"Would I have to wank you off, like?" I checked, cautiously.

"Not if you didn't want to. I could take care of that bit myself."

"I always said I'd never session with anyone I know. Is this gonna affect our working relationship, Jez?"

"Of course it ain't."

I pondered on Jez's request for all of two minutes. I did quite fancy him; we had a brilliant rapport, and we *would* still respect each other afterward and keep working together photographically. It *would* be a change sessioning with someone whom I knew I felt comfortable around, plus it would be foolish to turn down another hundred quid in the bank when money was so thin on the ground. I quickly calculated in my head the cost of Morgan's impending school trip to London and how much I still needed to pay off. The session fee should just about cover it.

"Yeah, go on then, I'll session with you."

Jez broke into a wide smile and we high-fived each other. What did I have to lose?

Jez and I settled on a Saturday to do the session, and I decided that I was cool with doing it at home because I knew him well enough. Now and again, if he was in the area with his photography work, he would bob in for a brew, so I guessed that it would feel the same as those times. I decided that I would wear a black corduroy A-line mini skirt which buttoned down the front, and a plain white spaghetti-strapped vest with no bra. It was a simple combination that looked understatedly sexy because the areola of my nipples were just visible through the material. Jez had emailed me beforehand, to stipulate that he wanted me to surprise him with whatever implements I would use on him. In other words, he wanted me to have the responsibility of choosing. That was not the easiest of tasks. Because he had previously mentioned whisks, I instinctively visualised my kitchen layout and listed the utensils in my mind. *Spatula, whisk, two-pronged fork, potato masher… yep, all of those will do.*

When Jez turned up, it was just like any other day when he had done the same. We had a coffee and a gossip on the sofa for a while, but this time was different because afterward we put down our cups and headed upstairs to my bedroom in silence. I gestured to him to lay down on the bed and pull down his jeans, which he dutifully did, still in silence, and with a serious, nervous expression on his face. I hadn't witnessed this side of my mate Jez before, and I suddenly felt powerful. His eyes didn't leave mine for a second as I climbed onto the bed, pulled myself into a kneeling position and said sternly, "Now I'm going to abuse your cock because this is exactly what you deserve."

And up said cock rose, in an action resembling the Titanic's back end just before it had split in two. I had never seen Jez's willy before, and I angled my head to one side to view it with blatant fascination. It was of average size, with a cocoa-coloured uncut shaft, and a bulbous, contrasting pinkish head. Standing proud as Punch, it bent slightly to one side to mirror the tilt of my head.

I slid out a big metal spoon with holes in from under the duvet by the side of my leg, where I had strategically placed it. It was the spoon with which I usually drained my Brussel's sprouts. Jez's eyes widened in anticipation, and his bottom lip quivered with nervous excitement. I felt nervous too because I didn't know how hard I should hit his appendage. I had never done anything like this. Before I could risk over-thinking and bottling it, I drew my arm back and landed the spoon right on the side of his penis. It kind of bounced off and his poor member slapped against his leg with the impact. This was more difficult than it had sounded because it was almost impossible to keep this love truncheon of his upright so I could get a good aim! I got the hang of it after a few thigh-whacking mistakes. Jez never uttered a sound when I was smacking him about like this, and it looked pretty damned painful to watch!

"You can go harder if you like."

So, I did. My nerves dissipated, and I brought the spoon down even harder.

"Harder. You can go as hard as you want."

I set down the metal spoon on top of the duvet and pulled out my next weapon – the big, two-pronged fork. I never knew which part of the fork would catch his privates each time I swung it. Sometimes it was the sharp prongs, and sometimes it was where the neck of the fork met the main body of it. Grazes appeared on Jez's foreskin. He gritted his teeth and winced, an unhinged look in his eyes as he watched his skin break open. He looked up at me with the expression of a man consumed with an unfamiliar dark lust.

"Harder!" he instructed through clenched teeth.

I did as I was told. I wasn't sure whether I was the Domme or the Sub at this point. He was now ordering me rather than asking me. In the fetish scene, this is commonly known as 'topping from the bottom' and is usually looked upon with disapproval.

By the time forty-five minutes was up, Jez looked like a man possessed. His penis was more or less lacerated, a concerning shade of magenta and less recognisable as a penis than it was at the start of the session.

"I need to come, Sinead. I need to come now. Have I taken enough abuse? Do I deserve an orgasm?"

I wasn't sure what the script should be. Did he want me to say "yes" or "no"? I went with an uncertain-sounding, "Yes." It sounded more like I was asking a question than agreeing.

I didn't have to say it twice. Jez grabbed his hand and frantically began shaking his penis up and down so fast that I could hardly see it. He grunted rhythmically, his breathing growing faster and faster until it reached a crescendo. Thick, globular, white semen pumped out of his penis and down his battered and bruised shaft for what seemed like an eternity, until Jez signalled the end, emitting a loud sigh of satisfaction. He stared at me for a couple of seconds in what appeared to be shock and disbelief.

"Fack, Sinead! *Fack*, that was good."

Naturally, over the following week, I reflected on the session and tried to assess the feelings it had evoked in me. I didn't feel aroused about what I had done with Jez, but I couldn't deny that it had given me a slight rush of something. I sensed that he had viewed me differently throughout the session, and I liked the feeling of his approval. I had a faint feeling of shame after he had gone home, but it wasn't pronounced enough to deter me. I felt more relaxed with Jez, and a bit more like 'me', as I knew that he knew who I was underneath the Mistress façade. In my naivety, I didn't expect it to affect our working relationship. My mum had wisely said to me on a few occasions, "Whatever you do, never shit on your own doorstep, Sinead."

Well, that's exactly what I had done by sessioning in my home with someone whom I knew on a personal and professional level. My reply whenever Mum offered me this wise advice was, "I don't want to learn from your mistakes, Mum. I'd rather learn from my own."

Well, just look at me now, eh, Mum?

Jez enjoyed our session so much that he arranged to come up again. And come up again he did; in more ways than one. A month later, during our cuppa at the start of our second session, Jez took me aback with a query, "How much do you usually charge for a happy ending?"

Well, I nearly spat a mouthful of my coffee over the cheeky sod!

"I bloody don't! God, what do you take me for?"

"I was wondering because I was gonna offer you an extra fifty quid to give me one."

I had the usual angel and devil on my shoulder, fighting this one out. As you've probably guessed, I agreed to do it. I figured that it would only be like what people did with their so-called fuck buddies in casual relationships. It's not like he was a client I didn't know. Why not? I couldn't scoff at an extra fifty quid. I needed to buy the whole of the new reading list for uni the following week, so really it had come at just the right time. I made sure I impressed with my super-duper pottery technique the first time I brought Jez to a climax. Luckily, he didn't have that horrible smell about him when he ejaculated. Maybe because we had a bit of chemistry between us. I felt a little grubby afterward, but I tried to see it as a bit of a novelty and told myself once more that I was the powerful one in this arrangement. I was an independent businesswoman and feminist with no ties to any man, and therefore I could do whatever I chose with my body. It was just an arrangement between two friends, no big deal, blah, blah, blah.

Anyone smell bullshit?

Jez came up to see me at home three times more after that for the same arrangement. Each time I tried almost successfully to push the feelings of self-disgust, parental guilt and shame to the very back of my mind. I focused on the money and the knowledge that I would soon be out of this game for good. The third and final time that I saw Jez was on another of our session days. By this time, any novelty aspect that usually distracted me from thinking about my actions had worn off. I was also running out of implements with which to beat him. There were a lot of factors that made this last time feel different. The sight of his penis repulsed me; especially when it was all purple and cut up. I watched the clock in my bedroom, thinking, *Not long to go and then I can get rid of him.*

When we talked afterward and beforehand, the conversation had become stilted or would all be innuendo on Jez's side. He came up to visit me roughly four times in four months, in which time our usual banter and gossipy connection had disappeared. He had started to just view me as an object, which was clear by the question he asked me after I had brought him to climax half-heartedly for a fourth and final time.

"Would you consider having sex? With me, like? Name your price."

I stared, open-mouthed in disbelief.

"What? You know I don't do that kind of thing, Jez. I'm just a

Domme and you know that domination is not prostitution."

"But we're mates. It wouldn't be like that. Come on, we both fancy each other a bit, don't we? It's just that I know you need the money. You'd be helping me out, and I'd be helping you. Just think of it that way."

I didn't know what to say. Half of me felt embarrassed, and the other half was already paying off my debts in my mind. It *would* be a big help, depending on how much I charged. *Nobody would have to know,* the little voice inside my head kept saying. I told Jez I would think about it and let him know.

I did a lot of soul-searching over the next few days and felt very low as a result, for the first time in ages. *What the fuck was I thinking?* Essentially, I was already charging a hundred and fifty quid a time for a wank. An elaborate wank, but still a wank at the end of the day, no matter how I tried to dress it up. Yeah, it was a lot more than an Escort would receive for a similar service; but I didn't want to be an Escort, and that's a bit like how I had begun to see myself. I felt cheap. This didn't feel empowering anymore, I didn't feel dominant or sexy. I felt like a slut. I had noticed that for four months I hadn't shot at Jez's studio. Usually, I had one shoot there every two months. I had stopped viewing him as a mate; he was just another paying customer. Had he stopped respecting me as a model, and now just saw me as useful for a bit of hands-on fun? Probably.

I concluded that something had to give, and I knew that it was this head-fuck of an occupation. I knew I had to stop before I undid all the good work I had done on myself throughout uni. Because of this continued personal development, I had become re-sensitised. Becoming so self-aware was both a blessing and a curse. I recalled how firmly my boundaries were set when I first embarked on my vocation as a Mistress. They had crumbled after only two or three weeks in the business. Had I held my self-respect and worth in such low regard? It seemed so. I felt like shit. Six days after our last session, I emailed Jez to tell him I wouldn't be taking him up on his offer of paying me for sex. So much for it not affecting our professional relationship, because I never saw or heard from him again. Not that I cared; I was content to not have him in my life as a reminder of the depths I had nearly sunken to.

CHAPTER 23

Psyched

After I had made my decision to exit the fetish scene as a Mistress, things seemed to happen quickly, and my mindset changed back into a healthier one. The day soon came when I had planned to message all the gentlemen whom I had been role-playing professionally with, to inform them I would be retiring. I didn't expect to feel sentimental, but I burst into tears midway through composing the group email. I had made quite a few friends, and it was the end of an era for me. I had no second thoughts about quitting, but I felt melancholy and reflective all the same. Most of my subs were supportive of my decision, but some didn't take it so well. They were only used to sessioning with me and found the prospect of finding a new Mistress daunting.

I still needed to be bringing in a wage if I wanted to keep a roof above mine and Morgan's head. The natural entrepreneur in me reared her pretty little head again, and I went into making video clips to sell. It was relatively easy because I knew the ropes from old modelling shoots and I already had a decent video camera. It was so easy that I wished I had thought of it years ago. I would book various Dommes happy to work on camera, and I would ask trusted old Subs of mine to come in and pay the ladies to punish them. That meant that my overheads were just the studio fee and online store fees. I had the perfect base because the online portal I had used for webcamming and advertising my domination services also had a store where you could sell photos, videos, and various items for sale. I had knowledge of basic editing skills which Alan from the studio had kindly shown me, so it was a no-brainer and just what I needed to keep my hand in, whilst not having to do the dirty work myself anymore. I shot, edited and produced all the videos myself. I decided not to focus on a particular niche, but to include any and every fetish that came through the studio door. There was something that appealed to everyone. Mistress Olivia's Fetish Playground went down a storm, and I sold enough clips to keep myself afloat. It was exactly what I needed at just the right time. I thought of it as a prime example of synchronicity rather than coincidence.

By this point I was now on a placement as a trainee therapist at the same university I was studying at, and I had to provide a support service to students who were having a hard time at home or with their courses. It was right up my street because I seemed to have a natural affinity with teenagers. Perhaps that was down to my ability to draw upon my own teenage experiences so readily. I had always been a very adaptable person and because of my young outlook, I already spoke the teen lingo, which I suspect made me very relatable. I thrived on doing this kind of work and felt that I was already starting to make a tiny bit of difference in the world. It's amazing how many pro-dommes I met with various therapy qualifications. I knew of quite a few. Although very different occupations, there were many similarities.

The placement was to last around a year, which meant that I could get my head down and work at home without having to session all the time. I now focused much of my free time around coursework, and the end of the tunnel felt that bit closer than it had three years before. I don't mean to sound all cheesy, but it was though I was on some kind of inner journey to find myself, and I had felt so much better about who I was as a person.

I had casually dated since my split with Gigolo-Jack, but nothing had ever lasted. I had what I called my 'five-weeker', where I would somehow date a guy, feel that I was falling for them, and then suddenly change my mind within the space of five weeks on average. I either didn't fancy them enough, they were clingy or just didn't feel right for me. The situation happened repeatedly, so many times that I grew cynical and worried that I would never meet the right bloke for me.

Most of the fellas I dated for this short time were lovely guys and were unfazed when I disclosed the details of my unconventional field of work. I think upon getting to know me, they realised pretty much straight away that I was a decent person with thoroughly monogamous principles. They knew that domination was just a job and nothing more, and I didn't feel that I had to justify it any further than that. The men I dated knew that I wouldn't be stuck in the adult industry forever, so thankfully overlooked my work. Maybe if I had given the relationships chance to bloom, they may have changed their views, but I never let them get close enough to find out. I wouldn't have wanted to have brought someone new into eleven-year-old Morgan's life without knowing that they were the right guy for me, so as far as he knew, I just had a few male friends, albeit a quick succession of them. I still wasn't into one-night stands, as I had always enjoyed something more meaningful with people whom I felt comfortable with. There was one exception to this, and that was if the person in question was female.

I decided that with me being single and nothing working out with guys, whilst I was on the path of non-commitment and spiritual growth, I would explore this ever-growing liberal side to my personality. My feelings about my sexuality, whatever that was, were conflicting, to say the least. Even in today's society where bisexuality is deemed acceptable, I had shed many tears of frustration. Sometimes my thoughts were cripplingly depressing because I couldn't understand them or what they meant. I noticed a pattern that on certain days of the month I would feel repulsed by the idea of same-sex interactions and other days I would feel that it was something that I needed, on a strong, instinctive level. This mood seemed to fall around my ovulation time. How messed up is that? The prime time for mating with males, yet I was feeling urges for girls. Those were the days where I would spend hours online looking for an explanation that I could never find. Even on the Kinsey scale, I had varied results each time I took the test.

I read that there was a saying: 'people come out twice' – once to test the waters with those they know, and once more on a more honest and truthful level. I suspect that's probably true, but it didn't feel relevant to me because what would I say when I couldn't fit myself into a neat little box with a label? I couldn't even explain it to myself, let alone to anyone else! I figured that life would be easier if I were gay, as I would at least be able to give my sexuality a name. I have never been religious in the traditional sense, but the times I prayed to God to please make me completely straight are more than I can count. I worried that I would never feel whole, with my body pulling me in two opposing directions from one week to the next.

My first ever full-on sexual same-sex experience with was with a girl I found on a swinging website, who felt a similar way to me. I knew I only wanted a one-off experience with someone I'd never see again, so I thought the internet would be a good place to start. After two months of chatting about tastes and personal boundaries, we met up in a pub and got very drunk, which helped immensely. We then went back to mine and did what we had set out to do. It felt relaxed, funny and a bit sexy all at the same time.

Whilst I enjoyed the intimate experiences with women, I never grew romantically attached. With a man, romantic feelings would always creep in.

The women I usually had one-night stands with were also predominantly straight, so there would be no risk of me leading anyone on. It was an interesting phase in my life and something that I was glad to get out of my system as much as possible; although I knew that it would be something that would always be within me. It was just nice to know what it was all about and to find out whether the reality would live up to the fantasy. I found that the more experience I gained, the less frustrated I became. As a knock-on effect, it made me a bit of a girl's girl socially and increased my connection and empathy with other women. Because bisexuality covers such a broad spectrum of preference, and 'hetero flexible' sounded like a maths equation, I adopted a description that felt the most comfortable and fitting for me; 'a bit gay'. The realisation that I am actually blessed, not afflicted, was a very liberating and emotional one.

It seemed I wasn't cut out (ha!) to be a full time scissor sister, after all. I accepted that I would probably always find myself attracted to women on some kind of snuggly and intimate level, but that it was predestined that I would fall in love with a man. Not just any man, either. I had set clear boundaries for myself by now and had a strict criterion for what I could tolerate, accept and what I wouldn't even think of entertaining. I wanted a man who had a heightened sense of self-awareness, someone spiritual, creative, gentle but not a pushover, physically attractive to me, and whom I had fantastic psycho-sexual chemistry with. The question was, where on Earth was this man and how would I find such a mythical beast as this? Little did I know that I was getting warmer by the day and that the answer would be right under my nose.

My home life and social life were good, and I was moving ever closer to my chosen career. The only thing out of sync was my love life, i.e.: I didn't have one. Late one evening in the middle of June, I was on the sofa at home with the laptop resting on my knee, taking a break from my coursework and browsing on social media. A message popped up from a profile I didn't recognise. It was from a guy called Reece who appeared to be in his early thirties, like me. I was cautious with randomers messaging me, because I still received the occasional unsolicited dick pic. I wasn't in the mood for one at that moment. My head was already bursting with Freud and Jung and God knows what. I definitely didn't need a horny douche-bag thrown into the mix. I decided that I would ignore it until the next day, but on closer inspection, this guy looked pretty cute!

"Hi, how are you? I hope you don't mind me saying that I think you're really pretty. We seem to know a lot of the same people. I wonder if we'll ever meet so I can get to know you. Reece x"

It felt like a long time since someone had called me pretty. Compliments usually thrown my way were, 'fit' and 'sexy'. I took some time to look through Reece's photos and check out his credentials before replying. Yes, I was right about his age, we did have a few of the same friends (God knows how we had never met), and he was as fit as a butcher's dog. *Oh, my heart!* There wasn't one thing I didn't find attractive about this creature, from his thick, light brown wavy hair (very grown-up-Simba but with more loin than lion), soulful, kind-looking brown eyes and a bit of designer stubble. Yep, he was fit with a capital F. I was instinctively cautious though because I knew from experience that him being a fittie didn't mean he would automatically be a decent bloke.

I eventually replied after much typical femme-stylee online stalking. Within one week we had shared mobile numbers, and we spent the following two weeks playing text tennis with one another. It turned out that Reece was in a popular rock band from in the area. I knew who they were, but not enough that I would have recognised him at first glance. We spoke on the phone the evening before we were due to meet for our first date. I had imagined Reece's voice to have a southern twang, like a posh media student or something; but it pleasantly surprised me to hear his broad northern accent. It was just like mine. His voice was soft, had a calming quality about it, and felt strangely familiar. I felt bewitched by the sound of him, and his pretty face; but it was his sweet nature and the articulate language he used that I found to be the most captivating. After just three weeks of chatting online and then over the phone, I was dying to meet him as much as he wanted to meet me.

I had to have a few words with myself to stop me from wearing my heart slap bang on my sleeve, because I had learned from experience that men loved a challenge with a prize at the end. I vowed to myself to not make the same mistakes as I had with my previous partners – no jumping into bed straight away and giving myself too freely. If he turned out to be a dickhead, that would inevitably lead to me feeling used, cheap and rubbish about myself. I knew in my heart that I needed to remain patient and not chase this man; but I had already grown romantically attached to what could be just a fanciful illusion. What if he didn't live up to the image I had of him in my mind? What if I didn't fancy him when we met? I rang

Louise in my excited state as soon as I had put the phone down from talking to Reece.

"God, not another one, Sinead! Is there anyone you don't fancy lately who has lasted over five weeks?"

She was right. I had encountered a lot of blokes in the past few months whom I had fleetingly found attractive on at least a psychological level, but then they didn't live up to my romantic idealisations. Dating and I was a poor combination.

"But I'm meeting him tomorrow, Lou. What if I don't fancy him when I see him?"

"Oh, you will. I can feel it. Anyway, he's cute, so why wouldn't you?"

Good old Louise, always there to tell it like it was when I needed her.

No matter how much I tried to think rationally, my heart couldn't help getting carried away with itself. I had healthier values now, but that huge part of me that enjoyed giving and receiving affection and intimacy kept breaking through and taking the driving seat. It was a part of me I couldn't deny. I got the most awful adrenaline rushes whenever I thought of Reece, and I would forget to eat sometimes because my body was on such high alert with all the attraction chemicals coursing through it and killing my appetite. I was undeniably and shamefully infatuated with a man I had never met. Thoughts of Reece would flood my mind even when I was indulging in a spot of self-love. I didn't fantasise about dirty, wanton sex with him though; I would imagine him cupping my face in his hands, looking directly into my eyes and kissing me gently. I know, it makes you want to barf, doesn't it? I know exactly how pathetic it sounds because I felt embarrassed to be even feeling and thinking like that.

On the day of our first date, I was calm, perhaps because Reece and I had already spoken on the phone at length the night before. I had decided beforehand that I would take a casual approach with my appearance this time. Usually, I dressed up to the nines for dates, but I had a feeling that this man would be special, and I wanted him to see me for me, rather than an enhanced, cartoon-like version of myself. I wore a tight black t-shirt, blue jeans, and black wedge sandals. My hair was down for a change and I wore natural makeup, no false eyelashes or anything fake. I felt relaxed, and surprisingly, I felt attractive.

We met in a local backstreet café. As I turned the corner of the street, I saw Reece standing outside waiting for me. He looked taller than I had expected, about five foot eleven at a guess. Other than that, he looked exactly as had I imagined he would, and identical to his online profile photo. My heart did a little backflip as I clocked him, standing there in a pair of baggy combat pants and a white t-shirt, with a maroon-coloured checked shirt over the top; looking confidently casual. He had his hair swept back in a low ponytail with a few tendrils that had come loose, framing his masculine, handsome face. *Fit, fit, fit!* Looking at him made my ovaries sing, even from afar. As I got closer, Reece noticed me and broke into a big, warm smile, holding his arms out to welcome me with a friendly hug.

We found a quiet spot in the café, away from everyone, ordered two hot chocolates with marshmallows, and began getting to know each other properly. Conversation flowed easily, and we found that we shared a lot of the same interests such as poetry, musical tastes, and spiritual ideas. We even bounced off one another with our shared, politically incorrect sense of humour. Reece was also on a somewhat personal journey after a couple of relationships hadn't worked out for him. He lived alone on the outskirts of a nearby city, didn't have any children and had an established career as a musician. *Perfect.*

Louise was right – I fancied him like mad! I felt that the only thing that could stop this progressing further would be my job and my past. No other men I had dated had kicked up a fuss about it, but Reece seemed on a different intellectual level to those other guys, and he seemed to have self-respect in droves. This was a guy who knew what he wanted and what he didn't. Jesus, he was like a Nicholas Sparks[42] film character and could have his pick of the crop. Would he want to date an ex-Mistress with a child and plenty of emotional baggage? I knew that I had to be honest with him from the start so I would leave the date knowing where I stood.

It's now or never.

"Reece, I've got something to tell you about what I do for a living. You know I told you I was training to be a therapist, right? Well, that's true, but…" He interrupted me before I could finish.

"Sinead, I already know. I don't want to sound like a stalker, but I did a bit of a search for you online to check that you weren't a psycho or anything. I saw your name on some video credits where women were beating the shit out of men and other stuff. It didn't take long to figure out that you made fetish films."

It felt like in a split second, all the blood had drained from my body. I could only muster one word in response, which was a very flat sounding, "Oh."

"Did you honestly think that would bother me? God, Sinead,

---

[42] The novelist who inspired films such as The Notebook, responsible for giving millions of women the world over, unrealistic expectations of ever finding such a flawless man.

everyone has a past. I've not been an angel all my life either, I can see who you are and if I thought you couldn't be trusted, I wouldn't be sitting here drinking hot chocolate with you now. Speaking of which, do you fancy another?"

It turned out that Reece also had a big interest in psycho-sexual behaviour and following my disclosure, we had a riveting conversation about fetishes. He was a sexually and emotionally mature guy, and I liked that. There wasn't an ounce of sleaze about him. Funnily enough, Reece had a little secret of his own. He had a foot fetish that he had only recently come to terms with, following years of shame and confusion. Yep, you couldn't make it up. And there I was, thinking he was whiter than white! Of course, this was something I understood the dynamics of. Our finding one another seemed to be a well-timed twist of fate. Or was this actually my penance for all the past mischief I'd got up to in life? The reality being that having a boyfriend with an interest in feet would mean stepping up my personal grooming routine. I imagined a lifetime commitment of toe hair waxing, pedicures, and expensive monthly French manicure appointments. *Fuck's sake.*

We had drunk four cups of hot chocolate between us and been there for three hours before we decided that we had better end our date before we got kicked out of the café. It must have looked very obvious that we were on a first date because the waitresses were whispering, giggling and looking in our direction. Reece pulled out my chair for me like a true gentleman and we left the café, still heavily engaged in conversation (naturally, me with a pocket full of condiment sachets that would come in handy for when we ran out at home). There was so much I wanted to learn about him! When we reached my car, we stopped talking and began uttering our goodbyes. Reece pulled me towards him for a hug, our eyes met, and yep, you guessed it – we kissed for the first time. The only way I can think of to describe the kiss, is that it felt like coming home. We stood there in a tight embrace for about five minutes afterward, neither of us wanting to pull away from the oxytocin overload. We arranged to meet again a few days later at Reece's house.

Within a month we were an established couple, and our relationship progressed quickly. Every minor thing about Reece attracted me, and I couldn't pick out one individual part I liked the most, it was just a kind of all-encompassing attraction. I realised that when someone was right for me, all previous criteria went out of the window – height, weight, penis size, job, age… none of that mattered anymore because it was just him. This time I wasn't projecting any fantasies and idealisations. I was speaking the truth when I told my friends I had never met a man so similar to myself regarding work ethic, emotions, and beliefs. Having a bloke just like me in every way would do my head in; but having the same core values is something I view as pretty essential.

Reece was like a hybrid of the few good qualities each one of my old boyfriends had possessed, with all the bad bits removed, and a few of his own magical attributes sprinkled on top. It was as though I had bought a design-your-own-boyfriend kit. The Universe had listened, and it had rewarded me for all I had learned on my journey.

We were great companions and had the most fascinating conversations. This was really it – I was in love, and together we were a dynamic couple. Morgan loved Reece, and Reece was great with him; attentive and caring. Morgan was a perceptive lad and could pick up on fakery well, and he could tell that Reece's attention on him was sincere. My whole family was taken with him too because they could see how good he was for me and how compatible we were. I think even my mum fancied him a bit; and who could blame her?

We knew within that first month that we wanted to spend the rest of our lives loving each other, if possible. It felt as though there was something bigger than us both, making some universal shift, leading us in the right direction together. It felt beautiful and terrifying simultaneously, that feeling of not being in control and being vulnerable. Sex was on another plane completely because it just seemed so natural and primal. Every sexual act between us was instinctive, as though we had been familiar with the workings of one another's insides and outsides, for years. Before Reece's arrival in my life, I hadn't known that this kind of spiritual connection was even possible. There was no guilt, shame or hesitancy as we explored one another's bodies and pushed our sexual boundaries in all our expressive, beautiful, fucked up, kinky glory. In fact, the word 'kink' didn't cut the mustard as a descriptive term when we were between the sheets, because when kink was paired with the love and sensuality that we shared, it became something magical and indescribable. If I thought I had experienced good sex in the past, then this was something else altogether.

On occasion, we experimented with MDMA together – the main ingredient in ecstasy tablets, without all the other crap mixed in. It fascinated me to discover that in the 1960s they had used it in psychotherapy to enable families to open up to each other in sessions. I read that it was now being researched as a possible treatment for depression, and I was curious. With Reece and I, the effect was an altogether empathic and spiritual one, and before making love, we would discuss things we had never dared speak about to another living soul. When couples say they know everything about each other, they usually don't. Most people hold at least one thing back for themselves, for fear of judgement. Reece and I learned everything about one another's pasts, our darkest desires, and our greatest fears. It left us with a deeper bond than either of us had ever thought possible. We were grateful for the experiences as we felt they had affected our bond and understanding of each other positively. Although controversial because of its current illegal status, trying MDMA as a couple was something we have never regretted.

Reece moved in with Morgan and me a year later. It felt like the next natural and logical step for us all. Our home was a happy environment with an air of unity and peace about it whenever Reece was around. Even our garden seemed to flourish like never before, because Reece was most comfortable when he and Morgan were in the garden, planting vegetables and flowers of all colours. He was an excellent role model, and I imagined what it would be like if Reece and I had a baby of our own.

It was an eventful year filled with family time at home, accompanying Reece to gigs with his band, and the three of us going for days out and making memories. By the end of the year, with Reece's wage, I could stop being active in the adult industry altogether, while he supported us all financially. I kept the video clips up for sale online for a while so they would keep on generating us a small amount of money with which to supplement our family income, but I gave up filming and updating the online store.

I sold all my domination implements on eBay, except for a few of the more fun items – two pairs of handcuffs, a blindfold, a little leather strap, some bondage tape, and a few other little bits and bats. Well, you never know when these things might come in handy, do you? Reece used a few of my canes as plant supports in the pots in our back garden. They didn't half look funny because it was blatantly obvious what they were originally intended for. These were big, heavy canes of the crook-handled variety, that you would never see at your local B&Q. God knows what the neighbours must have thought, although I bet our nosy-parker postman spotted them straight away! Having the canes there seemed symbolic, like having a little graveyard for my old trappings, showing me daily how much I had achieved, and also perhaps to serve as a little warning that I should never take my new life for granted.

It took me a good two years to stop jumping every time I heard a noise in the night, thinking Jack was breaking into my home. By the time I had completed my placement at uni and was busy putting together my final piece of work to prepare for graduation, I felt like I had wiped my slate clean and that I was finally free to start again. My approach to life in its entirety had dramatically altered, so the ending of this life-chapter perfectly synchronised with the birth of the new, upgraded version of myself. I realised that I enjoyed living a refreshingly drama-free life. It was as though I had been redeemed from all the ugly, self-indulgent mistakes I had made and had somehow become pure of spirit. Pure of spirit; but still dirty of mind, however. I hadn't completely relinquished my naughty streak. I realised when two people are so in love, kink could be an intimately enriching form of sexual creativity – an emotional outlet not dissimilar to drawing, painting, or writing poetry.

After one particularly beautiful, filthy afternoon love-making session, Reece and I lay on our bed, collectively catching our breath. He turned onto his side to face me, gifting me with a bit of man cleavage eye candy. His tousled hair hung over his dewy, flushed cheeks, and he smiled at me with a sigh of satisfaction and contentment. Brushing his hair out of the way of his eyes, Reece tucked his hair behind one ear. God, he was gorgeous. I used to find such perfect looking men characterless and irritating, but the only thing

Reece irritated in me were my reproductive organs! His stoned-looking post orgasmic gaze conveyed the depth of his adoration for me.

"Babe, promise me we'll never stop disrespecting one another."

I smiled, and leaned in for a meaningful kiss to seal our pact.

"Never."

It wasn't always rosy with me and Reece, but it was heavenly compared to my previous relationships. In the first couple of years, we went through the usual horrible transitional shite that most couples inevitably have to face. Even if you don't end up with a knob-head, you still have to be tested with a lot of the crappy relationship stuff. Y'know, the honeymoon period insecurities, extreme jealousy, bloody awful rows, tears and communication breakdowns – the lot! I learned that if you can get through all that and still end up with two of you in the relationship, then you've probably got a good chance of going the distance.

We learned a lot about ourselves and each other from this rough patch and emerged with shit-hot communication skills which gave our relationship a new strength. In the past, we had both been cheated on, but the emotional baggage from those relationships soon disappeared. It was a liberating feeling for me to finally not feel threatened by male sexuality, and vice-versa for Reece. We were two sexual individuals in our own right, who also enjoyed partaking in sex with each other now and again. With that acceptance came mutual trust… and a lot of fun between the sheets!

Reece and I learned so much about how to conduct ourselves, how to tolerate and accept each other's differences, and how to pick our battles wisely. What remained was a strong-as-steel union. So strong that we decided that we may as well get engaged and try for a baby.

CHAPTER 24

What doesn't kill you

It's funny how quickly time can fly by when life is exactly how it should be. At the low points in my life in the past, time seemed to drag on endlessly and without meaning. Now I wished it would slow down a little so I could carefully savour every moment. It was as though I had blinked and suddenly had a different lifestyle. Fast forward another year, Morgan was thirteen and had just started high school, and we had four people living in our home, because we had made our family complete with another gorgeous boy – baby Roman. He looked just like Morgan, which was strange to say they both had different dads. The pain of childbirth was so much easier the second time around, probably because I was older and knew what to expect. Roman was the apple of all our eyes. Such a cute little thing, with dark brown hair and chubby cheeks. Morgan took to being a big brother like a duck to water. Initially, he wasn't very keen on extending our family, but once he recognised that Reece and I weren't replacing him, he came round to the idea. Reece was also a natural at being a dad, and he doted on Roman. I had attempted many times to describe to him the feeling of having a child of one's own, and he now understood the overwhelming love that I had been talking about.

I received my degree certificate two months after Roman was born, which was perfect timing. I had nearly thrown the towel in on more than one occasion. If it hadn't been for Reece giving me the occasional metaphorical kick up the arse, I don't think I would have seen it through. It took me a while to come to terms with knowing that I had worked this hard and achieved so much on my own – that nobody else was responsible for my new qualification, just little old me. When I finally came to accept this, my confidence soared. Now, that is some amazing shit that you cannot fake. I had gone from a little kid with no self-esteem, to an unshakeably confident woman, brimming with self-respect and glowing with pride.

I took two years out after qualifying to stay at home and care for Roman until he was old enough to go to nursery school, and during this time Reece and I got married. It was a relaxed affair in a manor house close to where we lived, with Morgan and Roman as page boys. Mum, Matt, and Dad were looking on, with eyes welling up with emotion as we took our vows, along with everyone else who was important to us. Alan from the studio was our photographer and did us a great deal in exchange for us feeding him. The reception meal was a huge Sunday roast, followed by a massive free-for-all party that went on until the early hours of the morning. Thank God for babysitters is all I can say because Reece and I still knew how to go on a bender!

By the time Roman was two, I was ready to spread my therapist wings and give working independently a shot. My ambition when I had first started my degree was to one day go private, so I started there, rather than working for an organisation first. I knew it wouldn't be easy at first and that being a therapist is something you learn on the job. I realised that we can only learn some things through life experience, and not in a classroom. Y'know when people say you don't learn how to drive until you've passed your test? Well, being a therapist is the same. You never know what will come through the door next. Like being a Domme, actually.

I found an office to rent in a building close to where we lived, with the other offices occupied by various holistic health and well-being practitioners. There I was, renting out a room for counselling when not so long back I had been renting out a studio room for sexual services. Reece and I were still living hand to mouth with only Reece's wage as our main income and a family of four to feed. I turned to eBay and the local charity shops to furnish my counselling room with two big, comfy sofas, a little table and framed paintings of landscapes to hang on the walls to give it a relaxed vibe. Who would have thought the young girl who used to hang around on the street outside Oxfam, while her mum went in, so that her friends didn't see her in there, would one day be such a charity shop fanatic? I can't keep out of 'em nowadays!

The final thing I had to do in preparation was to hang a sign on the door. I stepped back and admired the shiny gold lettering and felt overcome with emotion. It read, 'S. Winters. Rise Psychotherapy'. That was me – I had done it! Within hours of my first advert going up, I had received my first enquiry. Then another, then another, and another. Before I knew it, I had twenty clients a week through my door. I had my own private practice as a psychotherapist at last. I was thirty-eight years old and every one of my dreams had come true all in one go. I considered myself to be one lucky bugger, indeed.

I settled into my new role in no time at all; and I dealt with everything you could think of – anxiety, abortion, bullying, employment issues – you name it, I worked with it. Unsurprisingly, the areas in which I excelled the most were Domestic Violence, Relationship Issues, and Sex Therapy. I already had a tonne of experience worth its weight in gold, what with nearly every fetish and sexual issue known to man crossing my path at some point. In essence, my training as a sex therapist had begun at age fourteen, mediating between Mum and Dad. The aggression I had experienced with my ex-partners was coming in useful too. I didn't need any formal training to empathise with my domestic abuse clients, because I already understood why they stayed in their relationships for so long. Now I was using my past to make a difference in other peoples' futures.

I would still have the occasional nightmare that Jack was hunting me down and Reece would have to comfort me. It must have hurt seeing someone he loved still being affected all those years later. Maybe I would suffer from those nightmares until the day I died, but at least I would wake up knowing that I was safe with a man who would never raise a hand to me. I could live with that.

I couldn't help but feel thankful for every single time someone else had made me feel like crap, and also every time I had been responsible for making myself feel like crap. It was as though every event had been carefully masterminded by the universe, to lead me to this point. I thought of myself as that teenage girl who used to fantasise about being an agony aunt for Just Seventeen magazine's problem page. I had finally made something good of my life; but I wasn't advising in a magazine, making money for the people who ran it – I was advising in my own office as an independent self-employed agony aunt. I was helping people turn their shame into pride, just like I had done for myself.

I had a lot of time to reflect on my progress when I was at work, whilst waiting for clients to arrive. I usually made sure I arrived at my office a good hour before my first session, so I could sit quietly with a cuppa and get myself into the right headspace. I would sit and ponder on my life, wondering if I would do anything differently if I had my time on Earth again. Yes, there would be a lot of things I would go back and change if I could, but if I hadn't chosen the route that I had, I don't think I would be as tolerant, patient and understanding as I am today.

In my case, all the struggles had been worth having, because I could now pull myself out of the darkest times quicker and easier. If I hadn't suffered at the hands of Tim and Jack and had not had therapy to re-shape my values and heal, I wouldn't have felt inspired to train as a therapist at all. If I hadn't been in those relationships, would I have learned to appreciate what a good man looked like? I may not have ended up with Reece. Perish the thought. Maybe I would have viewed the work of a therapist as 'just another one of those boring office jobs', rather than the dream job I see it as today.

If I hadn't done my stint in the adult industry, would I have been able to view sex workers without judgement, and be able to view them as regular people with intelligence, fears, hopes and dreams? And what about the clients who came to me with scars on their arms and legs from self-harming? If Jack's abuse hadn't dragged me to the depths of despair and I hadn't mutilated my body that dreadful night, would I now just see self-harmers as attention-seeking Emos[43] instead of understanding that there is always an underlying cause?

I considered how my life's journey had also helped me to empathise with clients in other areas too, other than sex and violence. If I had never had both good and bad times whilst taking drugs in the past, would I have pre-judged the drug addicts who entered my office, secretly wondering how anyone would be so stupid as to make that decision to try drugs in the first place? Surely, I wouldn't have gained a thorough understanding of how maybe they thought it

---

[43]Emotive Rocker. Stereotypically with a dyed black, floppy fringe and black, gothic-style clothing. Emos have a stigma relating to self-harm – particularly cutting their arms in a bid for attention.

would help them cope when life felt otherwise unbearable? With suicidal ideation, would I have viewed such thoughts as a selfish cry for attention, had I not have been there myself when I was drowning in debt and despair?

Whenever I had these moments of reflection, I would always arrive at the same conclusion; that maybe regretting events and viewing bad decisions as mistakes isn't the way forward, but that learning from them is. I considered all the positive lessons that I'd gained from each not-so-great time. Take lap-dancing, for example. I learned how to be comfortable with my bare-naked body, wobbly bits included, which is something that many women wish for but never achieve. Regarding sexuality, maybe if I hadn't had confusion in that area, I may not have been able to comprehend why a person couldn't just happily choose which sex they preferred to be with.

In making poor judgements during my time as a parent, I gained a new understanding and respect for my parents. They were both brought up by unloving parents in dysfunctional home environments. I could see how easy it must have been to get things wrong, as well as right, without having had decent role models to learn from. I felt grateful that partly through my parents, the life lessons I had gained were enabling me to raise my sons to view women as equals and to always treat them with consideration and respect.

Morgan was a floppy-haired, kind-natured sixteen-year-old lad by now, who loved rock music and animals, and had a shy, grungey-looking girlfriend. He had finished his GCSEs recently, and I wanted to buy him something special. True to our family's form, he asked for a pair of Dr. Marten boots rather than the latest Nike trainers. He didn't know about my crazy past but had grown to be very proud of what I do for a living. Little Roman had grown into a cheeky three-year-old and was at nursery school, enjoying the simple life while it lasted. I would still call Louise up regularly for a good moan and a laugh about the old days. It wouldn't be her advising me, but the other way around for a change.

I was proud of my roots and upbringing. If my experience of being a kid had been easy, I may well have grown up to be a self-entitled little brat who didn't appreciate the value of money or understand the importance of being nice to people. I would never have developed this grit, determination and ballsy attitude. My parents had helped me to become the unique, open-minded, non-conformist and kick-ass woman I am today. My relationships with Mum and Dad were now much closer and healthier, as the time we spent together would be more about quality. Mum had become my best friend in the true sense of the phrase, with no enmeshment, and a healthy mother/daughter boundary line.

One thing that had remained consistent was my sense of humour. Not taking myself too seriously and being able to laugh at my sheer stupidity and dumbass-ness had helped me to always see the funny side of things, no matter how awful they would sometimes seem. Freud would have said that my humour was a defense mechanism, but sod Freud. Rumour has it he was no angel, either, as well as being a bit of a wrong 'un, sexually. Maybe he just didn't appreciate comedy? I would much rather have made light of a shitty situation than have felt sorry for myself any day; because bitterness and baggage had never got me anywhere.

So, I had swapped domination sessions for therapy sessions, and I was now practicing CBT all over again; but this time it stood for Cognitive Behavioural Therapy rather than Cock and Ball Torture. It took me a while to not feel like chuckling whenever a client asked me, "What does CBT stand for?"

I had recently been considering hosting therapy sessions through Skype. Some people would feel self-conscious at the prospect of being in front of the camera, but it didn't faze me one bit. I guess that once you've been naked in front of one, all feelings of embarrassment go out the window!

My story has certainly been no rags to riches one. Back when I had been a single parent, I always seemed to chase money and compromise my morals to make ends meet. There had always been an easier way that I just couldn't see. My story had been more about how I'd learned to be comfortable in my rags and change my definition of what it meant to be rich. I would probably never be wealthy in terms of wads of cash; but I was rich in wisdom, which I considered to be priceless.

Although I had started my life on a run-down council estate, I would reflect on how greedy, image-conscious, judgemental, pretentious and superficial I had become under the influence of men like Tim and Jack. I was still skint from time to time, but happier than ever. I learned that sometimes a truly happy ending could come free of charge. The only trouble is that happiness can be short-lived because you can never predict what may be just around the corner. Mum in her infinite wisdom had once told me it was always best to prepare for worse-case scenarios… So, if by some cruel twist of fate it all goes tits up, I know there are always a few canes at the bottom of the garden, that I'm sure would come up as good as new with a bit of elbow grease[44] and some linseed oil.

…Oh, and I still look banging in a PVC catsuit. Never say never.

---

[44] Persistent, hard work.

EPILOGUE

It was a normal dark, winter night for me in most respects. My youngest son, Roman, was fast asleep, tucked up in bed. My husband, Reece, was out on a zombie-shooting activity evening that he'd got on Groupon[45] for a bargainous price, and I was at home, curled up on the sofa, watching my favourite film – Rita, Sue and Bob Too. I cracked open a bottle of wine, pressed pause and headed outside to have a smoke on my doorstep. I called my best friend, Louise, on the telephone, to pass the time. For the next half an hour I sat there, gossiping and reminiscing with her about some of our funny memories.

"Oh my God, I could write a book about my crazy escapades!" I joked, almost choking on my wine.

"I know! You couldn't make your life up!" Louise laughed.

"Should I?" I teased.

"Yeah, why not? Do it."

I broke into a mischievous smile.

Reece came home, later on that night, looking tired, but excited, and told me all about his zombie-bashing experience. I listened intently, trying not to look shifty.

"Anyway, what have you been up to?" he asked.

---

[45] A website where you can buy discounted goods or services. Groupon are best known for their vouchers for experience gifts, such as racing driving and fine dining.

"Well…" I chimed. He knew that something eccentric was going to spill out of my mouth. When I was in that kind of mood, anything could happen. While the cat's away and all that… "I'm gonna write a book!"

Reece looked at me, rolled his eyes, shook his head and chuckled as though nothing I could ever come up with would surprise him.

I had no idea how to go about doing this kind of thing. I had enrolled in a creative writing course at night school about fifteen years back, but I only went to one class, because of my usual self-doubt. I thought about the time when I had attended a one-day life-coaching course just after I had broken up with Crazy-Jack. I had thought it would be a good idea, as I knew I wanted to make some life changes, but I wasn't sure what path I wanted to take. The results of the final exercise I had to do that day had surprised me. After writing all the things I felt passionate about, I was instructed to stand up and take individual paces forward until I reached the wall at the end of the room. With each step I took, I had to imagine that I was moving towards my goal. When I reached the wall, I turned around, faced my coach, and declared, "I want to write a book."

I was as shocked as he was. I didn't have a clue what I wanted to write about, I just knew I wanted to write something. During all the drama and studying towards my degree, this dream had been long forgotten. Well, now I would do it. Yep, it was time to fulfil yet another ambition.

Around the time I started writing, Sub/Dom relationships were causing a bit of a media stir, because of the popularity of a world-famous book, turned film. You know the one. The bored mums and housewives who were reading this theme of chick-lit were being lulled into this notion of romantic idealism. Many seemed to think that Dom/Sub relationships were all about being rescued and being constantly raunchy. But I knew that if you stopped to look at the grass from another angle, and on a rainy day – it wasn't always all that green. More often than not, it could be wilted, grubby and dismal looking. It's not a world inhabited by real-life Mr. Greys[46], that's for sure. Well, unless you count Mr. Grey-and-wrinkly. There are more of those than you can shake a whip at!

It took me about twenty minutes to come up with my first few words:

    Give me your riches, bitches. I have a book.

Hmmm, this would not be as easy as I had first thought; but I couldn't resist a challenge.

No, Sinead, I scolded myself, *this is not the time to pull out your stupid sense of humour. This is a serious project.*

Delete, delete, delete. Start again. *Sigh.*

I built myself a little nest of blankets and cushions in the living room, downloaded a free, dodgy version of Microsoft Word, and set to work. This was no easy task, as I had little Roman constantly round my ankles, and CBeebies would be on the telly at full volume. I found that the urge to write felt akin to being hungry. Ravenous, in fact. I relished every spare moment that I got and felt relief as soon as I began typing. I had never felt such focus whilst immersed in a creative process. I was born to do this.

The housework was no longer my priority, so I had no right to moan at Reece for his untidiness anymore. He could be a scruffy

[46]Christian Grey was a sexually dominant character with a penchant for BDSM, in the book-turned-film Fifty Shades of Grey, by E. L. James.

bugger, and I was quickly coming down to his level. Upon seeing the laundry piled high and crockery teetering in the kitchen, Reece chuckled.

"Now do you understand why most creatives and artists live in shit-holes?"

"Nice try, Reece! It still doesn't mean you can leave your scratty undies on the floor. I wouldn't expect you to pick up my knickers and sniff them to see if they're dirty or not."

He gave a little predatory smirk, and I raised my eyebrows in mock annoyance.

"Oh, very funny, you little perv. Now help a girl out and load the dishwasher, would you?"

I stand by my belief that men are disgusting creatures. I've seen plenty of proof.

I just knew that I was on the path meant for me. Reece was great and brought me coffee on demand. (I made a mental note that he was obviously after my imminent fortune.) I dug out my old diaries, poems, and emails, and put them into some sort of order so I could use them to jog my memory. There in the safety and comfort of my happy home, coal fire blazing and candles burning, with the smell of coffee and contentment surrounding me, I typed out the story of how I slid partway down the slippery slope of the sex industry.

JUST FOR SHITS AND GIGGLES

Here is a small compilation of the varied messages I received. I had a feeling there would one day be a good reason I had kept these emails for so many years!

Hi Mistress,

I have a fetish for sniffing dirty, white briefs. Also, little white trainer socks and trainers, all preferably worn to the gym so they're very sweaty. I also like to worship legs and tickle feet, if possible. Would you please laugh at me whilst I'm sniffing your socks and knickers?

Callum x

♥

Dear Mistress Olivia,

Well, I am a complete novice to this, but I know that I am looking for a version of SPH (Small Penis Humiliation) - Verbal insults about me and my penis. I don't want any anal penetration and no ball kicking. I am just looking to be humiliated while I jerk, and then possibly be tied up with you jerking me to a finish while abusing me. I hope my questions are not too stupid and I look forward to hearing from you,

Greg x

♥

Hello Mistress,

Would you consider having a slave over maybe a long time, maybe two to three days where the slave will be your personal maid/butler? Mostly you would ignore me. I would be very interested and, of course, be prepared to pay more.

Jemima

♥

Hi Miss Olivia,

I would enjoy watching you smoke. Not many ladies who offer this service 'do it for me'; but few Dominas are as beautiful as you. I just want my head in one of your clouds of smoke.

I also like other things such as humiliation, face slapping, human ashtray, stocking worship, shoe/boot worship, etc. Do you offer any of these services?

I hope you don't think I'm weird? I wouldn't blame you, to be honest, I sometimes think I am LOL.

Yours hopeful,

Jaden

♥

Hi,

I am just writing for your help and advice. I have had the obsession in the back of my mind for a while and I'm just writing to see if you can help me out. I want to be a slave - every other weekend and at special events. I'm very obedient and will do anything you tell me.

Please, I am not a moron or anything. I have messaged you because you seem to be the best in this area. If there is a way to earn a bit of money, then that is okay, but mostly I want to do this for fun.

Your willing servant

♥

Hi there!

Just wondering if you could accommodate a

nappy lover? I'm not into the adult baby theme, I just like wearing good old-fashioned terry-towelling nappies (With nice PVC or rubber pants, of course!)

Please let me know,

Neil x

♥

Dear Goddess,

Do you ever sell your worn panties? If so, I was thinking about white full-backed cotton panties. I would be willing to pay forty pounds.

Simon

♥

Dear Mistress Olivia,

I require a strict mistress who enjoys giving severe canings and to teach me to worship and obey the superior sex. I prefer you to be in tight jeans or shorts. They would show off your wonderful figure and curvy bottom! I am not into PVC or bondage.

Yours,

Daniel

♥

Hello Mistress Olivia,

I am a twenty-six-year-old cross-dresser and would like a three-day meeting with you at the end of July. I am contacting you now because I want to pay for it weekly.

I would like to get a beauty therapist to do my makeup and nails, also a shopping trip.

I am a willing slut maid.

I am a builder as well.

All my love and best wishes,

Andy

♥

Hello Mistress Olivia,

I wondered if you would have any use for a Bondage Gimp. I enjoy being placed in heavy bondage, gags, and genital restraints. I am willing to be left for long periods or whatever would make this scenario work best for you.

Hoping for a quick reply,

John the Gimp

Did I fulfil any of the more 'interesting' requests? Now, that would be telling! I'll leave it to your imagination...

A WORD FROM THE AUTHOR

Thank you, whoever you are and wherever you are, for reading my book. I hope it gave you a few belly laughs. If I have successfully entertained you, please share the fun, smut and chaos by passing it on to a like-minded friend. I would love to hear any comments and it would mean the world to me if you would kindly take a moment to leave an honest online review.

Finally, although this book is mainly light-hearted, if any of the serious issues raised are affecting you or someone you care about, here are some useful contact details:

- If you, or someone you know, are experiencing domestic abuse in any of its many forms, the Women's Aid website has a wealth of information and a team of dedicated support workers. You can contact them through their website: www.womensaid.org.uk

- If you are finding debt difficult to cope with, National Debt Line is a charity giving support and advice. You can contact them at: www.nationaldebtline.org

- If you are experiencing symptoms of depression relating to confusion about your sexuality, or simply need support, the LGBT Foundation helps thousands every year through their helpline, on Tel.: 03453303030 or email: helpline@lgbt.foundation.

- For victims of historical sexual abuse, please visit: www.thesurvivorstrust.org

- If drug addiction is a problem in your life, or you feel your usage is getting out of control, please visit: www.actiononaddiction.org.uk

- If you are feeling suicidal and don't know where to turn for help, the Samaritan's helpline is free to call, on Tel.: 116 123.

The above organisations are there to help. Please share the burden and know that you're not alone, no matter how hopeless things may seem now.

I wish you all the best on your own life journey wherever it may lead.

Sinead

Printed in Great Britain
by Amazon

44081892R00169